FUNDED!

"Anyone with a big dream—that needs funding to get off the ground—should read Lucy's must-read guide on finding fellowships, raising money and winning grants. She shows you how to get your hands on the resources that can turn seemingly lofty goals into reality. Under her informed guidance, readers will also better figure out just what their big goals are and how to fulfill their deepest passions."

—**Kimberly Palmer**, author of *The Economy of You*
and senior editor at US News & World Report

"As a long-time director of university study abroad programs, I helped many students and professors find international opportunities and funding sources. That job will be a lot easier with the publication of Lucy Gent Foma's new guidebook. She does an outstanding job of describing the nuts and bolts of applying for international funding, but also helps newcomers to this field focus on their passions and goals, and match them to their skills and strengths. This is an essential guide for students, teachers, professionals, artists, and anyone who yearns to travel and work for a better world."

—**Ken Carpenter**, PhD, Founder of
Casa Xalteva Study Center, Granada, Nicaragua

"With this book, Lucy Gent Foma has pulled together much of the best advice on grant writing and put in one place, ready to be put to use. *Funded!* is full of useful ideas and encouraging words, and there isn't a grant-writer I know who couldn't use a few of those. If you are considering seeking fellowship funding, I suggest starting here."

—**Stefan Senders**, PhD, Cornell University Fulbright Undergraduate Advisor

"*'Funded'* is both a useful primer for first-time grant and fellowship seekers as well as an inspiring reminder for veterans who may be re-entering the application game."

—**Alexandra Huddleston**, author of *333 Saints: A Life of Scholarship in Timbuktu* and recipient of a Fulbright Islamic Civilizations Grant

"This is a brilliantly written, clear, and well organized guide to fundraising. Lucy's personal success and detailed description of her process make this not only a treasure chest full of useful information, but also a very interesting read.

The mastery of this book is how Lucy entertains the reader with stories which lead them through practical exercises without making the process tedious. I was pleasantly surprised by how engaging the book is.

Her story is a perfect model for how any individual can plumb the depths of their unique personal experiences to find their true passion. Just as in Lucy's life, the practical methods for finding funding came out of a personal exploration. She demonstrates how to track the path from your own interests out into the practical world."

—**Catherine Hebenstreit**, author of *Waking in the Dreamtime* and Life Coach

"*Funded!* offers invaluable insight and a systematic approach to the world of fellowships and funding for those who wish to follow their passion and make a difference in the world. Lucy Gent Foma demystifies the process of winning grants and awards and, through her genuine accounts of personal experiences, provides companionship to the reader in his or her quest for funding.

The honesty and authenticity of Lucy's writing, combined with the very thorough and practical process she has laid out impresses me."

—**Ayla Schlosser**, Founder & CEO, Resonate

"In Lucy Gent Foma's book, *Funded!*, she has masterfully crafted a format where the practical recommendations flow according to a clearly organized structure. Simultaneously, her own and other individuals' rich personal perspectives make the information easy to remember and apply, which is essential for busy readers."

—**Merideth Paxton**, Research Associate at the University of New Mexico

"If you're someone who has aspirations to explore and contribute to the world, the tools in this book can help make your dreams a reality. By skillfully interweaving reflections from her own experience as the recipient of nearly a quarter of a million dollars in scholarships, fellowships and grants; tips from other successful awardees and reviewers; and insightful leadership development exercises, Lucy equips us with the motivation, resources, and action steps necessary to successfully pursue funding our passions."

—**Benjamin Gillock**, Faculty, United World College-USA

"No matter what your academic or financial background, your goals are worth pursuing and your dreams are within your reach. This is the message that reads loud and clear from the pages of *Funded!* But this book is not just motivational, it is practical! Not only a great resource for fundraising personal projects but a great resource for personal leadership development, I highly recommend this book to all the youth and young professionals we train through our programs. Too often access to financial resources is limited to those who know about them and feel entitled to them; which too often means those who already have economic privilege. Lucy's book makes these resources and the process to get them much more accessible to us all."

—**Bianca Sopoci-Belknap**, Executive Director, Earth Care; Chair, Sustainable Santa Fe Commission; Program Director, New Energy Economy

FUNDED!

HOW I LEVERAGED MY PASSION TO LIVE A
FULFILLING LIFE AND HOW YOU CAN TOO!

LUCY GENT FOMA

New York

FUNDED!

HOW I LEVERAGED MY PASSION TO LIVE A FULFILLING LIFE AND HOW YOU CAN TOO

Published in New York, New York, by Morgan James Publishing. Morgan James and The Entrepreneurial Publisher are trademarks of Morgan James, LLC.
www.MorganJamesPublishing.com

The Morgan James Speakers Group can bring authors to your live event. For more information or to book an event visit The Morgan James Speakers Group at
www.TheMorganJamesSpeakersGroup.com.

Shelfie

A **free** eBook edition is available
with the purchase of this print book.

CLEARLY PRINT YOUR NAME ABOVE IN UPPER CASE

Instructions to claim your free eBook edition:
1. Download the Shelfie app for Android or iOS
2. Write your name in **UPPER CASE** above
3. Use the Shelfie app to submit a photo
4. Download your eBook to any device

ISBN 978-1-63047-708-0 paperback
ISBN 978-1-63047-709-7 eBook
Library of Congress Control Number:
2015911709

Cover Design by:
Chris Treccani
www.3dogdesign.net

Interior Design by:
Bonnie Bushman
The Whole Caboodle Graphic Design

In an effort to support local communities and raise awareness and funds, Morgan James Publishing donates a percentage of all book sales for the life of each book to Habitat for Humanity Peninsula and Greater Williamsburg.

Get involved today, visit
www.MorganJamesBuilds.com

Habitat for Humanity®
Peninsula and
Greater Williamsburg
Building Partner

To Lola Moonfrog, Marta Townsend,
and my family,
who saw travels and accomplishments
in my future before I did.

TABLE OF CONTENTS

ICON GUIDE

 Measure Up: Sample winning proposals and personal statements will give you a sense of what your own project should look like.

 North Star: Advice from past scholars, mentors, and reviewers target the key advice others have gleaned from going through the process. Follow the advice to get to your destination.

 Origin/Destination: Not everyone's path follows the same route. Here you will learn how others navigated the process.

 Checklist: These are things to be sure to do or include along the way to getting funded.

This image indicates a worksheet. Completing worksheets will leave you with the foundation for your application. These steps and exercises will help you practice the lessons throughout the book.

PREFACE

Since graduating from Smith College I've been awarded nearly a quarter of a million dollars in fellowship, scholarship, and grant monies—including a Fulbright Fellowship and a Rotary Scholarship. I worked as a microfinance fellow and environmental studies teacher in Cameroon, researched traditional dance in Senegal, traveled the world, and was able to graduate with my master's degree from Cornell debt-free. Now I want to share my secrets.

Funded! How I Leveraged My Passion To Live A Fulfilling Life And How You Can Too! is both a how-to guide for people looking for an inspirational career, and a professional development book that will transform readers into the change agents they want to be. It includes anecdotes from other successful grant and scholarship winners—as well as my personal story—and step-by-step advice, worksheets, and exercises showing you how to tell your story in a compelling way, find a mentor, line up contacts, and develop your passion.

The book is based on a simple precept: a person doesn't have to be an extraordinary student—I was waitlisted at Smith, and struggled in academics for much of my life—to pursue and win these awards. All it takes is strategic planning and a particular writing skill set, both of which I can help you acquire.

Funded! is not the only book on the market about this subject, but it provides something new and necessary. There is a woeful lack of resources for personal fellowships and funding outside of the undergraduate and non-profit sectors—and also a lack of information about this growing source of prize money. *Funded!* fills that gap. These days, people want creative and personalized working situations, and fellowships are a perfect way to achieve them. College and high school students are a built-in audience, but I also wrote the book for people of all ages seeking nontraditional careers—a fast-growing group.

INTRODUCTION

It's a quarter to five in the morning, and the mist is lifting from the base of the valley as the sun warms the cool night air. The chicken coop by the outdoor kitchen smells crisp instead of ripe, chilled overnight by the surprisingly low temperatures. The sun hasn't reached the north side of the house, where the heavy metal door closes with a clang, despite my effort to shut it quietly. I'm the first person awake and out of the house this morning, as usual.

As I turn the corner and make my way down the steep dirt driveway, which is a little slippery from the daily monsoons, the sun warms my face. A spectacular view greets me: a deep, lush valley full with banana trees and high-altitude tropical plants; a waterfall that drops into the town is barely visible in the distance. I smile to the morning, barely able to believe my good fortune.

I'm quick but sure-footed as my Tevas grip the stony path down to the main road. My Timbuk2 messenger bag—packed with my computer, snacks, water, and spare clothes—digs into my lower back as I bounce along, ready for the day.

I've never felt a greater sense of purpose than when heading to these early-morning meetings in villages around the Northwest Province of Cameroon. Although I'm only a rising senior in college, I feel like I'm really helping people.

My job consists of granting and reporting on small business loans that transform modest gardens into crops of produce that can support families.

In town, the taxis are scarce this morning; hardly anyone needs them at this early hour. I have to wait five minutes before I can hail one. Anxiously checking my watch, I worry that my co-workers will leave without me. I'm heading to our meeting spot, an office in the central commercial district of Bamenda, and from there, we'll take motorcycles to navigate the back roads destroyed by rain. Tediously winding between giant, muddy potholes, it takes us a full hour to go twenty miles. As we pull up to the village meetinghouse, all the members are already seated and ready to start. They've lost an hour that they could've better used to prepare the day's food or tend to their farms, and they want to get business out of the way as quickly as possible. This morning, we are efficient. We sing the anthem, everyone checks that they have brought their money, and the group remits the collective repayment for the loans they owe to GHAPE, the Grounded, Holistic Approach to People's Empowerment Microfinance Institute. As everyone waits patiently, I check off each loan with my co-workers, marking down the debts in repayment ledgers. We're done in an hour. It's only seven in the morning, but we've finished a significant part of the day's work, and I'm ready for breakfast.

As a first-time Kiva Fellow, I couldn't have asked for a better experience. Kiva, an online lending platform for microfinance institutes around the world, had just started a fellowship program, which sends people into the field to report back on in-country office operations. As the only undergraduate accepted into the Kiva Fellows Program's fifth class, I felt more than a little intimidated by my charge, but seriously motivated to do my best. This first positive experience and success at winning a fellowship set me on a path to apply for and win other fellowships, scholarships, and grants that I would never have dreamed of reaching for.

Back in 2008, going to Cameroon over the summer ignited my passion for writing additional applications. The following year, Smith College awarded me a Ruth Dietrich Tuttle prize for a project I envisioned that summer. In 2010, I went to Senegal as a Fulbright Scholar and a Rotary Ambassadorial Scholar. In 2011, I started my graduate studies at Cornell University, where I won two grants for independent projects in the community. In 2012–13, Cornell awarded me one of five Foreign Language and Area Studies grants, which covered my tuition, plus a living stipend. After graduating in 2013, I became a Transportation Scholar with the National Parks Foundation, working in Bandelier National Monument, close to my hometown of Santa Fe, New Mexico.

I've had a lot of help along the way, for which I am very grateful. Although I was never the perfect student and barely had the confidence to apply for the first Kiva fellowship, I somehow have ended up with a number of large scholarships under my belt. It was not luck; it was practice and assistance from friends and mentors.

I wanted to write a book about all that I've learned during this process for two reasons. First, I see so many passionate people who would be perfect for these scholarships if they only knew how to apply. I want to help people get the money to fulfill their dreams. Second, I want to record my own lessons and adventures for myself so that I don't forget.

CHAPTER ONE

HOW I ARRIVED HERE

I just had to let them laugh at me first, and then I could do the dances I knew.
—**Elise Smith Gent**, my mother, a dance teacher for thirty years

Oshogbo, Nigeria, 1997: The twenty-year-old, tin-walled minivan rumbles and shakes as we swerve between people, potholes, dogs, and goats on the road. You'd never guess we are only going twenty-five miles per hour by the way the Raggedy-Ann vehicle whistles and groans under the strain. The entourage, which includes my mother, father, brother, grandmother, a friend, and me, unloads from the minivan into a village, where we're immediately swarmed.

They would show me a dance move, and as I made my best effort to move my white butt like they did, everyone would laugh uproariously!

When we look at candid pictures that our self-appointed documentarian takes, we see many amused faces, some with mouths wide open, mid-guffaw. Other onlookers appear confused about why these Americans are voluntarily making fools of themselves.

> *After all the laughter, they seemed to like watching me dance. They even asked me to teach them these dances I knew from Guinea. Although if they didn't like what I was doing, they would just sit down and watch me again.*

This was our "Big African Adventure," as my family refers to it now, where we learned that, although we'd never know what it was like to be African, we could appreciate our role as Americans who have learned to make this culture our own.

Santa Fe, New Mexico, 2015: My mother has been dancing her whole life, beginning with her childhood training at The School of American Ballet in Manhattan. She studied dance at Bennington College and discovered African and Haitian dance after meeting my father in New Mexico in the early 1980s. She transformed her passion into a thriving practice as a dance teacher for thirty years. Although she's a seasoned pro, she prepares for each class as if it's her first, meticulously reviewing her new dance combinations and fretting over creating something that her students will like. At least twice a year, she donates performances in which she has invested hours of time choreographing, teaching, and rehearsing. When I ask her why she never charges anyone for these many hours of work, she says, "Because I am so lucky to get to do what I love every day."

Before Santa Fe's historic Railyard district became the town's new urban mecca, my parents bought and renovated an old warehouse right beside the tracks. Coal-blackened earth surrounded the building, and the chain-link fence that enclosed our small, pothole-ridden parking lot turned muddy during summer monsoons. My father renovated the whole building, taking the time to disassemble, re-sand, and re-glue each piece of a salvaged basketball court floor—perhaps not saving money, but saving many trees.

Together, my parents created a light and open dance studio, said to be the best in New Mexico, where my mother could teach her African dance class. It just so happened that, years later, the back door of their building would open to a famously thriving farmer's market pavilion, commuter rail line, bike path, walking promenade, and extraordinary park.

For the past seven years, every Monday, Wednesday, and Saturday that I missed dance class, I sat in vigil, noting the designated times when I knew everyone was arriving, starting the warm-up, dancing across the floor together, and finally closing in a circle. My heart and soul were with them, even if I was hundreds or thousands of miles away. Dance class is where I am whole, being with new friends and old, witnessing families blossom, and supporting those in distress. It's more than exercise or cultural transmission; it's a community.

Hundreds of people have passed through my mom's class over these several decades, including one young man from Nigeria who became a dear friend. Olabayo came from a family of artists and quickly became part of our own family. He lived with us on and off while he attended the College of Santa Fe. Olabayo became so much a part of our life that we decided to travel to Nigeria in 1997, when I was ten years old. This was not a trip to enrich my mother's dance repertoire; it was for my family to learn about our friend's background.

Among my most vivid memories was the first night we arrived in Lagos. The burning piles of trash along the road provided more illumination than the streetlights on the highway. I covered my nose, worried to see that people were sitting in the wafting, toxic, black smoke of burning plastic.

Bamenda, Cameroon, 2008: While I was traveling around the Northwest Province, working with farmers and small entrepreneurs as a Kiva Fellow, I started to notice that people were cooking their food in plastic baggies instead of the customary banana leaves. These non-biodegradable pieces of trash were then burned, because there was no formal waste management system. Again, I would cover my nose and cringe when I saw people sitting in the smoke, unaware of the harm in which they were placing themselves. I decided that I could do something about this, starting with the next generation: the children.

My newfound love and I worked for six months creating an environmental education program for the summer after I graduated from college. He did the logistical part, meeting with school administrators in Cameroon, while I proceeded with fundraising in the United States. I applied and competed for funding from many sources, ranging from grants for recent college graduates, to online social entrepreneurship competitions. Finally, I received the Ruth Dietrich Tuttle Prize from my alma mater, Smith College. We were able to teach classes for our Go

Green Africa project as part of a pre-existing program of holiday courses, giving us access to students without having to recruit them independently.

This process of discovering what I wanted to do to serve an observed need, followed by investigating and pursuing funding, all while connecting with mentors and contacts, demonstrated the successful and rewarding procedure I have followed many times over the years. This is how I went about funding my passions, and after reading this book, you'll know how to do it for yourself. Whether you had an experience as a child that has fueled a path through your life, like dance did for my mother, or you are exploring a new field, this book will tell you how to get funded.

You Don't Have to Be an A Student

"She didn't even have a 3.5 GPA," snidely remarked a girl in the Smith College fellowships office, as if that person was kidding herself if she thought she would even have a chance at a fellowship.

"I don't have a 3.5 GPA," I said, leaving the other applicant awkwardly seeking another conversation topic. I had to make a strong case for why I deserved those first fellowships, because it wouldn't suffice to hand over my transcript, which bore a D⁺ from my first semester of economics. And I didn't get the Fulbright the first time I applied. It took almost two whole years of application refinement, some rejection, and a lot of resilience to finally become a Fulbright Scholar.

If you're reading this book, it's because at some point in your life you've had a dream about doing something fantastic, like winning a scholarship to study in a foreign land. What was that thing? Fashion design in Africa? Youth culture in South America? Renewable energy technology in Asia? Studying art history at a small liberal arts school? Being the first in your family to go to college? What was that dream that you saw yourself fulfilling, and what did that feel like?

I often see students (and adults) with dreams for projects or travel, who either don't know how to get to the point of applying for grants and fellowships, or feel like they're not exceptional enough. You *can* follow your dreams. Anyone can win grant monies and fellowships if he or she knows how to go about it. It's a science and an art, not luck.

Start firming up that goal now, because you'll need endurance to get through the application process. Sometimes, in the tedious moments, you may want to quit, but having a goal and a vision for your future will pull you through those moments.

The process of applying for grants, fellowships, or scholarships includes the following steps:

- **Envision** what you want to do
- **Review** your project with a mentor or group of mentors
- **Work** to become a competitive applicant
- **Research** fellowship and grant opportunities
- **State your intention** concisely
- **Network** with contacts or partners
- **Write** your proposal
- **Compose** a compelling personal statement
- **Edit** your application
- **Prepare** to fulfill your dreams

The chapters of this book are laid out in this order so that the sequence of steps becomes solid in your mind. Read the whole book before embarking on your own project, so that you are prepared mentally and emotionally for the whole process. If you absolutely can't wait to get down to the work, skip to Chapter Ten, the "Cheat Chapter." I discuss the details of each step and examine how some people have handled the process differently in each chapter.

Since I have written this book from personal experience, I have included my own reflections, which I hope will help and inspire you. There are also exercises and worksheets for you to complete throughout the chapters. By the end of the book, you should have a good idea of what you're planning on doing, where to look for support, and the beginnings of your application, which you can tailor and refine prior to submission.

Learning how to apply for fellowships changed how I saw myself in the world. As it turned out, I was the type of person who could learn new languages, travel alone in foreign countries, and win thousands of dollars in grant money to pursue my interests in West African dance, microfinance, environmental issues, and city planning. I could not have imagined all these possibilities before learning how to write grants and apply for fellowships.

By the time I was a junior in college, I had come a long way toward believing that I could realistically apply for big scholarships like the Fulbright, but I was still far from the perfect candidate. I have always been a B student, occasionally turning in late papers and prioritizing life's lessons over those in the classroom. For example, when it came down to making the choice between traveling to visit friends while abroad in Brazil or taking rigorous classes, I chose to travel because I didn't know the next time I'd be in Brazil.

I don't think I'm very different from many other students.

If you've never won a prize in school, it doesn't mean that you can't win a fellowship.

All you need is a dream and a passion. The rest is strategy. You may crave travel, but feel like it's out of your reach. I am here to tell you that it's not.

My original dream was to go to Senegal and study Sabar, the traditional dance from that region of West Africa. My mother passed that passion down to me. My first memories include performing with my parents at age five in a modified, black sports bra decorated with cowry shells. I had been studying West African dance with her for about eighteen years when I applied for the Fulbright. Dance was always something I did in addition to my academics and professional development. It was never the focus of my life, but it anchored me throughout all of my other interests.

After my first year of college, I went to study Sabar with the family of Aziz Faye, a dance teacher in the United States. In general, West African dance incorporates fluid—but exuberant—arm and leg movements. It's more jumpy than dance in southern and eastern Africa. Sabar is even jumpier, with your legs flying as high as your ears, and staccato arms slicing through the air. As a gangly, twelve-year-old girl, my initial encounter with this particular dance form was love at first jump. Our family was at a dance camp that Aziz had organized in Los Angeles. The challenges of the more complex rhythms and odd time signatures enraptured me, while it felt natural to use my long legs to fly through the air. In Senegal, my love of the art form grew because I met the wonderful people who carried its tradition. The young and old all gathered to dance and celebrate, showing off talent and passion in the form of a living and vibrant legacy. Taking this leap of faith, going alone to an unknown country and traveling—literally and figuratively—way outside of my comfort zone, laid the groundwork for my future.

Despite never having won so much as an essay prize in school before, I applied for a fellowship that was way out of my league: the Kiva Microfinance Fellows Program. After leveraging the few experiences I had and researching the fellowship thoroughly, they offered me the position. But instead of posting me in Senegal, they sent me to Cameroon. This serendipitous turn of events changed the course of my life by setting me on the fellowships path, introducing me to my love, and kindling a sense of self-direction that I never had before.

After the Kiva fellowship, which gave me confidence and ignited my interest, I started looking into other opportunities. I researched my college's fellowship programs, which were notoriously successful at turning out scholars. During my two years on the Smith College campus, I had heard about the program and wondered what the hoopla was about. Thinking it was a long shot, I attended an information session.

Although the Smith program was completely voluntary and extra-curricular (albeit a very demanding extra-curricular), I think the skills I learned about applying for fellowships from program director Don Andrew were the most valuable and tangible proficiencies I gained from my whole college experience.

**All the scholarships and awards I have
since won have built upon one another.**

I couldn't have gotten into Cornell if I hadn't been a Fulbright Scholar, and I wouldn't have been a Fulbright Scholar if I hadn't been a Kiva Fellow and won other prizes and grants. This prestige and monetary payoff has done more for me than any of my college classes. I neither consider myself smarter than other people, nor am I a particularly great student. It was all in the help I received learning how to write applications.

Writing this book is my way of paying it forward, giving the gift of knowledge to all those who don't have access to fellowship advisors. Friends and unknown peers have approached me for help on applications. Since both Smith and Cornell list my name on their fellowship websites, students at both schools ask me to give them advice or read and review their applications. I'm always happy to provide this service because I benefitted from many generous peer and faculty revisions. I was fortunate to get the chance to work with an excellent fellowships advisor, which was one of the best experiences of my entire college career. Had I not pursued this option at school, I would be living a different (and far less engaging) life right now.

"The best (Fulbright) advice was to be yourself and they will love you for who you are. So I tried to speak with my heart and it worked. Don't be afraid also of being creative. Fulbright is not only about academics...I think it's more than that!"

—**Bénédicte Nègre Vermongen**, Professeur de
FLE et de Lettres Modernes and former Fulbright Scholar

"Pay attention to those things that you can identify as bringing you happiness, contentment, and piquing your interest. What makes you so giddy your knees shake? What are you reading about or doing in your free time? These reflections can just as easily come from times when you're not doing the right things as when you are. Don't be afraid to blaze new trails—the perfect job for you might be something that you need to create for yourself. This won't come overnight, but don't be afraid to use all your other experiences to dream up

and work towards your goals, even if they might lead you off the beaten track."

—**Gemina Garland-Lewis**, former Thomas J. Watson Fellow and National Geographic Society Young Explorer Grantee

"Challenge yourself. If you're going to apply for a scholarship to study overseas, select a country that is less traveled. In your lifetime, you will have plenty of opportunities to visit France or England, but how often will you be able to go to Mali or Guyana? Studying in a less obvious place will enrich your life in ways you cannot foresee."

—**Artis Henderson**, former Rotary Ambassadorial Scholar

"Before going abroad, I wish I knew that there are so many different scholarship opportunities! Coming from a society where scholarships are few and far between, I had no idea about the range of scholarships one can apply for in the United States, and that it is indeed possible to receive scholarships and grants!"

—**Vidhee Garg**, Scholarship recipient at Mumbai University and Cornell University

I used all my friends' advice when I was in the beginning stages of dreaming about where my life might lead with a fellowship. One of the most important pieces of advice I can pass on to you is to be yourself: write with passion and enthusiasm about what you want to do; it will make you a unique applicant. You'll learn how to do this in Chapter 2, when you build up the enthusiasm and combine it with the details of your dreaming process in Chapter 4, like Gemina and Artis encourage. It is possible to win grants and fellowships, as Vidhee reassures. This book is a practical and inspirational guide, and whether you want help with the entire process, or just tips on specific elements, *Funded!* will help you succeed.

SECTION ONE

FIND YOUR STORY AND YOUR PURPOSE

The next three chapters will help you prepare emotionally and mentally for the process of applying for fellowships, scholarships, and grants. This work is not mandatory; perhaps you already have a good sense of where you come from and what you want to do, but these are some tips I've developed with the help of friends and mentors to help you clarify your personal mission.

CHAPTER TWO

TELL YOUR STORY

I n this chapter, you will explore your passions and learn how to tell your story in a way that supports what you want to do. If you want to teach a kids' program, describe how your background made you care about youth education and how you've pursued this field in your other work. If you want to study science in Argentina, talk about what made you passionate about science and why Argentina is the most logical place for you to go. All applications need a good personal story that grabs the reader's attention and clearly paints a picture of you as the perfect candidate.

"Be coherent. Always know where you want to go with your story and don't go astray. Make sure that the story is something the reader can relate to. The best storytellers are those who can connect with their audience. Don't

be afraid to add personal tidbits; lend your personality to your story. Make it unique."

—**Vidhee Garg**, Scholarship recipient
at Mumbai University and Cornell University

"Demonstrate your passion for the specific work and commitment to give back to society, that's how it worked for me."

—**Shweta Dhoubhadel**, Sustainable Development Professional
and former Fulbright Scholar

Connect with Your Audience

Caroline was a Fulbright Scholar in Azerbaijan and has since worked for the United Nations in New York and started her own non-profit in Eastern Europe. From the first day I met her, I was so impressed by how well she knew her origins. Her mother had moved to Hawaii when she was pregnant to give birth in the ocean with the dolphins. Her father had conducted his own Fulbright research in the Middle East while finishing a PhD. They lived in a tree house on the island of Molokai and her strict Christian upbringing led her to start college at a California school that outlawed dancing, citing a Biblical ban on having that kind of fun. This is how she explains her drive:

About what has always helped motivate me, I guess that I've always tried to surround myself with inspirational people. It sounds cliché, but I strongly believe in the Law of Attraction, and how it can be such a positive force for expansion. Another motivation stems from the influence of growing up in Hawaii, which was truly formative to helping me contextualize a purpose for my life. I was raised in a small shack without electricity in the jungle. I was raised alongside the indigenous islanders, most of whom lived under the poverty line and were socially and economically disadvantaged. At an early age, I came to the realization that if I wanted to create positive change in my community, I would first have to start with myself. It was this affinity that helped me to develop a passion for empowering individuals and communities, so that they are better able to participate fully in society and influence their own development.

Caroline cheerfully and doggedly articulates her determination to make a positive impact in the world. Having a purpose seems to give her joy and helps make roadblocks surmountable. Of course, this is my interpretation and, like anyone else, she probably feels discouragement from setbacks; but knowing where she comes from and where she's going directs her life goals.

The Personal Narrative

The personal narrative offers the strongest connection you can make with other people. Learning how to tell this story is one of the first obstacles to achieving your dreams. Like most stories, a personal history makes the most sense and is easiest to follow if it's told in a chronological, linear way. To uncover how this story begins, you must look at where you are presently and then work backwards to see how events linked together to get to your present circumstance. Reliving events, incidents, and experiences in your life can be a fun and instructive exercise. These meaningful moments help you make sense of life experiences, and can even uncover universal truths about the lessons you've learned by enabling you to glean insights you had not formerly identified.

> **Eventually, sorting through your past helps you learn important things about who you are and who you would like to be.**

The process of remembering events in your life often results in a cascade of forgotten experiences that can be tied together to make a cohesive story. These tangible moments also help you tell a more vivid story about yourself. Caroline could have vaguely alluded to her unique upbringing, but she instead chose to describe her parents' backgrounds and what it felt like to be a child growing up on Molokai.

My father's words, "I encourage you to go make the world a more beautiful place," will always be formative. Born deep in a jungle over a waterfall in Hawaii, I was raised without electricity on Molokai, an island untouched by even traffic lights. I spent my nights with my father, a Princeton PhD who ran for Congress, and my mother, a former Peace Corps volunteer, reading books by candlelight and listening to National Public Radio. Drawn to the Middle East because of the lullabies in Arabic that I heard my father—a former Fulbright Fellow to Jordan—sing to me as a little girl, I spent a semester abroad in Egypt.

Your specific story makes you more interesting, and helps those people who are reading your application relate to you more easily.

Acknowledge the Problems

Acknowledging your problems and failings makes you a stronger, more resilient human being. I know how devastating life's low points can be, but sometimes after I've come through them, I realize that life's highlights wouldn't be as great if I didn't have the comparative lows. As psychology professor and gratitude expert Dr. Robert Emmons explains:

> [T]elling people simply to buck up, count their blessings, and remember how much they still have to be grateful for can certainly do much harm. Processing a life experience through a grateful lens does not mean denying negativity. It is not a form of superficial happiology. Instead, it means realizing the power you have to transform an obstacle into an opportunity. It means reframing a loss into a potential gain, recasting negativity into positive channels for gratitude.[1]

I gradually learned how to put Emmons' lesson into practice in my own life. For example, when I was pregnant, I was extremely tired and had frequent headaches. Now, when I have some energy and my head is clear, I take a moment to give thanks for my health. When I didn't get the Fulbright the first time I

---

1   "How Gratitude Can Help You Through Hard Times," Robert Emmons, accessed June 10, 2015, http://greatergood.berkeley.edu/article/item/how_gratitude_can_help_you_through_hard_times.

applied, I was temporarily devastated, having worked so hard on the application and visualizing how success would feel. Yet, I eventually came around to view the rejection as a motivational catalyst to do better the second time around. Allowing space for failure has subsequently enhanced my motivation. I had realistic expectations, knowing that I would be lucky to win a Fulbright. I don't base my self-worth upon any one achievement. I will achieve my end-goal in some other way even if my current method does not work out. Like when I wanted to study dance in Senegal, I applied for the Fulbright, but I also applied for other grants and scholarships. My chances were slim, so I did not put all my eggs into one basket. Instead, I figured out a couple different ways to reach my goal.

TIP: Because I don't expect to be successful all the time, I feel liberated to go full force into my ambitions.

Your Narrative Arc

Start by jotting down all the experiences that relate to your story. Create your story map, even possibly going so far as to make little pictures to help you align the beginning, the conflict, the climax, and the resolution of your tale. Connecting these pictures together will reveal the chronological series of events that perfectly explains who you are today and where you are going. Building this history makes your future trajectory more evident as well.

When I was writing my personal statement about dance, I knew that I wanted to explain how I was positioned to be the perfect dance scholar in Senegal. I wrote on a notepad all the highlights in my life that related to Senegalese dance: performing at the age of five with my parents; hosting African dance guest teachers in our family home; traveling to African dance camps across the country; traveling to Senegal after my freshman year at college; spending my junior year break in Senegal again; and all the dance performances, volunteering, and guest teaching I had done in the interim.

My background created a very logical story for the reader, which showed how qualified I was for the project I proposed.

I learned this skill from reading other successful proposals, in which the personal statement made it obvious that the applicant's entire life had led up to this moment of getting the Fulbright.

"Whether you know it or not, you have a story. You have something that makes you unique. What about your experience in this life sets you apart? (Go with your gut here—overthinking this will likely get you nowhere.) What gives you a new perspective on a topic, a project, or an opportunity? What about you shows how you would truly engage in a new experience or tackle a new problem?"
—**Gemina Garland-Lewis**, former Thomas J. Watson Fellow and National Geographic Society Young Explorer Grantee

You may be having a hard time identifying how your story fits together at the moment. If this is the case, ask yourself, "What do I love doing?" Or, "What is my underlying motivation for doing this project?" As I mentioned, when I was first applying for scholarships, I knew that I just wanted to get back to Senegal to dance, but I didn't think that asking for money to just dance was a worthy or credible request. I kept trying to think of what I thought would be valid purposes for getting to Senegal, knowing that if I could just get there under some other pretense, I could dance on the side. It took months and a significant amount of external validation from my mentor for me to finally realize that I could just ask for money to do what I wanted to do: dance. Think about what you truly want to do and, most likely, that is the thing for which you will be most qualified.

**Personal Statement from my successful
2009 Fulbright application:**

Creating a Sabar dance program in Senegal will extend what I came to know growing up in a dance community. My good fortune to experience the success of artists—both my parents and those my family sponsored—ingrained in me the importance of having a consistent dance space and program within which people can flourish, as I would like to establish in Dakar. My apparently diverse interests, spanning economics, travel, languages, dance, and community engagement, are related. As I've explored each of these aspects of myself, I've come to understand that their synthesis formulates a successful community.

Being raised in a dance community, the rhythms of the drums I danced to as a child reverberate in every step I take. From the age of three, I've trained in ballet, modern, jazz, Middle Eastern, samba, and folklórico. My mother taught me Haitian and West African dance, as she has done with others for over twenty-five years in Santa Fe, New Mexico. My ardor for West African dance took me to Senegal in 2006, where I found that Sabar is the dance that belongs in my body. As a future dance teacher, I will continue to study West African dance and I am committed to upholding the traditions of the communities that formed me.

My experience has taught me that artistic endeavors are really community endeavors. Dance, by nature, is a community undertaking, making me an advocate for supporting my local and extended communities. In Santa Fe, I am bringing education about sustainability to public schools with Earth Care International. I was a teen fundraiser and ambassador to the Bioneers Conference for Warehouse 21, a teen arts center. In summer 2009, I organized and administered the Go Green Africa conservation education project in Cameroon.

My interest in social structures and artistic communities led me to understand that economics is fundamental to social justice and wellbeing, so I studied economics at Smith College. My personal interest in making my passion a feasible profession necessitated an understanding of finances. I was a Kiva Microfinance Fellow in Cameroon, acting as a liaison, field journalist, and internal auditor.

My life-long interest in culture, and my travels to Africa and South America have shown me that forging relationships and connections with people I've met is the most valuable experience in life. To better communicate and further myself in Senegal and abroad, I started studying languages. Speaking the native language not only cultivates trust; it will also help me to conduct the academic research needed to complete my project. Language, dance, and music create common cultural and personal understanding between global citizens.

Because my family has hosted many West African artists, I've seen the value of enduring personal relationships with artists. Watching my mother create and sustain an evolving community helped form my personal capacity for leadership. My skills as a listener help me facilitate a vision that is grander than my own individual idea. As idealistic as I am, I am also results oriented, and my passion drives me into situations where I need to be flexible and self-reliant, while still depending on other people. My love for Sabar and my personal history uniquely prepare me and give me the tenacity to see this project to fruition.

I know that I stand to benefit enormously from the opportunity to experience a Fulbright scholarship in Senegal. I've had the great good fortune to be formed as an artist and as a human being in a nurturing African dance community. Through this fellowship, it's my intention to help be part of a collaboration that provides the same kind of opportunity for Senegalese and foreign artists and academics to grow and prosper in the Sabar community.

What eventually seemed like a very obvious path leading me to a Fulbright Fellowship to study dance in Senegal was completely unknown to me at the beginning of my application process. It took a lot of soul searching and a very wonderful mentor to help me discover this thread that ties my life together. Up until that point, I had just been doing the things I loved to do (along with the things I had to do), and somehow all these activities added up to make a complete picture. I've followed the unifying thread of dance into multiple other aspects of my life, but since my Fulbright experience, I've also found other threads that have taken me on interesting and fulfilling explorations. I now intentionally follow the things that interest me because I know they tie together somehow in the end.

Where do you come from? This can include everything from where geographically you and/or your parents were raised to what core beliefs you have. Write down what constitutes your background.

_____
_____
_____
_____

What are your traditions? Do you regularly perform spiritual or physical rituals? Think about their origins and why you continue to do them.

_____
_____
_____
_____

What do you want to do in this world? Which people or things do you care most deeply about serving? Is it your home community, kids, the environment, animals? If you have a deep-seated desire to help this entity, you will be a much more convincing and credible applicant.

_____

_____

_____

What motivates you? How—and why—have you overcome adversity or specific challenges? Was it an altruistic drive to right an injustice, or an opportunistic motivation, like getting experience so that you can get a better job? Identify your underlying motivations so you can tap into them for inspiration. It helps if you can pinpoint specific instances where you felt this motivation and can recall the sequence of events.

_____

_____

_____

Where do you want to go? This could include a literal, geographic destination, but you should, more importantly, describe where in your life you want to be in five or ten years. What do you envision yourself doing in the near and far future? Envision a goal so you can create a story that moves from your background/origins, to where you are currently, and finally, to where you are going. This will be your story's arc.

_____

_____

_____

Can you begin to see how your motivation can be traced to your background? Can you connect your future goals to what you want to do in the world? How have your traditions informed the actions you take? Answering these questions will help you begin to build the résumé of your life and the elements that you can draw upon to create your application profile.

Your Angle

Even if you're not aware of it, you tell stories about yourself. We all do. In choosing *how* you tell your stories, you also choose *where* your path takes you. In writing this book, I've uncovered some elements of my own story that I didn't realize I held. For example, I used to think that I could not write and that I could not remember stories about myself. The ways you describe yourself socially and internally relate back to the story you hold, deep inside, to be true. To begin uncovering this story for myself, I had to look at where I was in the moment:

- What am I doing with my life?
- What are my priorities?
- What do I love to do?

From there, I looked back into my past to uncover how I came to my current situation and where my values came from. Finally, I asked:

- Where in my life were the turning points?

If you're anything like me, your story may start to look like a zigzag smorgasbord of unrelated events and activities. It helps me to focus on one individual thread at a time. For example, I have danced throughout my life, but it has had nothing to do with my interest in social activism. I have histories in both areas, but I have to consider the dance story separately from the social activism story; otherwise, the picture gets too garbled and I can't make a coherent storyline. Beyond being useful for writing personal statements on applications, I think understanding how you see yourself and letting go of harmful beliefs about yourself make for important spiritual and self-esteem-building work.

Soul-searching for what you want to do with your life:

"I'm going to give a personal account here: Every time I'm approaching or I cross a major milestone in life, I question myself, my decisions, my existence. Then I panic, cry, moan, and complain. Then I realize that what I want is to be happy, and that I'm the only one that can make myself happy. That gives me the strength to question myself, and I start to find answers. And I look everywhere for answers, literally.

This happened when (1) I graduated college; (2) I'd been working for two years after college, and wanted to do something else with my life; (3) I entered grad school; (4) I finished grad school and was looking for jobs; and (5) I'd been at my first job after grad school for over six months, and I felt constrained.

I ask myself three questions: Why am I unhappy? What can make me happy? How can I get there?

And then I brainstorm, scribble, read, and write. It helps me when I read biographies, some select self-help books, and write down important thoughts. It helps me chart a path, know where I'm headed, and how I can get there. Most importantly, it helps me realize that there is always a way, if I look hard enough. I can do great things with my life, irrespective of where I am. I just need to think.

Have a ten-year plan, but make sure you leave room for exploration, and room to grow laterally."

—**Vidhee Garg**, Scholarship recipient at
Mumbai University and Cornell University

Make an Effort and Clear the Way

Not only must you focus on what you are attracted to; you must also start to make the effort towards achieving it. The way to truly ask for what you want from the universe is to put yourself in the position to receive it. I mean put aside all the petty things that don't matter as much and take the lead in making your goal come true.

I graduated from college in 2009, which, due to the collapsed economy, was probably the worst year to start a professional career in recent history. Jobs were scarce. I applied for a couple of positions and unpaid internships, and received no offers. I decided to devote all my attention to getting funding for my Go Green Africa project that summer in Cameroon. In my free time, I researched and applied for grants to get money. It turned out that this project was perfect for a prize from Smith College. This was the first grant or prize where I received money for a project of mine and it ended up being a major stepping stone on the way to getting a Rotary Scholarship (which was also my ticket to getting a Fulbright).

My friend took another route to getting a job. She went to Monster.com, Craigslist, and any other online job-finding website she could find and sent out her résumé for every possible opening. She was looking for work in New York City— one of the better job markets in the country at that time—but she wasn't getting any bites. I recall one day at lunch when she reported back to our group of friends that she'd had a slightly perplexing interview that morning for a secretarial position at an electrician's office. "When they asked me why I wanted to work there, I didn't really have a reason," she recalled. Of course she didn't! She was studying government, had traveled internationally, and spoke three languages, but had no interest or experience as an electrician's secretary.

After sending out hundreds and hundreds of résumés for weeks on end, her parents finally told her that she should take a break because she was wearing herself out. If nothing worked out by the end of the semester, they would support her until she found something. I think that focusing your intention and making time for the thing you really want to do brings better results. If my friend had stopped focusing on just getting any job and instead figured out what she really wanted to do, she probably would have found a job sooner.

My husband tells a story about his Catholic boarding school in Cameroon, where the night before final exams, students would pray for good grades. This is a humorous story because no higher power or universal force can work entirely on its own. You must take responsibility for the trajectory of your life and show some effort. In addition, focusing on the scarcity in your life will never bring abundance. Someone who just complains about how unfair the world is can never expect his or her situation to change. Instead, by acknowledging and being grateful for the things you do have in your life, you show that you deserve more good things. I've found this to be true on a personal level with friends and family, but this gratefulness and humility is immensely valuable in the application process, too.

> **When I write applications, I always mention how lucky**
> **I am to have had the opportunities to go to college and**
> **graduate school, and to study abroad on fellowships.**

In addition, I try to strike a careful balance between humility and confidence when mentioning my qualifications for grants, while also describing how I would benefit from the award. People respond well to someone who acknowledges the positive things in his or her life. Who likes to spend time with a friend who complains all the time? Nobody. You—and the people around you—become happier when you dwell on what you have, not on what you lack.

Describe three definitive events in your life that relate to your field of interest. Choose one from each period of your life: formative years (ages 1–10), adolescent years (ages 10–20), and young adult years (ages 20–30).

1. _____

_____

_____

2. _____
_____
_____
_____

3. _____
_____
_____
_____

Now describe a component of your current work that relates to your field of interest.

_____
_____
_____
_____
_____
_____

Tie the three period examples together in a chronological string, culminating with your current work to create the sequence of your story.

_____
_____
_____
_____
_____

From the exercises and anecdotes in this chapter, put together your own story. Start by describing what you want to do with you life. Then, trace that interest back into your past and possibly into your family's traditions. Did you overcome a struggle that instilled a passion for your work at a young age? **Describe how it felt to come through that challenge and how your subsequent actions directly resulted from this moment.** Then, draw that interest out into the future you see for yourself. Tell the reader about the definitive moments that made you who you are. You now have a rough draft of the personal essay that will accompany many of your applications. Test out your story on someone you trust, ask him or her how it sounds, and clarify as needed. In the next chapter, you'll learn how to prepare yourself for the process of going after your dreams. It took time for me to build the confidence and support I needed to be where I am today. Learn from my mistakes and get funded faster!

CHAPTER THREE

PERSONAL TRANSFORMATION— HOW IT HAPPENED

"I wish I knew that the experience is always transformative—even if it's not always fun. Going abroad can be difficult—there's homesickness, and illness, and the struggles of adapting to a new place. But each of these things changes us as a person—for the better, I believe. It's good to remember that your life will be richer when it's all done, even if in the moment things seem rough."

—**Artis Henderson**, former Rotary Ambassadorial Scholar

"Believe in yourself! Nothing is impossible. If you want something badly enough, and if you work hard enough for it, you will get there. Dream big. But again, this has to come from within."

—**Vidhee Garg**, Scholarship recipient at
Mumbai University and Cornell University

Y ears after we graduated from college, one of my best friends confided in me that, among our group of friends, I had changed the most since we were freshmen. At age eighteen, I thought it was not cool to try too hard in school or with friends. A hard shell had built up to guard my sensitive, curious, and enthusiastic nature, obscuring my genuine self. This particular friend helped me start to crack that exterior. "Sally is scared to talk in front of you. She feels like anytime she says something, you shut her down." I had not realized that just three months into college I was in danger of losing the close friends I had. I did not even realize I was lashing out at the people I loved. Thanks to her honest and gentle feedback, I started to soften and trust that my friends were not constantly searching out my flaws.

I recovered my self-esteem in large part because of the wonderful friends I made at college. This confidence bloomed through positive encouragement from teachers, like my Portuguese advisor, who asked if we could visit and check in when I started missing my morning class. These same teachers believed that I had a shot at winning a Fulbright when I first applied, in turn making me believe I could do it. Even though it took perseverance and applying twice to eventually get the Fulbright, I became a more resilient person because of my struggle.

My friend's shared insight was a really kind and genuine statement. I'm somewhat surprised when I think back to how I was as an eighteen year old that I lucked out with such a great group of friends from the very first days of school. I wouldn't be the person I am today, more loving and compassionate, without their support. I think my friends were the beginning of the transformation that led me to being a successful candidate for the Fulbright and other awards.

"While it's important not to be consumed with comparing yourself to others ('Just look at what they accomplished by the time they were my age! I shouldn't even bother!'), knowing more about what others do can definitely help inspire us to develop and pursue our own passions ('Wow! They did something I find really inspiring—maybe there is a way for me to pursue this after all!').

To be fair, some people are much more driven by competition than collaboration, but in my experience you'll always get the best results in the end—in all parts of your life—with collaboration. You might strive to accomplish something to do it better than anyone else has done, and this can be great fuel. Just be sure that you're conscious along the way that building bridges is much more important than burning them."

—**Gemina Garland-Lewis**, former Thomas J. Watson Fellow and National Geographic Society Young Explorer Grantee

Affirmations

In my college dorm, there was a girl who was a saccharine optimist. She was part of the Ada Comstock Scholars program, which admits students of non-traditional age into Smith. She was about four years older than everyone else in the house, but her frilly bed skirt, bubble gum pink wardrobe, and pink, rhinestone-bedazzled cell phone (à la Paris Hilton) made her seem more like a teenager. Upon first meeting Angel, you might cringe and expect you knew everything about her, but once you spent more time with her, you'd find that her sincere happiness and joy for life were contagious. Each house at Smith (they called both the dorms and the converted New England houses, *houses*) had its own unique character. Sessions House was one of the oldest buildings in all of Northampton, built around 1700, with horse-hair insulation, which resulted in a thirty-second burn time (meaning the house would burn to the ground in thirty seconds if it caught on fire). The secret staircase built into the house was for escaping Indian raids on the settlement from that era. Most of the residents of current-day Sessions were more often crunchy, alternative, lesbian types. I fit right in with my dyed and braided hair, Birkenstocks, and henna tattoos. Angel didn't fit in at all, but somehow she'd been placed there with the other thirty of us.

The thing I liked most about Angel was that she decorated the downstairs bathroom with positive mantras. Cut out of colorful craft paper, or drawn in curly crayon letters were affirmations like, **"I am strong," "I deserve love,"** and **"I am healthy and happy."** I don't know if I'd ever seen mantras before, but it struck me that saying these positive things about myself—especially in the mirror—could be a powerful practice. Angel's bathroom mantras planted a seed in me. Two years later, when I was working on my first Fulbright application as a senior, I wrote affirmations of why I believed in myself in my journal.

> Saturday September 13, 2008: This weekend I'm finalizing the proposal and personal statement to go over again on Tuesday with Susan to have approved by Donald by the 22nd. After that, all I have to do is my language evaluation, get a sponsor in Senegal, and fill out the online part of the app. It's so close. All my friends and family are convinced I'm going to get it. It's mine. They're proud of me already. I deserve it. I've worked harder on this than I've worked on anything in my life and my heart and soul are in it and I'm the perfect person to get it. It's mine. I'm winning this Fulbright. My proposal is going to win. I've been revising and fine-tuning it for two months. It's rock-solid. I will make it work.

A couple of months later, I wrote some inspirational advice that I heard from Sarah Jones, an actress who came to campus for Otelia Cromwell Day at Smith. These themes have come back into my life time and again as I keep reminding myself about who I want to be.

Saturday, November 8, 2008: On Thursday I was having a really hard day with my friends but it was Otelia Cromwell Day, so there were some amazingly inspiring women here, including Sarah Jones, the amazing actress from New York, who I knew about because she sponsored Equality Now. They said some powerful things that I need to remember.

- Shine
- Be Recognized
- Have Limits
- Love Myself
- Enjoy Myself
- Take Care of Myself
- Respect Others
- Listen to What is Needed
- Listen to Feedback
- Do What I Love

One of the environmental activists also said something really powerful to one of her audiences:

"Don't Waste Me."

I've been doing a job search for next year and made an affirmation poster from adjectives I saw in job descriptions for positions I want. They are:

- Passionate
- Intelligent
- Resilient
- Humorous
- Tenacious
- Humble
- Graceful
- Warm
- Energetic

These are the adjectives I want for myself.

Write three adjectives that you want people to use to describe you:

_____

_____

_____

Now write down a compliment that someone has given you recently. It can be about anything: how you look, one of your qualities, or about an action you took, like helping a friend:

_____

_____

_____

Beginning to write these affirmations was a big turning point in my life. A couple of years ago I got a letter in the mail from myself as a seventeen year old. My high school has a practice in which the seniors go on a class retreat before the start of their last year. At some point during our camping trip into the Pecos Wilderness back in 2004, we all sat down and wrote letters to ourselves about our expectations. One letter would be handed back to us at the end of our senior year and the other would be sent to us in the mail more than five years in the future. Here's what I wrote in the first letter:

Mainly, my hope for myself in the next year is to find something unique about myself that I am proud of and that I like. I hope that I find respect for my friends and they find something in me that they respect because at the moment, I don't have that. The final thing that I can think to remind myself about is not to get discouraged about not getting into some of the colleges I apply to. It is inevitable to get rejected from some schools, so don't let that become a huge mental barrier on the road to success. I know, for myself, some of the small disappointments in my life have made a huge impression on my self-esteem and confidence. So don't let that happen. It is only college and I will be happy almost anywhere I end up.

I only got into one of the colleges to which I applied (University of Vermont) and I was waitlisted at Smith. It took being waitlisted to really make me know that I wanted to go to Smith. I wrote them another letter and had another teacher send them a strong encouraging recommendation after that. Finally, they accepted me.

The second letter that I sent to myself as a college graduate, which arrived out of the blue one day, said things like, "I don't know if you'll have any friends" and "I don't know what you have done with your life." I assume I was trying to sound mature and not overconfident, but reading myself as a teenager made me sad. I didn't have confidence enough to even assume that I'd have friends, let alone have achieved anything. If I could have gone back and hugged myself, I would have. I wish I had been able to be gentler with myself at that tender age, but by the end of high school I was so guarded about expressing who I was that I didn't have that ability. Even now, it takes constantly reminding myself that I can only be a good friend and family member to others if I'm a good friend to myself. I need to love myself first in order to love others and receive the love around me. These are life-long lessons that I think everyone has to work on, so I'm forgiving when I forget and tell myself mean things.

"I'm a big believer in this: Everyone has their good times, and their bad. If you're doing everything right and nothing is happening, it's probably just a

bad time. Be patient and persistent, and the good times will come along and soon enough, things will start to happen."

—**Vidhee Garg**, Scholarship recipient at
Mumbai University and Cornell University

My Journal Entry from Monday, April 13, 2009:

I found out today that I didn't get my Fulbright. I thought I would be devastated and think that my life was going to end, but after hyperventilating for a few minutes and walking towards Don's office [to tell him the news], I became calm and just began to reassure myself that everything would be fine.

Last Wednesday I found out that I wasn't going to get the money from Mountain Dew for my other project. I had been a finalist but I just didn't get enough votes to win. I took that news much worse. I cried on my bed for an hour, and then I erased my Facebook photo and laid on the floor sobbing with my door locked and lights off. Finally I called Okwen and cried about how nothing was going to work out. I really upset and scared him because he didn't feel like any of his attempts to appease me were helping. I said that I didn't know if I would live if I didn't get the Fulbright, which really hurt him. I made him feel like his love wasn't enough for me, which he told me later and which made me feel absolutely terrible. I dreaded hearing back from the Fulbright because if I didn't win with 1 in 2 chances [with Mountain Dew], how could I possibly win with 1 in 7 chances [with the Fulbright]?

Yesterday I went to Easter service and the sermon was about feeling how the love of God and those around us holds us up higher and makes us stronger. The Pope yesterday talked about the light of God being a gift and it made me remember my light that I envisioned shining through me when I prepared to go to Cameroon and how I couldn't wait to shine my light on all the new people I would meet in Cameroon last summer. I tried to remember how to be a beam of light as I walked around this morning, even before I found out about the news.

When I called Okwen to tell him [he was the first person I called], I was calm and upbeat. He was expecting a breakdown at any minute, I could tell, because he kept telling me that everything was going to be alright, not to cry, just to stay focused and to please not do anything to myself. He said he loved me so much. I then told mom and she said she wasn't upset if I wasn't upset and that a ticket to Cameroon would be more expensive but that she'd come visit anyway. I told her she was going to have to meet Okwen's family sometime anyway. I just told her that I had been reading this memoir of a child soldier in Sierra Leone (A Long Way Gone by Ishmael Beah) and it made my life look really good. I told her I was so grateful for all the things I have and it just means that whatever I do next, I'll just do better.

When I told Abby, Elizabeth, and Kearney at lunch, I explained that I just saw this as a learning experience that gave me a lot of feedback and that I'm really happy for those others who did get it. That this could just give me time to breathe and time to be with Okwen, and for him to get a really good start to his career. Elizabeth said she couldn't believe how well behaved I was and reflective so early after hearing. Kearney said she never would have guessed that I hadn't gotten it just by my reaction, by the way I was holding myself, and what a strong woman I was. Abby said that I should just continue to shine the light that I shine because I am so beautiful and wonderful things would come to me! Last night too, Caroline was saying that people liked me so easily because I win them over soon after meeting them with the "Lucy Light" that I shine wherever I go! They both could see my light!! I'm still shining, even though I've been having such a hard time lately! I was so happy to just have my friends at that point.

I clearly recall the day that I finally did receive the Fulbright a year later. I was preparing to go to dance class on a Saturday morning. Because of the farmer's market next door to the dance studio, I walked over instead of taking my car. Everyone else in the house had already left for class and I was rushing out at the last minute. I had picked out a festive outfit just because I was happy it was spring (an early April day): a hot pink shirt with a hot pink and white skirt that made me feel bright and pretty. I was rushing out the door towards the front gate when I saw that the mail had been delivered early that day. The mailbox was full, but a larger-than-normal envelope was folded over and sticking out above the rest of the contents. **I registered the envelope from afar because of its size, but then I started to wonder what a large manila envelope might contain.** It couldn't be anything from school, because I had graduated the year before. Then, all of a sudden, I realized that this would be about the time that I would be hearing back from Fulbright. As with college applications, the receipt of a large return envelope is a positive sign, while a small envelope is usually a negative sign (although this was not true with my acceptance as a Rotary Scholar). This was it! My heart started racing as it took more cosmic time than chronological time for me to walk from the door to the mailbox.

I picked up the envelope and saw the return address from the Institute of International Education (IIE), which administers the Fulbright program. Unlike the long span of time it took me to register the envelope's contents, I hardly remember how I got back inside the house. Tearing open the envelope, I pulled out an unfolded letter that started out, "We would like to congratulate you on your acceptance to the Fulbright program."

I started laughing and crying at the same time, hardly able to withstand the joy of the moment. I immediately called Okwen and was crying, "I got it! I got the Fulbright." I couldn't believe it; I was sobbing, but I had worked so hard for this. Barely taking the time to dry my tears of joy, I ran to my mom's dance class, eager to tell her the good news. Everyone was prepared to start, but I ran up to her and said, "I got it!!" Tears welled up in her eyes as she gave me a big hug and my sister-in-law, Nicole, came over to hug me too.

To explain the celebration, my mom turned to the class and said, "Both of my children are amazing. Lucy just found out she got a Fulbright." Everyone clapped as I began to settle into a haze of not really understanding what this meant for my life. I was so overwhelmed, but also wanted to relish in the moment of accepting the gift into my life and being with all the people I love most at my mom's class. I danced in a daze of gratitude for the rest of class and for the rest of that day.

Giving to Receive

The world works by the law of giving and receiving. Just as energy cannot be created or destroyed, the energy that we want to receive must be expended at some time. Giving may seem like the harder part of the equation, but actually receiving is a skill that we have to learn as well. Learning how to receive is in part learning that you deserve the things you work for. If you allow yourself to believe in yourself, you start to open the possibility that your desired objective will come to you. **This is a process of visualization. How would it feel to open that fellowship acceptance letter?** How would it feel to be working abroad or studying the thing you most want to study? Giving yourself permission to envision the perfect future without having doubt in yourself is one of the first steps to receiving that gift. To receive also means to be open to seeing opportunities come our way. This is a skill to be able to recognize when we have an opportunity coming to us. Sometimes it's really obvious, but other times it's not.

When was the last time you were disappointed? Did you apply for a job and not get it? Did you tryout for a team and not get picked? What was the situation and what disappointed you about the outcome?

_____

_____

_____

Now describe what you did in response? Did you feel angry? Hurt? Sad? Did you vow never to try again? Did you avoid all the people who love you?

_____

Now describe what transpired instead of your intended event? Did you get a different job that you loved? Did you move to a new place? Did you meet new people who you would not have met otherwise?

Look for the silver lining in your disappointments. Being able to see how events in the past worked out well, even if they weren't exactly as planned, help us have faith in the future. We can trust that disappointments are natural, but there can be hidden benefits behind them.

I never thought that I would be the type of person who would get scholarships to travel and study amazing things. **That was before I realized that winning scholarships is just a skill that can be developed.** The more you practice a skill, the better you get at it. I believe that I work hard and deserve the scholarships that I've gotten, but I believe there are many other people out there who deserve these scholarships as much as I do, but don't know that these opportunities are available to them. I don't think I am any more special or outstanding than the next person, so if I can do it, so can you. With some simple tips, practice, and reviewers, most people would have a good shot at winning some money to do what they want to do.

First, develop the confidence in yourself and start to imagine what you're capable of. Building the passion behind a project or a trip comes from dreaming up possibilities. In the next chapter, you'll take the affirmations and qualities you ascribe to yourself and make a plan. Dreaming just takes some practice, but once you learn how, you'll find it's a fun and inspiring process.

CHAPTER FOUR

LEARN HOW TO DREAM

"The world is your oyster. If you dream big, you'll get there. If you think small, you'll be stuck."

—**Vidhee Garg**, Scholarship recipient at
Mumbai University and Cornell University

W hen I was ten, our TV broke. "An act of God," my mother commented facetiously. On a stormy night, lightning struck our house and fried the poor thing. For years my parents had admonished against television watching anyway, only allowing my brother Hountor and me to watch movies. It went without saying that the machine would not be replaced. *Bored* was a dirty word in our house. "You're not 'bored,' you just haven't found what to do yet," was my mother's response in my more feckless moments. As I sat around that summer, pondering the possibilities with thirteen hours of daylight, I started daydreaming. I wished more than anything that my dad would build me a tree house. He had been a carpenter; it wasn't that he was unable. Maybe it was the lack of tall trees in our New Mexican yard. Over the years I had brought up the possibility of building some sort of platform in a juniper tree. Nothing had transpired. If only I had a tree house, I could live out the adventures of my childhood dreams!

Then it occurred to me, why couldn't I just build a tree house on my own? Yeah! I could build things; I had just seen my father remodel our house; I knew the process. A tingling itch overwhelmed me, and energy bubbled from my exponentially expanding imagination. I started moving around, fidgeting to circulate this idea fizzing in my head. I looked at our yard. The trees were still not suitable for a platform. I couldn't change that, but what about a playhouse on the ground? I sought out the pile of leftover adobe bricks from the remodel and calculated about how many were available. Just enough for an eight-foot by six-foot house, a little room for me to play.

Scouring the empty space in our packed dirt yard, I traced off the square footage and began digging a foundation. It was hard work! New Mexican earth is not soft. I soon enlisted my best friend Aaron and my little brother to help with the digging. We soaked the earth with water, eating watermelon while we waited for mud to form. Then we continued. All day for a week we dug and dug. It was finally time to start the actual building. By the end of the summer, I had convinced my whole family and Aaron to help out. My dad even got invested, going to the home improvement store to buy tarpaper for the roof and cutting custom vigas. We salvaged an old door and cut it down to ten-year-old size. As I sat on the flagstone bench, my feet resting on the brick floor I had laid over sand, and looked out the back window, I thought back to that tingling feeling that started the whole project. That was the beginning of my addiction to dreaming about—and completing—projects.

What do I mean by dreaming? I mean get back to your inner child and imagine all the things you could do if you put your mind to it. Where could you be in the next year? What could you be doing next August? The more you dream and envision possible futures, the closer you are to getting where you want to go. If you don't dream about what your favorite future would look like, then there's absolutely no way that you are going to make that vision a reality.

Put aside thirty minutes. If you want, listen to music, or something that you can tune out. Talking a walk alone is a great time to dream. Think about what you love doing. Was it something you did recently or has it been a long time? What is that thing?

_____

_____

_____

Now, imagine where you love being or where you *would* love being. Write down your ideal place:

_____

_____

_____

Can you see yourself *doing* what you love in the *place* that you love? Think about all the components: Who are you with? Where are you living? What exactly are you doing? When are you there? How did you get there? I find that once I start to think about the *where* and the *what*, the other parts come into focus.

_____

_____

_____

To start dreaming, I suggest taking some time to spend alone with your thoughts. Start by thinking about what you want to do.

- Is it a project?
- Do you want to travel?
- Study?
- If you could do anything, what would it be?

If you have had an experience in the past that you would like to revisit or recreate somewhere else, think about how the logistics of that experience made it a reality.

For anything you dream about doing, there is a high likelihood that there will be a grant or fundraising money available to do it.

It takes solidifying your mission to begin the search for the grant. Perhaps you already have a vision and that's why you're reading this book. But perhaps you just know that you want to start getting fellowships or grants and don't have a particular project in mind. I started my application for the Fulbright by just searching the things I liked to do and listing countries where those interests would apply. It can go either way.

You could also start the process by thinking about what you're already good at. As I explained earlier, it helps if you have a track record with the activity you're applying to do. Do you have experience working with kids? Or have you always been a gardener? Are you an artist? Or is mathematics your real passion? Any of these things can be combined with other components to become an excellent project or fellowship study.

"Brainstorm. Read the application requirements, and start scribbling on a blank piece of paper. Record anything and everything that comes to

mind—it could be a word, a phrase, a sentence, a graphic, a sound, absolutely anything. Let your imagination run wild, and make sure you catch most (if not everything) that's running through your mind. Then categorize these thoughts, and start approaching the application in a systematic manner."

—**Vidhee Garg**, Scholarship recipient at
Mumbai University and Cornell University

"What could you do with $10,000?" The minute I saw the email in my inbox from Smith College's career development office, my mind shot off in a dozen different directions. "Student Prize Contest winner gets $10,000 for her project; international development and health initiatives prioritized." Like a starved rabbit, the carrot of prize money got the wheels of my brain whirring. I had just been in Brazil for a year, and after that I'd been in Cameroon. I could definitely call up some of the contacts I had made to help me think of something to do with that money. What about that teacher I had met in Cameroon, who worked with the second largest middle school in Bamenda? I could do something with the kids there. What would be international development-related? Maybe teaching kids writing skills. Or, why not work on something about climate change? I knew enough about it to teach a course. I bet that would be a competitive topic.

I called Okwen, my then-fiancé. "What do you think about doing a summer program with middle-school kids, teaching them about climate change?" I asked eagerly. He has always been my sounding board for ideas, reciprocating with his own contributions and pointing out gaping holes my enthusiasm skips over.

"Well, that might work, but *what* about climate change? Are you going to teach science? You don't know very much science." That was a good point. I would probably end up teaching them the basic science and then all of the terrible ramifications of human activities. What a downer that would be! Without realizing it, I was staring at my wastebasket. **Visions of teaching eager students in a cinderblock classroom floated through my head.** I refocused my attention and saw a crumpled plastic bag in my garbage, a despised object that I almost always rejected when retrieving purchases from the store.

"What if I focused the project on educating kids about the dangers of cooking in and burning plastic bags?" I shouted out, an epiphany on my lips. That was it! That was a rationale good enough to win the prize. Never mind that, hours beforehand, I had not even thought of spending my summer that way. For the next month, I contacted schools in Cameroon, pitched my idea, and by the deadline, I had a fully formed proposal and two support letters from administrators. Little did I know that to eventually fund this project, I would have to apply for over five grants, but during the summer of 2009 my Go Green Africa middle school environmental program would teach over one hundred kids in Cameroon.

Imagine there is a $10,000 grant available for you to do anything you want. What would you do with the money?

_____

_____

_____

Now imagine that you have to convince the person giving away this money to give it to *you*. Most importantly, **why is your project the best project for this grant?** Why does it need to be done at all? Why are *you* the best person to do it? What will you accomplish that nobody else can? Bring attention to the qualities that make you unique. Who will benefit from this project?

_____

_____

_____

_____

Now, what is the breakdown for the $10,000? How and when will you use the money? Describe your general timeline and deadline for when you will be finished.

_____

_____

_____

You have just successfully completed an application form. This is how you start any application, just by jotting down notes about WHO, WHAT, WHEN, WHERE, WHY, and HOW you will accomplish what you want to do. From here, you elaborate on your goals and fine-tune your rationale to become as clear as possible for the reader.

Dreaming helps me when I try to motivate myself. Dreaming is a beautiful state of believing that anything is possible. When I think of all the things I could be doing with myself—anything in the world—I get really excited and that excitement can then propel me through the hardships of getting to my goals. Obviously, dreaming alone will not achieve anything. There has to be follow through and lots of action to make things possible. But when you have a motivating thought behind your actions, the hard moments are a lot easier. Dreaming can also be called *visioning*. Visioning can be done in groups, or individually. It's figuring out the big picture, without the details. If you get excited about a big project, like starting a school, or studying a foreign language and living in a different culture, then you can start to work out the details as they become necessary.

A key to writing successful applications is making a novel, but practical-sounding proposal. While I was working on my first applications, I thought I was somehow supposed to think of something that had *never* been done before (or at least not for a long time), but also make it fit into a ten-month research timeframe. How could these two expectations be reconciled? After talking to experts and my mentors, I learned that the reviewing boards know there's an element of illusion in these applications. They are looking for inspired and motivated young people who are a little naïve and think they can do anything. There will inevitably be things in the proposal that don't get accomplished. At the same time, if they're going to give you anywhere from a couple thousand dollars to fifty thousand dollars for a project, they want to have something to show for it and thus need some realistic expectations. You are aiming for goals that are believably accomplishable.

One way to evaluate the feasibility of your project is to conduct thorough research on similar projects.

> Many students don't have such focus, although most have some idea of the areas that interest them. Being faced with a blank piece of paper on which to describe your earth-shaking future research can seem daunting. The first step, then, is to find out what people have already done in your areas of interest. Make use of your university librarian, and be as systematic as possible. Note that no matter how clear you are about what you want to pursue, you will need to demonstrate your understanding of the existing literature. So keep track of what you read—you will be evaluated partly on the citations in your final proposal.[2]

Once I finally decided on applying for the Fulbright in dance, **I started to identify what exactly it was about dance that I loved.** At home, dancing with my Santa Fe community, I love that dance gives me a place to be with really good friends three times a week. We all dance to be happy and free our minds of the stress that can overwhelm everyday life. I also love how I push the limits of what I feel comfortable doing when I dance. I try to do a little better each time I practice, which means finding a new aspect or nuance of dance.

When I studied dance in Senegal, I loved how the traditional dance was a point of pride for people. It was something that made everyone excited, and attracted crowds on the streets. It didn't matter if some of the people were not actually *dancers*; it seemed that almost everyone knew at least a few dance moves. This heritage, which lives on in modern-day Dakar, is something that fascinates me because there is no single culture that unites people in the United States. I also knew that I wanted to be part of a family, the same way I had lived the first two times I was in Senegal. The reason I fell in love with the country was the experience of integrating with the family's daily life and learning different aspects of the culture

---

2   Michael Kiparsky, "How to Win a Graduate Fellowship," *The Chronicle of Higher Education*, May 11, 2006. Accessed May 1, 2014, http://chronicle.com/article/How-to-Win-a-Graduate/46782.

from multiple generations. How was I going to combine these interests to make a research proposal?

For one of my successful applications, I proposed to help create community dance classes like those I had grown up with. When I studied in Senegal, my classes were all private lessons. This was difficult both for me and for the teachers. For me it was hard because it was very individualized attention and didn't have the community feel that I wanted. It was also very expensive to pay for these individual lessons because I had to pay the teacher and all the drummers by myself. It was hard for the teacher because if I was not available, the class did not happen. Also, the teacher would have to spend an intensive hour with just one person, whereas if there were a few more students, that same hour would generate more pay for the teacher. I proposed to arrange dance classes for groups of people that would be more efficient and regular than what I had been experiencing. From my proposal and personal statement, it was clear that this was a project that I could complete because I had been raised in a community dance class that I saw my parents build and maintain over many years.

Dreaming about your project can be really fun.

You can think of all the things you ever imagined doing. Can you integrate arts and capoeira and mathematics? Can you think of a final performance or a capital investment that will culminate the project's efforts? What is the most creative way you can imagine your project raising extra money so it can continue after the grant is finished? All of these questions start my mind spinning off with possibilities. On the other side of this, remember that you'll have to provide a methodology and rationale for all these components to fit together.

Planning for the Future: Placeholders and Milestones

Plans change. When I was in high school, I thought that I wanted to work as an environmental lawyer. Then in college, I thought I wanted to get a Master's degree in Public Administration. I currently work as a transportation planner, but who knows what I'll be doing in fifteen years? What matters more than *what* I end up doing is that I continually make plans for the future. I build forward momentum. The details change, but I am always moving forward. As a graduate student in City and

Regional Planning at Cornell, I was awarded a Foreign Language and Area Studies Fellowship to study Portuguese. At the time I was writing the application, I intended to go into a PhD program to study transit in Portugal, but by the time I was finished with graduate school (a year and a half after writing the application), my focus had changed. It was important for the application and for my career planning to have a goal in mind, but most granting bodies understand that priorities can change.

Successful 2012 FLAS Application for Portuguese

Portuguese cities like Porto and Lisbon present interesting planning prototypes because they maintain ancestral layouts while finding new ways to accommodate larger vehicles and multi-modal transportation. Small, pedestrian friendly streets foster community-based interactions that connect people. However, they often compete with the need to transport mass populations with new mobility expectations. This conflict is clearly visible in places like São Paulo, an exemplar of the developing world's sprawling cities. Transportation systems are a major energy-consuming sector and the single largest consumer of petroleum. Thus, in the global shift toward sustainability, we have to rethink transportation. By becoming an expert in Portugal's innovations, I can be a more active participant in efforts to bring better solutions to the world's cities. I am applying for the FLAS Fellowship because I will not be able to participate in these advancements without further knowledge of Portuguese. I can take full advantage of a year of language studies to reach fluency because I studied Portuguese throughout all four years of college.

Over the next three semesters, I will immerse myself more deeply in Portuguese language, culture, and transportation planning. Portuguese Club will enhance my colloquial skills, while my Intermediate and

Independent Study courses with Professor Juran Oliveira will improve my technical use of the language. I will also take Transportation Engineering and its successor courses in the school of Civil and Environmental Engineering, and Environment and Social Behavior in the department of Design and Environmental Analysis. My term projects and at least 25 percent of my studies in these classes will focus on Portugal. The Metropolitan Transportation Authorities of Lisbon and Porto will be useful resources for my research on their evolving transportation processes. I will draw on contacts with professionals in transportation and land-use planning as well as professors with experience working in Portugal to be advisors in my research.

Streets were created in response to the physical challenges of land use, accessibility, and activity patterns, but can unfortunately present a whole new set of constraints on human interaction and a sustainable environment. Typically, these competing agendas have led to the loss of smaller streets and gathering places and, instead, to the creation of highways. I first became aware of this problem when I visited Salvador, Brazil in 2007. The streets of Salvador are more accessible to people than cars, largely because they were built hundreds of years ago in imitation of Portuguese cities. Since then, I have visited old urban centers in Latin America and small towns in the United States, studying how to bridge the human/transit gap of street design. I have invested in a Cornell Master's in City Planning degree in order to better address this problem, and I take on the challenge of dedicating my life's work to finding the solutions.

I intend to apply for the Clarence Stein Scholarship to cover travel expenses to Portugal to supplement my FLAS research. This combined work will better prepare my standing when I apply to the MIT-Portugal Transportation Systems PhD program after I graduate with my Master's degree in Regional Planning. As a transportation specialist, I plan on working as a consultant to global cities, promoting the methods and heritage of Portuguese transportation systems.

I want to make cities better places to live by connecting transportation and community needs. The FLAS Fellowship will enable me to pursue a career incorporating international and local perspectives into new systems planning, while significantly reducing my student debt. I hope to be able to take a public sector job once I finish my education in order to serve underprivileged communities. My life-long interest in cultures and travels to West Africa and Brazil has shown me the educational and emotional value of forging relationships. So, in order to communicate abroad, I studied languages. I used these skills to successfully conduct my Fulbright Research Fellowship and my Rotary Ambassadorial Scholarship in Senegal from 2010–2011. I also studied for one year in Rio de Janeiro and for one year as a master's student in development practice in Dakar. My prior experience demonstrates my ability to communicate, assimilate culturally, and research effectively in Portugal. My international studies, language preparation, and understanding of global cultures uniquely prepare me to fulfill a successful FLAS fellowship.

With the project that you've been conceptualizing in the past few exercises, what are the skills and experience you will gain after completing the project?

_____

_____

What will you do with these skills after you complete your project?

_____

_____

How will these skills make you better at your future job? What will you be able to do as a result that you could not otherwise do?

Dreaming about the goals you have for your project or course of study is important, but it's equally important to dream about your long-term future and where you are going in your life.

For long-term planning in life, it helps to have some ideas of where you'd like to be in the coming years. I never consider these plans concrete; they're more like placeholders that keep me in forward motion. Sometimes my plans have changed completely from what I originally thought, but the change occurred because I was heading towards a goal and found another intriguing path. It's like branches of a tree. **I have found my way through the tree of life by climbing up one of my chosen limbs and happening upon a more intriguing sprig.** This method has worked out very well for me so far, even when my desired goal was waylaid. For example, when I pursued the Kiva Microfinance Fellowship to go to Senegal, I got the fellowship, but was placed in Cameroon instead. Despite my deep regret at not getting to return to Senegal, I accepted the fellowship and subsequently started an environmental summer program in Cameroon the following year. It all worked out in an oddly perfect way because I followed through on what I worked to accomplish.

Choice

My husband and I participated in an online seminar given by Dr. Christine Carter and Fred Luskin through the Greater Good Science Center's "Science of a Meaningful Life" series. The seminar focused on the science of romantic relationships. We were in Senegal for my Fulbright at the time and had to go to a posh hamburger joint that had Wi-Fi. As we crowded in front of the screen, sharing a single pair of ear buds and praying the Internet connection wouldn't fail, I listened as Fred Luskin told the amusing tale of most of his marriage counseling sessions. He said that struggling couples come into his office together and act as if they had never seen their spouse before, as if that person had just wandered into their bed one day. "The fact is," he said, "we choose our spouses, flaws and all, and whenever we're complaining, we just need to remind ourselves that the person we married was the person we chose." I think this applies to both marriage and life in general. Sometimes we can't see what the future of a given choice will be, but if we've done a poor job analyzing our choices, it's our own fault.

"We all start out with different advantages and privileges, but that doesn't mean you're set in a certain track forever. Your dreams are just as valid and achievable as anyone else's, though that doesn't necessarily mean you won't have to work harder than others in some cases. Don't let this get you down, however! Focus on doing what you need to do to get where you want to be. Comparing yourself to others and preoccupying yourself with how unjust life can be will more than likely lead you nowhere. The only person you can measure yourself against is yourself—this is the one that matters. It can be hard not to get sucked into comparing our successes to those of others, but in my experience this is one surefire way to bring yourself down."

—**Gemina Garland-Lewis**, former Thomas J. Watson Fellow
and National Geographic Society Young Explorer Grantee

Once we begin to clear the path for our story to unfold, we can start to invite good things into our lives. The more spiritual, woo-woo side of my Santa Fe persona believes in the Law of Attraction. For those of you who haven't read or seen *The Secret*, the Law of Attraction describes the correlation between envisioning our goals and achieving them. When you think of the things you want and focus on them, the Law of Attraction will give you what you want. Likewise, when you dwell on the things you don't want, those things will show up in your life. I think that this principle is not as mystical as it may sound at first. The incidence of what we observe has to do with the frame of mind we use in our everyday lives and what we choose to notice.

For example, have you noticed that when you learn a new vocabulary word, all of a sudden you see it everywhere? Is this because there's some magical force in the universe bringing a word into your life? Probably not. More likely, the word has been around you all the time, but you just passed over it before because you weren't looking for it. In the same way, I think if we choose to focus on the things we want, opportunities leading us in that direction start to pop up. This happens in a seemingly magical way, but really, those stepping-stones to your objective have been there all along; you just weren't looking for them. This shift in your awareness is a turning point to becoming a "deliberate creator of your life," as *The Secret* proclaims.

TIP: Remembering that I have a choice is a key component to taking charge of my life. Everything I do is my choice. When I start to complain because I've overcommitted myself and have no time to do the things I enjoy, I remind myself that I was the one who committed to those obligations. For better or worse, I'm in control.

Ivan Ledyashov, Kiva Microfinance Fellow

Microfinance and Kiva came into my purview in junior year of college. At the time, I was working in a Web 2.0 company that democratized stock market analysis (for a fee). Social networks and any related technology fascinated me. At the same time, having worked for five years in corporations large and startups small that glorified profit-making, I was starting to have a hard time with my position of privilege, primarily because I didn't have enough outlets or time for my desire to help others. My desire, interests, and constraints finally coalesced when I read about Kiva for the first time. It was a perfect marriage of a web-enabled community that drove change from a shared understanding of empathy and pro-social altruism. I instantly signed up and gave.

After finding out that a close friend of mine did a Kiva Fellowship in Kyrgyzstan, I was catalyzed to contribute in person myself. This, along with being laid off and finishing my undergraduate degree, created a perfect opportunity to do this in earnest. Having primarily worked with bonds, which are loans that investors provide to companies, and having studied finance, macroeconomics, and investments, I was excited to continue gaining professional experience in the same vein, but at micro level I couldn't have imagined. The draw of employing my bilingual skills in a work setting, which I had never done, was also something I was looking forward to. I knew that my finance background, people skills, and fluent Russian could make me a very effective Kiva conduit. This, unlike any other job I'd had until then, made me feel empowered. Finally—but most importantly—I was enthused about the opportunity to help lenders in person, because I would finally be able to reconcile my nebulous charitable online contributions with facilitating physical changes to someone's livelihood on the ground.

Once my placement was confirmed, and I understood the unique political situation in Azerbaijan, along with the great responsibility vested in me to rehabilitate failing relationships with Kiva partners in the region, I reveled in the challenge the situation presented. On a personal note, my affinity and respect for the Caucuses region, its cultures and history—specifically for Georgia—greatly influenced my country selection for the Kiva fellowship. Although my final placement was in Baku, capital of the neighboring country of Azerbaijan, I also spent significant amounts of time traveling to and working in Georgia and Armenia. This worked in my favor because it allowed me to develop a much better understanding of the region as a whole, as well as what challenges are localized and which cross national boundaries.

In the half a year between being laid off and leaving for the Kiva Fellowship, I kept looking for jobs. However, the economy was in a downturn after the 2008 stock market crash, and the opportunities were sparse and lackluster. Pursuing a Kiva Fellowship at that time made the most personal and professional sense for me. Incidentally, after the end of my fellowship I was approached by a company I interviewed with before leaving for the fellowship. They found my Kiva experience, with its due diligence, financial and procedural audits, and international exposure not just relevant, but integral to the position they offered.

Look for the Goodness

"You did great mommy," the four year old exclaimed as his mom pulled a perfectly browned marshmallow from the fiery horno.

"Thanks sweetie," she replied tenderly as my husband and I cooed nearby, nibbling on the marshmallow-chocolate sandwiches we had made minutes earlier. We sat at La Posada's Tuesday evening s'mores station in the courtyard of their patio café. The dusky sunlight streamed through the lush courtyard, bringing the first tinges of cool air as the evening waned on that August night. The din of meals coming to a close, combined with the gurgling water fountain, completed a moment in time that I will not soon forget.

Witnessing this sweet reversal of roles between parent and child immediately plucked my heartstrings. How wonderful to hear the words of encouragement and positivity come out of such a tiny being! All the encouragement in his life must have grown out of somewhere. Positive observations make us happier as individuals, but they also make those around us feel happier.

As my husband and I prepared to become parents for the first time, we took a parenting class offered through the Santa Fe United Way office. Our class took place over three Thursday evenings. The intimate group included just the two of us, our teacher, and another father from India. I was surprised at the low attendance, especially considering the class was held at New Mexico's Children, Youth, and Families Department (CYFD). Since the class is targeted at parenting children aged two to eight, I think we were a little preemptive, but we vowed to take a refresher course in a few years.

The Positive Parenting Program (or Triple P) was originally developed out of Australia, where it is widely taught. The Program bases their practical strategies on more than thirty years of ongoing research aimed at confidently managing children's behavior, preventing problems from developing, and building strong, healthy relationships.[3] While I had already considered many of the strategies before, there was one particular lesson that stood out above the rest: Look for the Goodness. For the sake of our children, the class teaches that parents should point out good things in life, from the simple pleasures that make us happy to commenting positively on another person when we observe behaviors we wish to emulate. This structure of framing the positive things around us helps our children to see the world in an optimistic light.

That's not to say we should shelter them from negative experiences, but we should train them to notice when good things happen. Practicing this strategy also trains us to take the good things in life as gifts and not birthrights.

"Seeing with grateful eyes requires that we see the web of interconnections in which we alternate between givers and receivers," writes Robert Emmons, co-director of the Greater Good Science Center's Gratitude Project. "The humble

---

3   "Parents, Stay Positive," Triple P International Pty Ltd., accessed June 10, 2015, http://www. triplep-parenting.net/glo-en/home/.

person says that life is a gift to be grateful for, not a right to be claimed."[4] This practice is just that: a practice. We need to train ourselves to find the positive side of a situation.

Looking for the goodness relates to mindfulness, one of the habits that has been found to correlate with happiness. The Greater Good Science Center out of UC Berkeley hosts a subsection of research on raising happy children. I found out about this center from the author of the book *Raising Happiness*, by Dr. Christine Carter. Mindfulness, compassion, altruism, empathy, forgiveness, and gratitude are all traits that lead to happier children and happier people. Practicing the skill of recognizing the individuals and natural world around us makes us feel more connected and biologically trains our bodies to feel at peace.

When I was going to graduate school in Ithaca, New York, the endless gray days really got me down. On my way to the bus on these cold mornings, I started reminding myself to look up and observe the world around me, instead of charging head-down into the mist. I noticed that if I looked closely enough, I could see the tiny purple, green, and pink buds appearing on branches, sheltered petals wrapped tightly in the shell of the trees' bark. Daily, I watched as spring slowly unfolded around me, smiling to myself and wondering at the beauty of life's cycles. One day I walked down the street and, without consciously taking note of this phenomenon, I just started smiling. I couldn't stop myself, as if I had accidentally tapped into a cosmic current of happiness. Once we feel good, we start to be receptive to possibilities for growth and outreach.

I find being present enough to acknowledge the positive things around me is a good practice. I know I will be more productive at work, a better friend, and a better civilian if I am a happier person. Reflecting on my positive observation of the mother and her son this summer, I am reminded that looking for the goodness brings everyone happiness and fulfillment in what they do. **Look for the goodness in your life and follow it. Pay attention to what inspires you.**

Find Your Inspiration

One of the best ways I know how to dream or vision is to talk to people. If I have the seed of an idea, I like to talk to someone who inspires me or knows me really

---

4   "What Gets in the Way of Gratitude," Robert Emmons, accessed June 10, 2015, http://greatergood.berkeley.edu/article/item/what_stops_gratitude.

well. I pick someone who will be encouraging at first because big ideas can be fragile and they just need room to mature. I pick one or two friends (or family members) who are very enthusiastic about my projects and mention the idea. Hopefully they will think of ways to enhance it. Then, based on their suggestion, I think of something else, and so on. This process of discussing the possibilities helps me blow up that idea into a full project or concept. Just discussing all the things I could do makes me really excited, because in these first stages, I have to be an optimist who does not let negative or problematic thoughts even enter my mind.

Once I have really nurtured the idea into a full project and feel confident about some of the details, then I start to seek out the people who I know will challenge the idea. My husband is good at pointing out weaknesses or logistical problems. If my idea is like a bubble, inflating and growing more colorful in the first part of this process, then the second part of the process is giving the big, colorful bubble a designated shape and size, and anchoring it to the ground with ties and pegs. This second part of the process starts to make the idea more real and manageable than it was at first.

TIP: Avoid pessimists and worrywarts who will shoot down your dream.

Step 1: List three people from whom you want to solicit feedback on your idea (a close friend/relative who supports you, a professional who may know something about your field, a friend/colleague who inspires you):

_____

_____

_____

Step 2: Sit down with them over a cup of coffee or lunch (your treat).
Step 3: Present your idea and ask them what they think about it.
Step 4: Write down their comments, particularly how they think your idea could be improved and what steps you're not considering already:

_____

_____

_____

Recently I was talking with an artist friend who has started dance camps and been on arts boards. "I was approached by a cultural festival that wants to renovate the way they are working with the community. They want to completely switch up how they're doing things," she told me. "I have a vision to make a collaborative performance with artists from all across the dance genres in the area, picking an annual theme that will influence the pieces."

The second component of her idea was to have the proceeds of the event go to specific causes named by the dancers at the outset of each annual event. This is a great idea and a unique opportunity. She asked if I thought there would be grant monies available for such a thing.

"I definitely think there is money out there for an event of this kind," I said, but I recommended that she dissect the different parts of what could be funded through grants.

"There's the money needed for the artists to prepare the pieces and work with dancers to rehearse and put together costumes. Then there's the actual performance, including renting a theater, paying a crew, and promotion for the event. Finally, there's the part of funding the projects that the artists bring to the table."

I asked, "Is the outcome trying to get money for the artists' projects, or is the outcome to have a great performance that brings collaborative efforts together around a central theme?" When you break down project in to the different components, both timeline-wise and mission-wise, the funding sources become clearer. "You could get a theater grant for the production, but you could get an arts commission grant for paying the artists to create their pieces. Alternately, you could get a Chamber of Commerce grant for building the local economy, or something for the causes that the artists aim to use the performance money for. This will help when you start to research the grants available and align your project with the funding goals that the granting bodies describe." My friend said she had not thought about it in this way before and thanked me for my advice.

Creating Your Own Program

A project proposal is an exercise in **matching your own objectives with the funders' objectives**. You have to be able to mold your ideas into the guidelines you're given. That can include altering your own ideas a little so that they match what's being asked of you. When you're in charge of the program, you can make these alterations more easily than when you have to consult with co-workers or your boss. I know that I can be flexible with my agenda, but I can't make those assumptions about others. I've found this constraining when trying to get grant money for non-profits or other people's programs.

When I was doing my Go Green Africa program in Cameroon, I applied for grant opportunities that spanned environmental programs, youth outreach initiatives, race relations, and international development. For each of these applications, I had to make sure that I highlighted the part of my program that aligned with the granter's goal. In one or two cases, I had to add a couple of features to my program that made it compliant with an aspect I hadn't previously considered.

For the major source of funding that I ultimately secured, I had to provide a few sample lesson plans that demonstrated the scientific exercises I'd be doing with the kids. I hadn't done this for any other application, so I set about preparing a new program detail. I made appointments with a couple of professors at Smith and we developed some experiments that would demonstrate the atmospheric and chemical reactions that I would be teaching about. Having these materials ready in advance of the program implementation helped me enrich the curriculum and add another element that I hadn't previously considered. This application requirement might have constricted me if I were writing the grant for another person, but because it was for my own project, I had the liberty and flexibility to include a new element.

Personal Fellowships vs. Non-Profit Grants

I've talked with some other professional grant writers and tried my hand at getting grants for organizations. I find that writing my own program proposals is much easier. When you are writing a proposal on behalf of a non-profit or a group, you are usually less familiar with the program details and the benefits of that program. One grant writer I met in Africa said that when she wrote grant applications for other people, she had a detailed list of questions she needed answered before she could start writing. In her case, she was not an expert in every field that she applied for (education, food programs, health outreach), but she had to gain enough knowledge about those programs to make convincing proposals.

Another significant part of writing grants for other people is that you have to double check with them about their program's capacity. The worst thing possible would be to over-commit your client or partners. It is essential to find out how much time the staff could commit to the grant (if awarded), what reasonable outcomes could be expected, and how this program fits into the organization's other current programs.

When I'm writing my own proposals for projects or courses of study, I know what I'm capable of and how it fits into the rest of what I'm doing. I don't have to keep going back and consulting with other people about what I can do. When it's my own program, I also have the entire picture in my own head, so I've already worked out the details and have put a significant amount of thought into what I've planned. **When I'm applying for my own opportunity, I have a lot more enthusiasm because the payoff will be big for me, not for someone else.** It can take a lot of endurance to write and rewrite proposals, going back to the research, and double-checking with contacts and recommenders. It's harder to keep up the momentum when I won't even be the person who benefits from that work.

Another benefit of applying for fellowships, scholarships, and grants on your own behalf is that you will never need non-profit status. This has been a learning experience for me, as I've tried to branch out into grant writing from fellowship writing.

With organizational grants, foundations often want to see that you have 501(c)3 tax status.

Going through the process of becoming a non-profit takes time and energy (and follow-up, such as providing minutes from all meetings). If you have not become a non-profit, there are businesses that can provide fiscal sponsorship (for a fee).

Fiscal sponsors receive grant money on your behalf and charge you a fee for using their 501(c)3 codes.

You usually have to apply and be approved for this service before even applying for grants. Once you are approved, you have to pay a monthly fee to retain their services and then they take a percentage of the grant money if it's awarded. Depending on the size and duration of your project, this can be a good option that enables you to bypass the logistics of maintaining non-profit status yourself.

In coming up with a project idea, finding an eye-catching focus may take a bit of time. If you think you've found the subject that few people have explored, that may become your hook. For example, during one conversation a musician friend mentioned to me that Japanese people easily learn traditional Zimbabwean music because of a similarity in languages. "That's fascinating," I exclaimed, "I could see a Fulbright research project stemming from that."

> **Run your Idea by a number of semi-experts**
> **to help gauge the quality of your proposal.**

You don't want to spend all your time writing an application for a topic that turns out to be passé or implausible. Having a good mentor to direct you to readers, or become your main sounding board, is the next step. Chapter Five is all about finding your mentors and how to be a gracious mentee.

Filling out the worksheet below, which is based on Smith College Fellowship Advisor Don Andrew's advice, will help you develop the body of the application in shorthand so you can test out the concept. After you've finished, find someone who might be interested in this topic and ask them what they think.

WHO

What fields of study/work do you have experience with?

_____
_____
_____

Have you been abroad before? Where? For how long?

_____
_____
_____

Do you speak other languages (including the language of the country where you want to go)?

_____
_____
_____

How do you plan on improving your language skills between now and when you do your project (i.e., take a summer course, community college course, travel to the country in advance of grant, do a Rosetta Stone project, join a club)?

_____
_____
_____

WHAT

What do you propose to do?

_____
_____
_____

What is your driving concept/motivation?

_____
_____

What is your background related to the project topic?

What is the title of your project?

WHEN

When do you plan on fulfilling your project?

What do you need to do before going?

WHERE

Where is your project going to take place?

What do you know about the host place/country/community/setting?

How much time you have spent there?

_____

_____

_____

_____

WHY

What is a one-sentence hook that sells your idea? (Make someone want to learn more.)

_____

_____

_____

What question are you trying to answer?

_____

_____

_____

_____

What is the first sentence of your application?

_____

_____

_____

Why is this project/event/work important?

_____

_____

_____

_____

Why does this project/event/work need to be fulfilled?

_____

_____

_____

Why is the project good for the place where it will take place?

_____

_____

_____

_____

Why are you the perfect person to do this project? (What makes you uniquely qualified?)

_____

_____

_____

_____

_____

Why does it have to happen in your chosen place and nowhere else?

_____

_____

_____

_____

_____

Do you have advisors/mentors who can help you or write a recommendation for you?

_____

_____

_____

_____

All of these components will come together in Chapter Ten to make a cohesive, fleshed out proposal like Ivan Ledyashov's application to become a Kiva Microfinance Fellow.

**Excerpt from Ivan Ledyashov's Kiva Microfinance
Fellow Application**

MOTIVATION STATEMENT

**Please explain the reasons why you wish to become a Kiva Fellow and
articulate how these reasons are related to your past experiences
and life goals. (250–500 words)**

As a Kiva Fellow I hope to help entrepreneurs in Georgia or Armenia
obtain better access to credit. I intend to further Kiva's mission of
microfinance-driven and socially spurred international development
by becoming a catalyst in loan transparency. Entrepreneurs whose
businesses bring benefit to their communities and those who plan
to uphold their obligations to repaying borrowed funds are the
cornerstones of Kiva's success. I wish to help these entrepreneurs
succeed so that other borrowers can benefit from their Field Partner's
unreserved relationship with Kiva's lenders. Their stories and funding
requests need to be communicated to the Kiva community clearly
and concisely to promote faster loan disbursement and credit cycle.
Conversely, Kiva lenders ought to receive timely updates on the
status of their loans. Using my bilingual skills I hope to establish much
needed rapport between Kiva's English-speaking lenders and their
Central Asian borrowers.

Responsible loaning practices stimulate innovation and self-
reliance. They benefit all the parties involved, while building enduring
economies. Central Asia's small businessmen and businesswomen
need better access to credit. In such countries as Georgia and
Armenia, many small entrepreneurs are not considered creditworthy,

while the loans they qualify for carry prohibitive interest and fees. The default on such loans, which is expected and even preferred by some lending institutions, results in confiscation of borrowers' entire livelihoods to repay debts. Thus Georgia's and Armenia's small entrepreneurs face a double-edged sword when it comes to loans. They lose equally if they borrow and if they don't.

Georgia and Armenia possess time-honored cultures, strong national identities, and favorable geography. In the near future these countries will inevitably become top emerging economies. Their economic strength rests on the shoulders of their small businessmen. They create jobs, benefit their communities, and drive the GDP. Kiva's active relationship with MFIs in the region will make loan capital more readily available to them and, as a consequence, to the small entrepreneur. This, in turn, will stimulate and accelerate the economic development of Georgia and Armenia.

As a budding entrepreneur, I want to better understand the forces that make businesses successful. As someone interested in developing market demand for Central Asian products in the United States, I'm eager to educate myself on the culture of these countries. As a person with a fervent desire to increase the wellbeing of others, I strive to help people help themselves using microfinance. Being a Kiva Fellow will enable me to accomplish all of my goals. It will also enable me to further the mission of an organization I admire.

CROSS-CULTURAL EXPERIENCE

Successful Kiva Fellows must be open to cultures and ideas different from their own and may need to modify their behavior or appearance appropriately. Provide an example of a significant experience that illustrates your ability to adapt in an unfamiliar environment. Please highlight the skills you used and the perspectives you gained. You may draw from experiences in your work, school, or community in the United States or abroad. Please list the date(s) of your experience. (250-500 words)

At the age of eleven I immigrated with my family to New York from Lvov, Ukraine. Prior to our immigration we spoke to our friends in the United States, read their letters, and looked at the photos they sent us to better understand what life in America would be like. It seemed similar in many respects, except for language. There were still life's staples, like family, home, and food, but there were also nice extras, like cars and big-screen TVs. The transition to American life wasn't without a hitch. I could no longer find comfort in my childhood friends, as my problems appeared alien in the context of theirs. The experience taught me how to relate to people from different backgrounds and form lasting relationships. Now, eleven years later, I understand just how few parallels can be drawn between life in Ukraine and the United States. While daily life is similar, societal fabric and mentality differ greatly. In the United States, success stems from one's intellect and perseverance as opposed to cunning and cronyism. Moreover, individuality is embraced and upward social mobility is possible and expected.

My direct cross-cultural experience is also worth mentioning. I grew up in Brooklyn at the ethnic crossroads of Caribbean, Latin American, Southern Asian, and Hasidic neighborhoods. By being exposed to different cultures through friends and experiences, I have learned to always keep an open mind and take active interest in other cultures. On attending Baruch College for my BBA (repeatedly ranked as the most ethnically diverse college in United States), I further expanded my world-view. Throughout my entire college career I involved myself in AIESEC, a student-run organization that enables students to develop international leadership skills to truly become global citizens. Through group discussions and events at AIESEC, I grasped the significance of problems in other parts of the world, and how important it is to help people so they can help themselves. In my junior year of college I studied abroad and worked in the United Kingdom, and traveled through Europe. This experience improved my ability to adjust to diverse environments quickly and to adapt in societies with strong national identities.

KIVA FELLOW TYPICAL DAY

Describe your vision of what a typical day will be like for you as a Kiva Fellow and how that work furthers Kiva's mission. (100-200 words)

As a Kiva Fellow I will start a typical day by interviewing business owners. I plan to explain to borrowers that behind their loans are not big banks, but regular people like themselves. After I convey the borrowers' stories, requests, and updates to the Kiva community through journal entries, I will spend time on fostering lender-borrower relationships through more interactive media. Prior to lunch with my colleagues from the hosting MFI, I will work with them to post borrower profiles onto the Kiva website. Throughout the day I will dedicate time to observing the inner workings of the Field Partner, how they use Kiva's platform to achieve their objectives, and whether Kiva's policies are adhered to. In the afternoon, after a thorough analysis, I plan to meet with MFI staff to offer my recommendations and training in how the Kiva's platform can be used more effectively. In order to promote the self-sufficiency of the hosting MFI, I plan to create accessible documentation of their inner workings, in the scope of Kiva's policies and best practices, to be used throughout and after my tenure. Given the time difference, I plan to communicate with Kiva HQ in the mid-afternoon to receive updates and new assignments. As the working day draws to an end, I will work on Entrepreneur Press Profiles, ad hoc projects for the hosting MFI and Kiva, and refresh my knowledge of Kiva's policies and procedures. After work, I plan to offer my MFI colleagues computer and English classes, and work on the Kiva Fellows Blog.

PREPARE THE APPLICATION

Though the following five chapters are set out sequentially, the tasks In them should really be done simultaneously. Finding a mentor, doing the research, and lining up contacts are things that can stretch in overlapping time periods. As with my own process, you may find stagnation or sticking points in one of these areas; do not wait to complete the first task before moving onto the second and third. Work in all of these areas continuously and start immediately.

CHAPTER FIVE

FIND A MENTOR

"Mentors are an important component of figuring out what programs, scholarships, fellowships, or career options are good for you. Mentors have been through it all themselves—the ups and downs, the rejections, and the acceptances, and can offer great advice about a variety of topics relevant to what you're searching for. It's important to find a mentor who has time for you and who values this role. There are plenty of interesting people who we would love to connect with and learn from, but sometimes people just don't have the time and it ends up as a no-win situation for everyone. Be humble and appreciative."

—**Gemina Garland-Lewis**, former Thomas J. Watson Fellow
and National Geographic Society Young Explorer Grantee

n the short span of her weeklong visit to her parents' home, Allison scheduled lunch or coffee dates nearly every day. She wanted to reach out to as many of her father's oncology colleagues as possible. "I'm applying for medical schools and these people have the best first-hand knowledge of application tips and pre-med programs. They could give me advice." And perhaps one of them may even become her mentor, following her through the long and arduous process of getting into the program of her dreams.

What is a mentor? "Someone who provides advice and guidance important to your personal or profession development," says Anna Beninger, director of research at Catalyst Inc., which studies corporate mentorship. Ideally, mentors also have a personal interest in you and want to see you succeed. Unless you are in college or high school, mentors are not paid. They are helping you in good will or for the joy of seeing you succeed. A good mentor will be available to write recommendations, review drafts of written work, talk in person or on the phone with you when you need advice, and seek out a network of other professionals who can help you. Even if you are in a formal academic setting where you've been assigned a mentor, sometimes you'll find that you need a better mentor who will help specifically with fellowships and applications. Advising on class selections takes much less involvement than going through an application process, so you may find that your school advisor or mentor is not enough.

Suggestions for Finding a Mentor

- Talk with a teacher who gave you excellent feedback on written work, or with whom you've talked at length during office hours.
- Approach colleagues who have expertise your subject of interest, especially if there is a grant-writing section in your office.
- Talk with friends who may have experience in grant writing about advice they may have. A friend can be a mentor, too.
- Look up scholars who have applied for similar projects and ask them for their help. You can look through a school database or the grant/fellowship websites; often they will list past awardees.

- Look for someone who currently holds your dream job or who has modeled your ideal career path. Ask them how they got there and what tips they have for you.

How to demonstrate that you are a worthy mentee

DO: Come prepared to meetings with your mentor—have specific questions and an agenda with a recap of what you've done to date, current actions, and future steps to show that you are conscious and respectful of your mentor's time and energy. Often mentors get no financial benefit for helping you. Make their experience as pain-free as possible. If you get all the tedious details of your project out of the way, your mentor can help you with his or her inspiration and guidance, instead of doing your homework for you.

DON'T: Never formally ask someone to be your mentor. A mentor should develop naturally (like any relationship). Because a mentor could be in your life for years (and possibly be involved in your activities weekly), asking someone to commit to this open-ended—and potentially intense—role could scare people away. Never expect your mentor to do the work for you. If you need help, give him or her advance notice of what you need them to do and provide as many details as possible. Coming to a mentor the day before an application is due and telling them you need a recommendation letter is utterly disrespectful. Ask for something a week in advance (less than a week is too little notice, more than a week gives people time to forget your request).

This exercise is adapted from Pamela Slim's 2013 book *Body of Work: Finding the Thread that Ties Your Story Together.*

Identify a Peer Mentor Circle

Experiment with creating a peer mentor circle, composed of people who can give you support, feedback, and ideas.

Name of project:

_____
_____
_____

Objective:

_____
_____
_____

Your strengths as they relate to this project:

_____
_____
_____

Your weaknesses, as they relate to this project:

_____
_____
_____

Names of people you know who could help address these weaknesses:

_____

_____

_____

Means of communication you will use to solicit input from your peer mentors for this project (email, video conferencing, in-person meeting, etc.):

_____

_____

_____

Length of project:

_____

_____

_____

How you will thank your mentors:

_____

_____

_____

Where to Find Your Mentor

If you are having trouble thinking about where to begin the process of finding a mentor, start by making a list of people you know who have helped you in the past or who may be willing to help you now. Ask some friends or friends-of-friends if they have mentors and how they got them. You probably know somebody who has written a scholarship or grant application. Ask them who helped them or just ask that person if they might consider looking over your work. The more readers who review your application, the better, even if you don't think they would know what to look for.

Sometimes, even people you don't know well might be helpful—someone you've admired but don't know personally, someone you met at a coffee shop, or on a tour. Don't strike out the possibility that someone you know very little may actually be of great help.

—**Vidhee Garg**, Scholarship recipient at
Mumbai University and Cornell University

Don't be afraid to ask for help. Getting a second opinion on every stage, from the conceptualization of your application to final drafts of your writing, is important. This can be a challenge. Sometimes we find that we are afraid to ask for what we need. I think one of the reasons this is so hard is that we have to confront our insufficiencies. Am I really bad at getting things done in a timely manner? Maybe I need to ask a mentor to impose deadlines on me. Am I really bad at following up with people? Maybe I need to ask a mentor to remind me about whom I need to contact or respond to.

**Nobody likes to think about the things they do badly,
but those are the things we need the most help with.**

I have an ongoing problem with responding promptly to emails. I know I should respond immediately, even if it's a query to which I don't have an answer. Yet, my tendency is to let a day, then a week, then multiple weeks pass before I respond to some emails. This is improper correspondence etiquette, and yet it still happens sometimes. I get an icky feeling when this happens—probably guilt—but I have to address that feeling face-to-face and see what could help me overcome that challenge. I finally got an answer to my frozen feeling when I was interning with the city of Santa Fe. I asked one of my colleagues for a piece of information and he wrote back,

**"Hi Lucy, I don't have that information at the moment and I am
currently under deadline. I will get back to you by this Friday."**

In hindsight, I could have asked a mentor for help with this problem, because this type of communication is learned, not intrinsic. Remember that a mentor is there to guide you through uncharted territory. A good mentor can give you advice about these small skills that will make everyone's job a lot easier in the overall application process.

This does not just apply to applications. In graduate school, I was trying to find a sub-letter for my apartment during the summer. I posted my apartment on Craigslist and the Cornell off-campus housing site. Every day for over a month, I received multiple emails requesting information about my listing. A few times, I encountered individuals who began bombarding me with ever-more-detailed requests. I could tell that these people would be difficult to deal with and would make problems for my landlord and me. I was unclear about how to break off these correspondences and increasingly became more hesitant to respond.

Finally, in a frozen state of uncertainty, I asked one of my best friends, Vidhee, how I should handle this. She gave me some great advice. "You should be honest and let the person know that there are more serious inquiries about the apartment that you are going to proceed with," she said. I just needed some external perspective on how to handle this and she gave it easily. A mentor can be anyone, from a friend to an elder to a renowned person. The commonality is that they can give you advice and care for your work enough that they contribute their wisdom.

When I asked my good friend Ayla how she found her mentor, she said that she approached a woman at work. This woman was in charge of grant writing for their non-profit. Ayla had built enough trust at the organization to ask for projects that interested her. She knew that she was moving into a new phase of her life where she wanted to explore her own potential. A project had come up to work with women in Africa and, in preparation, she knew that she was going to be doing a lot of grant writing after she left the non-profit. Knowing this, Ayla asked for more hours working with the grant-writing department. She ended up getting to spend about a third of her time writing grants in the last months at her job. The woman in charge of this department took a liking to Ayla and has since helped her with reviewing grants. Finding someone compatible and eager to help a new grant writer happened naturally, but my friend had to put herself in the position to show that she eagerly wanted the mentorship. She proved that she was willing to put in the hours to learn this skill and took the steps to change her trajectory.

Leave Ample Time

A recent column about fellowships in *The Chronicle of Higher Education* advises, "Plan well ahead of your deadline, and build extra time into your schedule. Many people budget considerable time over their summer and fall for a November due date. One winner I know worked on his proposal for over a year."[5]

Working on my first Fulbright application was like taking an extra class during my senior year. I emailed Smith Fellowships Advisor Don Andrew, who promptly replied back to me with a list of demands. "Write up a rationale for why you think you are eligible for a fellowship," read his first message, along with a few pleasantries. I spent two days writing a stream-of-consciousness piece about all my talents and assets. It was a little over-confident. I may have erred on the side of boastful. He wrote back saying, "You will need to refine your reasons but I like your confidence." That began a summer-long email and phone correspondence from Cameroon in which Don would demand things from me, bluntly stating whether I was missing items or not following his instructions to the letter. His fierce insistence on attention to detail and timelines was clearly behind Smith's good track record.

Meeting Don's demands also began my training for reading written instructions very carefully. He had a system in which applicants would deconstruct an application in preparation for writing the first draft. I have difficulty reading directions, I think partly because I have minor dyslexia, but also because I am a slow reader. It took me two or three times to read through the directions and understand them.

The forms would ask for

- A one-sentence statement of intent;
- A short rationale for your application;
- Supporting research for your topic; and
- A list of contacts you have or will make in the country of application.

This made the core contents of the application clear before I put all the pieces together. It was also easier for Don to decipher my purpose.

---

5   Michael Kiparsky, "How to Win a Graduate Fellowship," *The Chronicle of Higher Education*, May 11, 2006. Accessed May 1, 2014, http://chronicle.com/article/How-to-Win-a-Graduate/46782.

TIP: It's much harder to distill a completed document down to its core essence than it is to start with the core essence, refine it as needed, and then integrate it into a piece of writing.

These documents went back and forth between Don and me for months, with his revisions, then my corrections, until I thought there was no possible way they could still need editing. At the point when he started to be satisfied with the content, he set me up with other professors at Smith who did reviews for me. I thought this process was so long at the time, but actually I was working on a much shorter time frame than many of the other applicants. Each spring, Don holds his information sessions about the Fulbright and other scholarships, hopefully catching a group of juniors who will work for at least six months prior to applying.

Sample Timeline:

January: Learn about fellowships that are due in the fall.

February–May: Work on isolating your research topic and getting a mentor who will help you through the process.

May–June: Write drafts of purpose statement and secure contacts that will write recommendations for you.

July–August: Request edits from readers to incorporate into your final draft.

September–October: Finalize and copyedit all application materials, have them *done* at least a week in advance of the official deadline.

For the final review, I sat in Don's office and made the very last corrections (adding a space here, taking away a capitalized letter there) with his oversight. Don then had me fill in all the relevant fields in the application online and print it out before submitting it to make sure that words weren't cut off or misspelled in the input process.

TIP: Trust and honesty are essential. You want a mentor who will tell you if you are arrogant or if your performance is sub-par. They are like parents, who correct you kindly, but truthfully. They should also be able to keep your confidence so you can trust them with real questions.

At the end of that last day working with Don, I stood up from his desk after we said all we'd needed to say, and he stuck out his hand to shake on a job well done. I walked over to him and gave him a big hug. I said, "I didn't come all this way for a handshake!" He started laughing and hugged me back. We had come a long way, from his interrogating and terrifying me over the phone to a hug. I really felt grateful for all he'd done for me and felt like he was more of a grandfather figure than a teacher at that point. He told another friend of mine who also went through the process that I'd given him a big hug. He said that old blokes like him needed that every once in a while, and I guess I made an impression on him.

TIP: Not all mentor relationships are warm and fuzzy. They may test your mettle.

I grew to really appreciate all Don had taught me over that time. From when I started working with Don and had only one fellowship under my belt, to fall of 2009, I had submitted over ten grant and fellowship applications. I felt like I had learned more useful skills from working with Don than from all four of my years at college. He was a very tough critic, but in my circumstance, that pushed me to do my best. In hindsight, I think he was tough because he knew that he had to weed out those who could not handle the pressure of investing that much time in an application.

I had one-on-one meetings about my application with Don for months, and when I wasn't on campus, we would have phone calls and I had to be prepared to defend every part of my application. Being in a meeting—on the phone or in-person—with Don was more stressful than when I defended my Exit Project in front of my committee in graduate school. He was ruthless and scrutinizes everything, from my ideas, to my plans, to my choice of words. It was not an easy process working with him, but we had built a rapport by the time I submitted that last application.

Three years later, in late August of 2012, my husband and I went back to Northampton to visit a dear friend who had moved back to do a post-baccalaureate in medicine before starting medical school. Classes had not yet started, and the Smith campus looked ready for a new year. All the grass between walking paths had been patched, the campus center sparkled, and the library was unnaturally vacant.

We strolled down the arts quad, where I spent most of my time as a student. I showed my husband the halls in which I used to take classes, pointing out windows to the rooms I knew so well.

All of a sudden, a bicyclist raced towards us on the chained-in path. My husband and I stepped aside to let the hurried person pass us. I tilted my head in acknowledgement of this person's passing before we moved on. Behind us, I heard a screech that would seem to throw a person from a bike, and I turned around. "Don?!"

Don Andrew had been the speeding cyclist who nearly hit us, but he had stopped a moment after seeing us. "Lucy!" He proclaimed, and gave me a big hug. I introduced my husband, barely able to believe that on the deserted campus we would happen to be on Don's route, as he was clearly single-mindedly heading to his office.

"I recognize your husband from your wedding announcement; how are you doing?" We chatted for a few minutes before he excused himself. He was off to meet a student about an application (before anyone else was even thinking about school, of course), and would be late if he stayed much longer. As we walked away, I felt a warm tenderness about this chance encounter. Clearly, working with Don over that long period of time had left both of us with something that hadn't been there before. I was glad that Don treated me like someone he'd love to catch up with on a busy day.

When I think of planning for my future goals, I think back to a strategy that another of my mentors uses. Marta's title—public school teacher—does not do her justice. With two master's degrees and an incredible lifetime of experience, I would describe Marta as more of a savant or mystic. I first met her when I was in high school, and she practically cornered me, unsolicited, and assuaged all my inner demons.

"You're more powerful than you let people see," she told me in a creepy, fortune-teller way. I glanced at her sideways, with what I hoped was a too-cool-for-school façade that hid my surprise at her statement. "People try to tear you down because your intelligence threatens them, but they haven't touched your source." This was coming from a woman I'd never met before that night.

She had the ability—at least with me—to see into my deepest insecurities and communicate that she related to my problems. Not until a couple of years later—and much trust building—did she become my mentor.

As a super busy teacher and mother of four, she had a way of organizing her projects that made a lot of sense to me. She had a poster board that she transformed into a large calendar. She marked important deadlines and progress dates that she wanted or needed to meet on a rainbow of sticky notes. On another board, she laid out a table of the projects she was working on and, in the corresponding columns, the key components she needed to gather together. I used this technique when I was applying to graduate schools and had to keep track of multiple due dates, differing application topics, faculty contacts at each school, and whether the program required my GRE scores. Visualizing all the details in a large, colorful format helped me clarify the requirements.

Finding a mentor is one of the first steps to seeking guidance not only for scholarships, but also for helping direct your life.

Finding the Right Mentor

The benefit of being tied into the college's fellowship program was that a network of professors and professionals was already established to review our work. The application process involved a lot of rewriting. "Rewrite, rewrite, rewrite" was our motto. Some of the faculty members were more helpful than others in giving detailed critiques, but even a few comments about my methodology, or questions asking me to clarify certain language, were helpful. For the Fulbright, the panel of reviewers comes from a variety of fields, so having a cross-section of reviewers who were not specialists in dance or Senegal was really helpful, because **they helped me discover what I assumed people understood.**

My undergraduate advisor, Marguerite Harrison, followed my progress and continued to write recommendations for me all through college and two and a half years after graduation. She generously shared her time with me, well beyond her professional obligation. There are other kinds of professors or mentors who will only stay with you for a shorter period of time. Maybe they'll provide feedback on just one or two applications. I have acted in this position myself, providing detailed feedback on one or two essays, but not holding someone's hand through the entire process. These people are almost equally as important as your mentor because they provide fresh eyes and different criticism than you or your mentor can provide. You and your mentor are too engrossed in the concepts and the process to see obvious problems.

- To find the one-time reviewers, it really helps to be tied into a network, either through work or school, or mutual friends.
- The easiest way to gather these individuals is to seek out the people who have applied for the same position in the past. They are the people most familiar with the application requirements and biases.
- Another way would be to approach faculty who have experience in the field for which you are applying.

If you don't have a college affiliation, you may consider approaching the institution from which you most recently graduated. For example, the Smith College fellowship office works with students up to almost ten years after graduation. In 2010 when I got the Fulbright, there was an applicant from the class of 2002. Depending on the institution, this service may be available to you.

Finding a mentor does not always happen on your first try. Sometimes I have started to work with someone before finding out that he or she would not be a good mentor. The process has surprised me at times. I learned this quickly with one of my professors in graduate school, whom I asked to write a letter of recommendation for me. This professor had led me to believe that he had a true, vested interest in my future and had taken a personal interest in my skills. Yet when I asked him for the letter—for which I had even sketched out the traits I wanted him to expound upon—he gave me one of the least personal letters I've ever received. This was a strong first indicator that he had neither the time nor the interest to work with me on my scholarship goals.

However, the professor who ended up becoming my graduate advisor ended up being a great recommender and mentor. Any time I stopped by Pike Oliver's office, he cleared his whole schedule to meet with me about any concern, whether it was minor or major. True to form, he ended up writing the most complimentary letter of recommendation I received in graduate school.

How to Treat a Mentor

One thing to keep in mind with mentors—and reviewers—is that they are doing this on a voluntary basis. You should be respectful of their time and energy, because not only are they are not being compensated; they usually have a lot of other things going on in their lives. Depending on how involved the person seems to be, you could ask them to review two drafts, or have two in-person meetings about your idea. A mentor who has shown real commitment to you will be available to meet with you throughout the process of seeing an application from start to finish. Even then, however, you don't want to inundate their email with every little concern you have. If possible, try to figure out the problem you're facing first before going to them. This will keep you on your mentor's good side.

The last thing you want is for your mentor to see an email from you and groan that you have another problem for them.

After working intensively with a mentor on a project, you may also want to give him or her a break from your projects. Seek out someone else, or just take a hiatus from applications for a while.

Smith Fellowship Advisor Don Andrew says, "I appreciate contact and being kept abreast of the student's activities—especially activities that will help win the fellowship: emailing, calling, visiting with me. That way, we maintain the conversation and I get to know the student to help her win the fellowship."

One of the best ways to find a mentor is to start close to home, with people you know and your professors. Meet with them, ask them questions, and talk with them. Recognize that one mentor alone won't know everything you want to know. If they can't help you, ask for a referral. Don't go in with open-ended questions; do some homework and have specific questions.

TIP: To utilize your mentors' and recommenders' time efficiently, try to get a recommendation letter that is specific enough to highlight the real attributes of your project, but general enough to use for more than one application. Also, have your mentor or recommender use a general heading and refrain from mentioning the granting body by name in the letter itself. This way, they don't have to rewrite the letter every time you apply for another grant. This will save both you and your mentors a lot of time and hassle.

"As for the mentoring role, I always think of it as a chance to share knowledge and experience. Like any relationship, it is a dialogue, centered on communication. The role of listening is key. I also think that, in a mentoring relationship, there needs to be a lot of attention given to consideration for one another. In general, a mentor has the capacity to relate quite closely to the person she or he is mentoring, so it's important to establish comfortable channels of communication. Sensitivity to deadlines *and common courtesy are key elements as well. Sometimes those being mentored forget to follow up to inform the mentor if they got the position. It's important to remember to thank those in a mentoring role. The mentor has to be able to look at the big picture, as well as be able to make sure the individual examples in the mentee's experience shine through, rise to the surface."*

—Smith College Professor **Marguerite Harrison**,
my undergraduate advisor

Do the Legwork for Them

When asking your mentor for a letter of recommendation, send him or her background information about the granting body and what particular traits they're looking for. Then, provide a specific list of characteristics about yourself that you want them to include. This is a sample email I sent to my former employer for my graduate school applications:

Hi Christina,

Thank you so much for being willing to write the recommendations. Please let me know if there's any part for which you'd like my input. Here's information about the deadlines and specific details:

Deadlines*:
- UC Berkeley: December 7th
- Harvard: December 15th
- MIT: January 3rd
- Cornell: January 10th
- Penn State: January 15th
- University of New Mexico: January 30th
- UPenn: April 15th

*All recommendations are online except for the University of New Mexico. For this one, please write a letter with "Lucy Gent Foma, Community and Regional Planning" written on the top left side of the page. On the envelope, please sign the sealed flap and send it to:

Community & Regional Planning Program
MSC04 2530
1 University of New Mexico
Albuquerque, NM 87131-0001

Program Names:
- UC Berkeley: MA City Planning
- Harvard: MA Urban Planning
- MIT: MA City Planning
- Cornell: MA City and Regional Planning
- Penn State: Recreation, Parks and Tourism Management
- University of New Mexico: Community and Regional Planning
- UPenn: MA Environmental Studies

Points to Include:
- Your personal impression of my intellectual ability/capacity for analytical thinking
- Your impression of my qualifications and potential to carry on advanced study in a specified field
- Your impression of my depth of character (motivation, intellect, and maturity) and commitment
- Your impression of my previous work/work effectiveness and potential for future productive scholarship
- Your impression of my ability to work with people and leadership potential on the job or in community activities

To Be Specific:
- Rachel's Social Activism class at Prep and working on Living Wage projects during high school
- Go Green Africa project in Cameroon

- o Working at Earth Care as a Sustainable Schools Intern
- o Working with the Sustainability Education Task Force; connections with the city of Santa Fe, Think New Mexico, and the Green Building Council (through Katherine Mortimer)
- o Working towards sustainability with food/facilities/curriculum
- o Going to Senegal for Fulbright/Rotary scholarships to research how artists can viably support themselves and how Senegal can become more environmentally friendly
- o Intent to come back and work in Santa Fe to build an integrated/ sustainable community

This is another email I wrote to my advisor when I was applying for the Foreign Language and Areas Studies Fellowship in Portuguese at Cornell:

Dearest Marguerite,

Thank you so much for all the recommendations you've graciously written for me over the years. Once again, you have been my most devoted proponent. I've attached my proposal and my résumé. The application is due February 6th to the Cornell Institute of European Studies: [insert address here]. My Cornell ID is [insert ID number here]. Please include some of the following points:

Points to Include:
- Your personal impression of my intellectual ability/capacity for analytical thinking
- Your impression of my qualifications and potential to carry on advanced study in a specified field
- Your impression of my depth of character (motivation, intellect and maturity) and commitment
- Your impression of my previous work/work effectiveness and potential for future productive scholarship
- Your impression of my ability to work with people and leadership potential on the job or in community activities

To Be Specific:

o   Volunteer work teaching English in Brazil while I studied abroad

o   Kiva Microfinance Fellowship in Cameroon (I was the only undergraduate selected)

o   Nomination to speak at Smith Elects the World (seminar) my senior year at Smith

o   Go Green Africa project in Cameroon, which won the Ruth Dietrich Tuttle Prize

o   Nomination to the Dean's list 2008–09 and First Group Scholar 2009

o   Fulbright Research Scholarship in Dance

TIP: Notice how I asked my two recommenders to mention different aspects of my background according to how well or how long they knew me. You want to space out your strengths between your résumé, your personal statement (where you can expand on particular points that you wish to highlight), and your recommendation letters.

The strongest recommendations address the exact points of the application, so if you can focus all your energy on one application, the outcome will likely be more positive. The above letters help your advisor or mentor by saving them the time of looking up exactly what the application asks for. It also saves them the stress of trying to remember exactly what it was that you were doing when they last talked to you. You have the best idea of what makes you eligible for the grant or scholarship, so don't be modest, let them know what you think of your accomplishments.

Some recommenders may ask you to write the letter for them and just have them sign. Although I think this saves the person time, I sometimes shy away from these types of situations because I would like the recommender to give his or her honest opinion of my work. Obviously I pick recommenders who I know will say good things about me, but if I'm just saying all the good things about myself and having them sign off, it feels a little deceitful. Perhaps in these situations, you could write a few sample paragraphs about your past accomplishments for them and then ask them to write a paragraph or two about their opinions.

At the very least:

- **Provide them with the addressee and general outline of the letter, so it makes it as easy as possible to fill in the blanks.**
- **Always tell them when the recommendation is due and where it should go.**

Again, be respectful of their time. You can't expect that they can drop everything at a moment's notice and write a nice letter for you. Give your recommender three weeks notice (and a friendly reminder at the beginning of the week that it's due) so they have some time to really think about what they're going to write about you. As Don Andrew advises, get a commitment from them to write the letter before you even ask for the letter.

Thank You Notes

The final important part about having a good relationship with your mentor is remembering to send them a thank you note or a small gift after they've written recommendations for you. Maybe consider sending them a box of candy from a local chocolatier—but don't send anything that could be confused with a bribe. When I finished my Fulbright applications, I sent a photo of myself with a big "Thank You" sign I had made. After I completed my Fulbright year, as a way of sharing my experience I sent a collage of pictures from my journey to all my mentors.

These gestures are considerate ways to show that you appreciate the time they have given you. I learned this in high school, but some people seem to forget as they get older.

Once you have started the scholarship, grant, or school year, you could also write an email to update your mentor.

Mentors get gratification out of knowing that your combined work has paid off. This doesn't have to be a very frequent occurrence, but enough that your mentor feels a connection to what's going on in your life. If you are in the same geographic location, take them out to coffee and catch up on what's new. These small gestures go a long way in creating a sustained relationship. Then, the next time you need a letter or help revising an application, your mentor does not feel used. The relationship can be more reciprocal than it initially sounds. The mentor gets the feeling of accomplishment from helping a young professional; but it is nice to see the outcome of the work, rather than just experience the hours of revision that go into an application.

Be a Worthy Mentee

To merit the honor of being a mentee, you have to show that you're worth the time and energy. You have to offer something to that person that proves their investment will not be wasted. This does not mean offering extravagant gifts. Instead, prove that you are keen and interested in working hard. If you are a willing pupil, who will take all the advice being provided, that will make you much easier to work with. The other way you put yourself in the position to be mentored is by **doing as much of the work as possible yourself**.

Insight from Professor Mike Manville,
my graduate committee member at Cornell

I'm not sure I have too much to say about mentees and advisees, other than the default position I take toward most of them is that most won't use me for much, and aren't worth a lot of effort. I don't mean that to sound cold—it's just that most students aren't in school to get a lot out of their advisors and they view their advisors simply as a source of signatures and administrative procedures. It's fine, and we are all happy with that, but it means that when I first meet an advisee I assume I will see them about five times in two years and have no substantive conversations with them. I'm busy; they're busy.

So if someone *does* want to work more closely, I look for them to make that clear to me, by taking the initiative and by showing that they have done some homework *on their own.* I can't tell you how many students come to my office saying something along the lines of "I was really interested in such-and-such point from class," and then they want me to do something for them/put them on a research project, etc. I try to help, but the fact is that if students get interested in something, they have the tools to learn more about it. The syllabus has readings that, in turn, have references—go look up those references. Use Google and Google Scholar. Chances are, the professor has written something about the topic. Review the professor's papers. *Then* go meet with the professor with a working, baseline knowledge of what you're interested in, as well as some intelligent, specific questions. Doing that sends the message that you are a worker, that you are a self-starter, that you are legitimately interested, and that you're resourceful. And suddenly you're someone we want to work with.

From that point on, it is a matter of sticking to things: if I suggest reading something, I expect an advisee to read it. They might not like it, may not want to use it in the way I think they should. That doesn't matter. What matters is that they read it and understand it and have something to say about it.

Just as I provide the recommender with a legible outline of what the scholarship wants, what the recommender should say about me, where the letter should go, and what the due date is, doing this legwork makes it as easy as possible to do the real work of a mentor. Mentors should not have to hold your hand through every step. They are there to give insightful criticism and contribute their credibility to your cause. They should not have to do research for you or double check the address on the envelope. **Use the valuable time with your mentor for what only they can provide: insight.**

You can also show you are a worthy mentee by being timely and comprehensive in your correspondence. This is something I'm still working on. You cannot expect a reviewer to give you thorough and quick advice without returning their emails quickly. If an advisor asks you to make revisions, do them as soon as you receive them and let your advisor know that you have followed up on their suggestions. Responsive and considerate communication makes you a serious professional. This is a good trait to have in life, let alone writing applications.

TIP: If you receive an email requesting information that you do not have yet, immediately email back and say, "I will have this information to you by tomorrow (or Friday, or next week)." This lets your contact know that you have seen and acknowledged their request, but you cannot provide an answer at this time. This is a good tip for all correspondence—professional and personal.

Now that you have made some inroads into finding a mentor (maybe you've reached out to some candidates, or taken a couple contacts to coffee), start working on making yourself the best possible candidate to win a fellowship. Before you get the big prize, you need to get your ducks in a row with some small projects, prizes, or grants. The next chapter will tell you how to prepare for big fish. In other words, gather some low-hanging fruit to buff up your résumé.

CHAPTER SIX

PREPARING FOR BIG FISH

Megan joined the US Navy after finishing college. She is a third-generation officer, so the profession runs in her family, but she joined later than her father and grandfather. In searching for a way to pay off her college debt, she found that the Navy was one of the best options: in exchange for five years of service, they would eliminate her student debt. However, after the five years ended, Megan decided to stay. The Navy offered some really interesting career opportunities, including the chance to live abroad. I met Megan when she was doing her "Third Junior Year Abroad," as she called it. She had been awarded an Olmsted Scholarship.[6] As Megan describes it,

> It's a military scholarship for officers only (in the Army, Navy, Air Force and Marine Corps). I learned about it when I was a brand new Ensign in the Navy, and because competition is keen, I had to make sure that I did well in "competitive" assignments before applying (essentially being ranked highly among my peers, etc.). I also needed to have good undergrad

6   "FY-15 Olmsted Scholar Program," United States Navy, accessed June 1, 2015, http://www. public.navy.mil/bupers-npc/reference/messages/Documents/NAVADMINS/NAV2013/ NAV13101.txt.

grades, a good GRE score, proficiency for language, and a desire to make the military a career (the scholarship wants to create future military leaders who take their skills back to the service after their Olmsted tour is up).

In addition to making myself competitive by taking "hard jobs" prior to applying, I also had to make sure that the timing worked out. Basically, I had to hit some career "wickets" prior to applying (it took me about ten years before I could apply!). Essentially the scholarship is kind of an unusual thing to do, so I had to hit some big career milestones (or "checks in the box") prior to applying to ensure that I was still competitive for promotion while I was off the grid for a few years in Senegal, and not doing something more typical of a naval officer.

Once she learned about the scholarship, Megan molded her career toward the end goal of applying for this amazing opportunity. That entailed a ten-year action plan, including getting certain promotions and credentials, all of which contributed to her strong résumé. Having a big goal like this Olmsted Scholarship or a Fulbright is a great way to keep focused on where you're going. The "hard jobs" that Megan refers to include volunteer hours and frustrating rejections that make you stronger. Perseverance is one of the key components of becoming a successful applicant, and that means working through the sometimes-unrewarding jobs and experiences so you get the big reward at the end.

There are very few cases where you can start your fellowship career by getting a Fulbright or a Rhodes scholarship on your first attempt. I am a dreamer by nature. As a child, I would think up inventions or careers where I was everything from an architect to a professor. All I need to start dreaming is for someone to bring up a possible adventure or project that appeals to my imagination. I start seeing myself in that position, what I'm doing, what time of year it is, whom I'm working with, and what kinds of projects could come out of it. Sometimes I dream too much and I need someone to ground my fantasies with logistical questions.

Amy won her Fulbright to China on the first try. We were seniors together in college, both taking an introductory physics class on solar power and sustainability. The class consisted of non-majors who wanted to know the rudimentary science behind innovative technologies. In Amy's case, she had a vested interest in the renewable technologies available in China, from where her parents had emigrated. Amy proposed to continue researching this topic for her Fulbright proposal—and won! At the time, it seemed improbable that she would get this stroke of luck, but as I talked to her about it more, and revised my own understanding of the grant process, I learned that she had done the legwork to be a successful applicant.

Like me, Amy had not known about fellowships and scholarships in high school; she heard about them through Smith's fellowship office once she was taking Chinese language classes. Her background with the language and the culture helped considerably. Before winning the Fulbright, Amy won the National Security Education Program to China scholarship, which paid for the fall semester of her junior year abroad in China. Following that, she was awarded the Critical Language Scholarship through the State Department, which she conducted during the summer of her junior year. Both of these impressive awards put her in a good position to apply for the Fulbright in the beginning of her senior year at Smith. When I asked her about the process of developing her proposal and applying for the Fulbright, this is what she said:

> I think I wanted to combine my interests in Chinese politics/policy and environmental studies. I found my professional contact through a relative who lives in China and is an environmental researcher/academic with some connections to professors at universities in Southwest China. I narrowed down my research project based on the relevant environmental issues specific to the area where I could get an affiliation. Initially, [my project involved] solar energy, but then it turned into anaerobic digestion, because I found another advisor who specializes in that topic and was more welcoming/easier to work with.
>
> It took me a lot of time to write my proposal (and rewrite it several times with the help of the fellowship advisor), so I suggest setting aside plenty of time to do it. Also, it helps to get feedback from other people to help you refine your idea.

The Overachievers

I went to Brazil during my junior year of college. Smith didn't have their own study abroad program, so students would apply to a number of approved, external opportunities, such as the one Brown University offers. Brown has excellent undergraduate and graduate programs in Brazilian and Portuguese Studies, and I was accepted into their program because Smith had prepared me well by requiring me take four semesters of Portuguese prior to my junior year.

Our group consisted of about eight Brown students, five Smith students, and one Yale student. The Brown and Yale students were still far more prepared than I was, even though I had taken two years of Portuguese. They had only been taking Portuguese for a year or a year and a half, but their classes were intensive. I learned a lot from this group. I really looked up to them because they seemed so certain about what they wanted to do. For example, all the Brown students immediately found causes to volunteer for. Although my high school had integrated community service into the curriculum (both for bolstering college applications and to give back to Santa Fe), I had not ingrained this important activity into my personal agenda.

Active volunteer work is a great way to
line up career and personal opportunities.

These activities show a level of community participation and, in the case of international study, interest in reciprocal cultural exchange. They also make me more grateful for my education and upbringing.

Many of the Brown students had goals of going to graduate school or applying for fellowships after their time in Brazil. Being able to cite extra-curricular activities that gave back to Brazilian society demonstrated how proactive and considerate they were as foreigners. It seemed to be part of their basic operating mode. They were always looking for opportunities.

One of my friends, for example, was volunteering to teach English to a group of teenagers who were preparing for the Vestibular, a harder version of the SATs that counts almost exclusively as their high school record for college admissions. Another friend was volunteering with an organization that did work with kids in the favelas (the slums of Rio de Janeiro). I finally caught on during my second semester in Brazil. I volunteered for an organization that raised money for arts projects in rural communities. I also started teaching English weekly for the Vestibular prep class.

Beyond making my résumé look good, the extra-curricular projects I became involved with started to enhance my own personal interests. When I started looking for opportunities, obviously I wanted to do something that I had some experience with, but I also wanted to learn more. Having danced my whole life, the arts organization fit very well with what I already knew. I had a passion for bringing arts to people. Teaching English was something I could do naturally because I'm a native English speaker. What I didn't anticipate was that down the line, when I was applying for grants to teach about environmental issues in Cameroon, I was able to cite my Brazilian teaching experience as evidence that I could communicate with students from different countries.

Being of Service

Volunteering can help you refine your mission. It can be an interim step if you know you want to do a fellowship, but are not quite sure which field to pursue. Did you come away from Chapter Four with multiple dreams? You're not the only one. I have many so-called irons in the fire. I'm constantly expanding my portfolio of activities. While I have diverse interests, it helps when I am looking for fellowships to home in on my "project for the moment." This doesn't mean dropping my other interests; it simply means focusing on one for the time being. **Being of service to the cause I care about, even if it's just in my free time until I can make it my job, sets me on the path to accomplishing my goals.**

Volunteering is also a way to stick with your passion. Inevitably, you will encounter setbacks during your journey to get funded. Chapters Thirteen and Fourteen will help you handle this, but in the meantime, remember that *giving* your time freely helps you remember what you love doing. Doing something without being paid always makes me happy, which is an added bonus. Whenever I come away from volunteering at a benefit, or chaperoning a school field trip, I feel good about myself. Who doesn't want a little happiness boost every once in a while?

Diversifying my portfolio of activities enriches my life because I like to split my energies into different fields. Currently, I have my professional career as a city and regional planner, but I also dance in a performance troupe and volunteer in classrooms and help find grants for bringing teacher-training seminars to Santa Fe. I always have both academic and artistic outlets for myself, because I do better in each when I balance these parts of myself. This is good not only for my personal wellbeing and state of mind; it's also good for whatever I may plan on doing in the future.

As I explained in Chapter One, we can pull different threads of our experience together to make different stories about our lives. In my case, I have an environmental thread, a dance thread, an academic thread, a social-activism thread, a language-and-travel thread, and a teaching thread. I can pull together long-standing and sustained activities in each of these realms to construct logical stories about who I am and what I'm doing with my life.

I couldn't have done this without pursuing opportunities to continue working in each of these fields throughout the years.

Sometimes I've overcommitted myself to too many activities, but they've all been things in which I'm interested. I haven't always sought these opportunities; sometimes they've come to me because someone knew I was interested in that field, or I was searching for something else and a grant opportunity came out of the blue. **Take these chances and create options for yourself so you always have something interesting to do.** I am a great believer in creating options.

"Always have a Plan B, Plan C, Plan D...you get the idea. If Plan A doesn't work out, there are other options. Look for those other options. This way, you'll keep doors open even if you lose out on some opportunities."

—**Vidhee Garg**, Scholarship recipient at
Mumbai University and Cornell University

Track Record

The next step to creating options for yourself is to look for small grants that will help you build credibility for the big grants. Especially if you have a big goal in mind, start building your grant and fellowship portfolio. Fellowship and grant review committees look for your track record with winning grants. These boards are impressed if you have a big fish on your résumé already, but they also recognize small awards or fellowships. Most applications have a section for past awards. You want to be able to fill out that section with more than one listing.

Typical grant applications also ask you to show what other efforts you're making to accomplish your goal. Have you already set up a website? How many hours have you already put into coordinating the event? What other funds have you raised to date?

Most granting bodies don't want to be your exclusive funder; they want other people to be contributing to your work as well. This desire is two-fold. First, granting boards don't want everything riding on them; they want to know that other organizations also think your idea is good. If other granting bodies have already invested in you, it shows confidence in your work and reinforces your idea.

The other reason granting bodies like to see evidence of additional support is that they want to know that you're really committed to your proposed project and have already sought out other ways to accomplish it. The collection of multiple grants for your project shows that you've already been investing in and thinking about getting it funded. This helps you build one application on the foundation of another. The more support you have, the stronger your next application will be.

The same goes for personal fellowships. If you have won scholarships and fellowships in the past, it shows a board that you already have the ability to carry out a scholarship successfully. **Once you have a couple of small fellowships, you become much more competitive for a larger fellowship,** like a Marshall, Rhodes, or Fulbright. Then, once you have a Fulbright or another big fellowship, it will always be on your résumé for future pursuits. An honor like the Fulbright not only helps you get other fellowships; it also helps when you're applying for graduate programs and jobs. Anyone looking at your credentials will instantly recognize the big names.

It doesn't even matter what area your fellowship was in. Hardly anyone asks me what I studied on Fulbright. The fact that I was a dance research scholar is almost irrelevant. What's impressive is the fact that I worked my way up to get it. The work to get that big fish started way before actually applying for the Fulbright. I had to invest the time and energy in winning the easier-to-get small grants and fellowships. The low-hanging fruit—those fellowships and grants for which there were fewer applicants—paved the way and built up my credentials for the big fish.

> **Lesser-known awards, scholarships, and grants—with small applicant pools and multiple winners—mean you have a high probability of being funded. Multiple small awards make you a competitive applicant for the large awards later on.**

For my first applications, I didn't have very many scholarships, but I had done other things that provided recognition. During the spring of my senior year, I started fundraising for my Go Green Africa project. The idea for the project came to me because I had received an email from our school career development office asking for proposals for student projects that could be awarded ten thousand dollars. I came up with the idea of teaching middle-school students in Cameroon about global environmental problems. I rallied the schools' support and prepared the application by the February deadline, but I wasn't even a finalist for that large grant.

I decided not to give up since I had already laid the groundwork.

I spent the next couple of months applying for grant after grant, for amounts of five hundred dollars up to fifteen thousand dollars. One of the grants for which I was a finalist was the Power in Numbers grant sponsored by Mountain Dew. I was notified that I was a finalist during spring break, but then I needed to win the most number of online votes in the next couple of weeks.

I went into hyper-drive.

I made little flags with the voting information, taped them to Dum-Dum lollipops, and spent my study breaks walking through Smith's libraries to ask students to vote for me. I ended up not winning that grant either, but I was sure to mention in following applications that I had been a finalist, because I thought it showed that a grant board approved of my idea. Mentioning near-successes counts as achievement. Finally, after months of applying for grants—and multiple failures—I applied for another Smith College prize, and won.

The Ruth Dietrich Tuttle Prize had a slightly different objective: to encourage further study, travel, or research in the areas of international relations, race relations, or peace studies. This prize funded about half of my project's expenses. By that point, I felt strongly enough about the project to use my graduation money to make up the difference. As I mentioned in Chapter One, I had used some of my high school graduation money to go to Senegal for the first time. That investment paid off ten-fold when I got the Fulbright in part because of my prior experience in Senegal. Getting grants is a huge investment of time and energy. Money is an investment of time and energy, too, and sometimes that's what's needed to get to your final goal.

Karmic Budgeting

If I were a better bookkeeper, I would strictly regulate my budget so these personal investments would not be necessary. But as I've learned from my parents, sometimes it's not about strict accounting. The balance sheet is rarely so neat and tidy. My mom, for example, is asked multiple times a year to perform for benefits or community shows. Of course, that means she has to schedule all the dancers, donate the time to use our dance studio, choreograph the dance, teach the dance, and on top of all that, she usually buys and/or sews costumes for the event. She is definitely not compensated for this effort, but she believes her efforts are worthwhile because she gets to do what she loves to do as a profession, and it's good exposure.

Other times, I've received more in return than I put in. The Fulbright scholarship is very generous. They adjust for the expected cost of living in the city and country to which you are going. They usually give ample amounts for living expenses, and furthermore, they give stipends to scholars who are traveling with dependents. The same could be said for getting all of my tuition and living expenses paid for by the Foreign Language and Area Studies fellowship at Cornell. I worked on the application on and off for a couple of months, and in return, I didn't have to worry about repaying years of student loans.

To get these big fish, I had to put in years of time and effort applying for many small grants to build up my résumé. If you have this goal, opportunities will start to pop up for you. Your Gmail ads will start pointing to fellowship apps. You can do a Google search for *fellowship* and your field of interest. If you are in a college or university, your school will likely have a fellowships website listing scholarships and their eligibility requirements. Some schools even have a fellowships office, where faculty members offer help, mentoring, and application revision advice.

In my experience, schools can be very different in terms of how involved they become in getting fellowships for their students and recent graduates. Smith College has a rigid program, where the fellowships advisor becomes part of your life for the duration of the application period. On the other hand, although Cornell offered to pair faculty with student applicants, the faculty members I encountered were not very responsive.

TIP: If you are working on applications without the oversight of an institution, you can sign up with online services that will email you deadlines and notices about upcoming scholarships and grants. You fill out a form with your interests, then the website generates a list of relevant opportunities.

Where to look for small grants online*:

- Fastweb.com
- GrantStationInsider.com
- Youth Service America Grant Opportunities (http://www.ysa.org/grants)
- CollegeBoard.com
- CollegeNet.com

- Scholarships.com
- ScholarshipMonkey.com
- FinAid.org
- StudyAbroad.com

*Keep in mind that website URLs can become obsolete, so it's better to know strategies for discovering the most current information.

Look for local grants and awards through your local Rotary Club, newspaper, economic development department, or other local organizations. These are the small fish that usually don't get many applicants and therefore offer better odds of winning. These opportunities are often spread through word of mouth, but you can also search online for local awards. Just start talking to people about what you want to do and maybe someone will know about an opportunity. The more networking you do and the more you interact with diverse sectors of the community, the more exposed you'll be to possible collaboration.

Look to your various local communities for opportunities to build connections and opportunities outside of fellowships. Investigate local non-profit organizations, foundations, or religious groups to find out about service projects or volunteering needs. Just make a phone call or email them asking how to get involved. It's that simple.

Take the First Steps

List a local cause you are interested in helping:

_____

_____

_____

Search for the phone number or email contact:

_____

_____

_____

Make the call or email a request for more info:

_____

_____

_____

For anything, from working in the arts, to healing, to justice work, chances are that someone or a group is already doing work related to your interest *in your community*. Discover what's being done and how you can get involved. Who knows? You might meet the person who will become your mentor or connect you to the perfect person who will help you get funded!

Cautionary Tales

I recall a couple of cautionary tales about overcommitting and having difficulty following through. The first example was from an environmental youth program that I worked with in Santa Fe. We were putting together an event for Youth Service Day. The organization had won a couple of grants to have a day at the community farm, where numerous public school classes would come and prepare the field for planting. There was going to be music and many associated activities.

One of the grants for the event was for about $500—not that much, considering entertainment, transportation, food, and promotional materials. It was one thing to use the money to pay organizational staff, but after the event, the grant board wanted statistics for the participants: ethnic representation, income levels, and ages.

To collect all that data on top of actually implementing the grant was a huge pain in the butt. **Was it worth it in the end?** Maybe, but I don't know what our other funding options would've been. Sometimes we can get big-eyed when we find a grant and not look very closely at what is required before, during, and after the fact.

Another cautionary tale came from a more recent experience. The Cornell Community Partnership Board was offering $2,000 student grants for projects in the community. The application process was not that difficult, because the board usually has to seek out applicants. But as I found out, the follow-through was much more difficult. The first year that I got a grant from them, I had planned to teach a children's dance class at the charter high school in downtown Ithaca. I spoke with the school's director and got a letter of support, but after I got the grant, my communications with the school fell apart.

Unfortunately, I was trying to coordinate the class from New Mexico, so maybe emailing back and forth brought about additional confusion. When I finally returned to Ithaca in the fall, I believed I would be teaching a weekly, hour-long class at a local theater. But the school's director hadn't scheduled the time slot, so I only had a thirty-minute window with the kids. Additionally, the school had told the students that it was a drum class—not a dance class—so I had all boys who were less interested in dancing than drumming.

It became clear that my original plan was not going to work out and it seemed like I'd have to give back the grant money. Luckily, the grant board had some other connections in town and made a call to a children's after-school program, which immediately took up the opportunity to add another class for the kids free of charge. Sometimes the headaches like these can make doing projects a pain; but in the end, I did get to teach the class I wanted to teach. And, I could add another grant to my list of accomplishments.

CHAPTER SEVEN

DO THE RESEARCH

"Fulbright likes to see that you know what you are talking about and you did your research. They like to see that you have experience in life and are active as a person, because Fulbright is not all about getting a degree."

—**Ronza Almadbooh**, former Fulbrighter

T he funny thing is, I'm actually writing this from the White House...because that's just how crazy taking advantage of opportunities can be!" This was the message I got from my friend Phoenix when he finally was able to respond to my request to contribute to this book.

I met Phoenix Mourning-Star when the Rotary Foundation honored us both as Rotary Ambassadorial Scholars. He was heading to New Zealand to study international environmental and human rights law at the University of Auckland. This is how he told his story:

I'm a farm kid. I grew up on a small farm in southern Michigan, showing horses, hogs, and cattle at area county fairs. I somehow got hooked on competing in freestyle downhill skiing and ended up dropping out of school at the age of fifteen and moving to the western United States. I lived out of a van to save money. I worked as a ski instructor, lifeguard, pizza cook. When I was old enough, I eventually worked at a couple of bars. But my real passion was skiing, so I had to learn to market myself: asking local shops to sponsor me, haggling for extra swag at tradeshows, sending out letters to companies. I had started doing this self-promotion before I was even seventeen years old.

By the time I finally started in academia, self-promotion was old hat to me. Having transferred every two semesters in undergrad, I never really took the time to understand how funding my academic career was so similar to my athletic career. That is, until I came to the end of my undergraduate degree in Mathematics.

Graduate school opened a lot of doors, including doors of self-doubt. But one place I found my foundation was in my passion to do good work. Being an outdoors person anchored my desire to be a good steward of the environment in any way that I could. So when my academic world finally met my past in the grant and fellowship realm, my life took a major turn—but in a very subtle way.

It came in the form of a research assistantship. For my first graduate degree, I was awarded a tuition waiver and a stipend to teach or do research. Something like the adage that you have to have money to make money. This was the start of a history of having funding or winning support. I hadn't really won any academic awards prior to this, so this initial award was a real surprise and game changer that opened my eyes to the marketability and the demand for people with science skills and training.

Eventually, Phoenix was awarded a National Science Foundation IGERT (Integrative Graduate Education and Research Traineeship) Fellowship to pursue his PhD in ecology and chemical/biological engineering. His work furthered his passion for the environment and his commitment to be a good steward of natural resources. "I wanted to do work for and with people who needed it the most. In 2010, when I was notified of the award, helping the people of Afghanistan seemed to be the best way to do that."

Phoenix researched the different issues facing the people of Afghanistan and realized that he would be most capable in helping to find and develop alternative, renewable energy opportunities. In the process of completing his dissertation on methods for creating a renewable biofuel from poppy seeds, Phoenix managed to obtain a tourist visa to Afghanistan during one of the most dangerous times of the insurgency. He landed in Kabul with no on-the-ground contacts and within a week, he managed to leverage a network of people and colleagues to work within Afghanistan's Ministry of Agriculture, Irrigation, and Livestock. One opportunity lead to another, and after investigating his options, he ended up thousands of miles away from where he started. Research isn't just reading; talking to people, asking for help, and learning how other people arrived where they are can be invaluable clues for your future pursuits.

Research Shopping Cart

The word *research* makes this process sound like homework, but investigating all the ways you could get money can be fun. The next time you find yourself taking a few minutes at work to check social media or shop online, take a moment to search a couple of keywords related to your project. Start a Research Shopping Cart, a collection of websites on the various aspects of fellowships (local/national/international funders, travel destinations, and articles/blogs on similar projects). Evernote is a great workspace that can help organize your notes about different fellowship opportunities and related research. As their website attests, "From short lists to lengthy research, no matter what form your writing takes, Evernote keeps you focused on moving those ideas from inspiration to completion." Compiling your few minutes here and there will build a cache of information that can become the foundation of your application. Make a deal with yourself: take five minutes (or even just three minutes) to do the research.

The next step is to gather as much information as you can about specific fellowships.

Once you've decided which fellowships to apply for, it's time to gather information. Find out which topics are most often supported, and which rarely get the nod.

- Don't forget to read all of the material supplied by the grant agency.
- Tailoring your proposal to the interests of the agency or foundation is critical.
- Parse the call for proposals thoroughly, and make sure your proposal deals with all the criteria.
- Read as many successful proposals as you can find.
- University fellowship offices may have archived proposals, organized by agency.
- Hit up previous winners in your department for their proposals, and ask for their advice. They may represent potential editors for your drafts.[7]

"Two bits of advice I followed were to get in touch with previous scholars in the same specific Fulbright scholarship (professional one in my case) and discuss the application with them. The second was my own hunch, and that was to focus on my personal essay and emphasize what I would do with my Fulbright experience, especially once I returned. Critical to both of these things was to first get my institution to support the idea of applying."

—**Mark Boland**, Principal Accelerator Physicist, Australian Synchrotron

7   Michael Kiparsky, "How to Win a Graduate Fellowship," *The Chronicle of Higher Education,* May 11, 2006. Accessed May 1, 2014, http://chronicle.com/article/How-to-Win-a-Graduate/46782.

"[I concentrated on] a well-planned and concise description of my proposed project and excellent letters of reference. It also helped (and may still help) that I picked a country to work in (Malaysia) that was not very competitive at the time—like, say, France—and thus I increased my odds of funding. But I wanted to work there anyway, so it was not solely a practical decision. Letters from former Fulbright Fellows that say things like 'Mr./Ms. X walks on water because...' are guaranteed to catch the eye of the application reviewer (as does making contact with them informally and diplomatically, well in advance of the application deadline). In my case, I was actually able to go and see the Country Program Manager, in person, as she invited me to meet her, and I happened to live four blocks away from CIES in downtown Washington, DC."

—**Peter Cohen**, East and Southeast Asia Analyst and scientist

My regular routine for my first summer in Cameroon included going to work between 5:00 a.m. and 8:00 a.m., depending on whether we had a community meeting that day, working until around 5:00 p.m., and then heading to one of the two reliable Internet cafés after work. On Saturdays, I would do laundry, hand-washing each item in a tub of cold water and wringing it out to dry, and then go to the Internet café. On Sundays, I attended the Protestant church with my host family at 9:00 a.m. After the service, which could last anywhere from two to four hours, I would head once again to the Internet café. It was okay that I had to go to church for the whole morning, because the Internet cafés didn't open until 1:00 p.m. on Sundays anyway (everyone was in church). I spent so much time at the Internet café because my Fulbright advisor was really putting the pressure on me to find my proposal topic.

I sat at the aging computers, hoping the power wouldn't go out because of massive monsoon-season rainstorms. The French keyboards took a little getting used to: the letters *q* and *z* were in opposite places, and the period key required shifting. It slowed me down a little and created frustration when all I wanted to do was get down to work. **Doing research on possible topics in countries where I might have a chance at being an eligible candidate was nerve wracking.** I had come up with so many different possibilities that y Fulbright advisor had shot down unceremoniously that I was starting to feel discouraged. For each idea, he had me fill out a form that included the country, topic of study, purpose statement, my eligibility criteria and rationale for doing that topic, and the beginning structure of a methodology. After all this, he would write back a single-word, yes-or-no response, and I'd have to start all over again from scratch. After a month and a half of this, he started to write emails that were a bit harsher. Maybe he was just bluntly letting me know that my time was running out to come up with a topic.

One rainy weekday night, as sheaths of water created a deafening sound on the tin roof, I tracked globs of mud across the Internet café floor and sat down to one of the final emails from Don, my scary advisor. I was weary from a full day's work traveling to a village in rural Cameroon. My pretty pink skirt was blotched with huge, dirty, water stains from the motorcycle ride through muddy, mountainous roads. I was both sweaty and cold; my blouse smelled from the non-breathable raincoat I had been wearing for about ten hours straight. I tried to focus on the immediate task at hand, which was to come up with an acceptable topic.

Then it hit me, like a wall that was right in front of me as I struggled blindly to find it. *I could just study dance in Senegal.* I bypassed the form this time and just wrote a couple of sentences to Don about why this made sense. He immediately responded with the most promising phrase yet: "That might work."

"During my sophomore year of college I was trying hard to decide between going to Australia with my school's program or SEA Semester. I decided to meet with a student from the senior class who had done both programs, just to see what her take was. Immediately upon telling her my dilemma, she said, 'Why don't you just do both?' To be honest, the thought had never really occurred to me, which seems strange in retrospect. I **could do both,** *I thought. And so I did. An important component of this for me—a student heavily dependent on financial aid from my school—*

was to go through programs that were either run through my university or officially affiliated with them. I looked into going to a different, unaffiliated university in Australia, and it would have cost me a lot—more than I could afford even with extra loans. Going through my school's existing Australia program, I was able to get the financial aid I needed."

—**Gemina Garland-Lewis**, former Thomas J. Watson Fellow
and National Geographic Society Young Explorer Grantee

Once you know exactly what you want your project to be, you can start looking for the funding. Ideally you want to give yourself many months to prepare for applying to grants. For the Fulbright, if you don't start at least nine months in advance, you may not have a finished product by the deadline. There are search engines that list scholarships, as I've mentioned already, but you can also access most university scholarship sites, which often have more pertinent information about student scholarships. You'll find that the lists are often long; there are tons of money out there waiting for you.

Do the research. **Not all of the scholarships are going to be applicable to you or to your project, but there will inevitably be a number of grants out there that are perfect fits.** Many of the student scholarships I found when I was looking for graduate funding sought out minority students or first-generation college students. "Women in the Sciences" is another big category. But then there are scholarships from local organizations or religious groups. These may apply to you. Sometimes you can tell just from the title of the scholarship whether it's right for you. Other times, you have to dig through the details. A clear scholarship or grant will bullet-point the list of eligibility criteria. Maybe you have to be an undergraduate at the time of application, or more specifically, a junior in college.

The first thing you want to do is read through all the available materials to figure out if A) you are eligible, and B) you have enough time to apply. This is the quick way to sift through the many pages or websites of fellowships.

Check off this list:

- Are you an eligible candidate?
- When is the due date?
- Do you have to be associated with a non-profit?
- What areas of funding are available?
- How many letters of reference/recommendation do you need?

If the application deadline is within a month, you probably don't have time to prepare everything. This is how I got really good at reading through pages and pages of instructions. The key is to get to know everything about the scholarship. What is the political slant? What is the organization's mission? Who has the board or selection committee awarded money to in the past?

For example, the Rotary Foundation is a very patriotic organization. The Rotary Clubs consist of a network of wealthier professionals who have joined the club to network with businesspeople (mostly men). Reading about Kiva.org informed me that young, highly educated, and motivated individuals ran the organization, and they were more interested in making social change than in making money. The organization is operated out of a small office in San Francisco; it was started by a couple from Stanford and co-founded by another Stanford alum. My application for Kiva described how I had been part of startups and non-profit operations in the past. **You want to know as much as you can about the organization and the application before you write or prepare anything, because it will save you a lot of time in reworking the materials.**

If you are a visual person, start making a board or a display that has the pertinent details about the grant you're researching at the moment. Here's an example:

Grantor	Geographic Focus	# Awards Available	Deadline	Typical Grantee	Eligible Topics
Kiwanis	Local	5 per club	March 1st	Dedicated hometown volunteer	Food banks, trash pick-up, fundraising
Rotary	International	3 per region	April 2nd	Americans who will become goodwill/ culture ambassadors abroad	Environmental awareness programs, vaccine/drug distribution

You want to have the basic information about meeting the application requirements: the deadline, the application materials, which recommendations you'll need, and where to send them (also specify whether these materials should be submitted electronically or as hard copies). This is similar to the list you should prepare for your recommender(s).

Then, for the details about the grant itself, find out what the parameters are, such as whether you're allowed to ask for funding for everything, or if it's just for travel, or just for buying supplies for a project. Maybe funding is only allowed for work with children or for art supplies. If you ask for something that's clearly not allowed, you will be rejected outright because the granting body can tell you didn't do your research.

Additional Information

Grantor	Application Materials	Number of Rec. Letters	Destination for Application Materials	Electronic? (Y/N) Sign-in and Password
Kiwanis	1000-word proposal, 500-word personal statement	1 letter from a Kiwanis Club member	Sara Smith 111 Main St. Santa Fe, NM 87501	N
Fulbright	1000-word proposal, 500-word personal statement, 1 language evaluation, college transcript	2: 1 from a teacher, 1 from international contact in field of research	http://www.cies.org/application-login	Y Sign-in: LGF Password: Funded!2009

Remember, grants and scholarships often have so many applicants that they are looking for reasons to eliminate contestants to narrow down the list. If your application shows some blatant oversight of the details of the grant, or typos and general carelessness, then your project can easily be eliminated. I remember the final stage of filling out my Fulbright application (after months of editing and preparations), and my advisor making me put a period as the first line of the electronic submission box. He explained that this makes it easier for the reviewer to read the sections that I'd written (as differentiated from the description for the box). Simple format things, like making the spacing easier on the reader's eyes can make the difference between being considered for a grant or not.

The second essential part of doing your research for a grant is talking to as many awardees as possible.

Sometimes this is not an option if you're applying for a more obscure grant or scholarship. Sometimes you'll find yourself applying for a position or opportunity that is the first of its kind. If at all possible, however, try to locate other people who have been in the same or similar position. They will know the ins and outs of the application and be able to provide insight into the granting body.

When I was applying for the Foreign Language and Area Studies Fellowship (FLAS) at Cornell, I had the benefit of knowing three students from the year above me who had been awarded. I started talking to them months before I even started writing or formulating my proposal. I met with each of them privately and asked them questions about the projects they proposed, which field of study they focused on, who they asked for recommendations from, and who reviewed their work before the submission. This really helped me to understand what the FLAS board was looking for.

I have also found that most people, if you ask nicely, will let you see their applications. Reading successful application essays can help you pick out the essential key points to include. They can also give you some ideas about how to format your application. Sometimes it makes more sense to divide up application essays into sections: objective, rationale, and methodology. Other times, you may not have very much space to include details about yourself and/or your project. This limited space requires you to weave your personal narrative and project objective together more seamlessly. Looking over past applications helps determine what's right for your application.

Once you have filled out your own informational sheet about the granting body and the grant in question, you will start to have a better picture of your grantor's needs. Again, reading everything available about the grant or scholarship, from the entire website to chat forums, makes you better prepared when it comes time to actually fill out the application. **This is essential, because you want to make your materials fit the application, a technique otherwise known as *framing*.** You want to pull out the pieces of your project that relate specifically to the grant. Having the overall project in mind helps with this because you can dissect how your project addresses the topic at hand.

I got the grant-writing bug during my senior year of college. I had spent the entire summer before my senior year working on my Fulbright application and when it was finally submitted in early fall, I just wanted to keep writing applications. Having just worked up the enthusiasm for my Fulbright project, I started to think about other ways that I could get funding to dance if the Fulbright didn't work out. In fact, Don Andrew advised everyone submitting for the Fulbright that we should all do our best to just forget about it, because it would take until late January to find out if we were finalists, and then, if we passed into the next round of review, it could take until June to be awarded.

Don Andrew's advice to forget about it

The Fulbright initial stage of review takes from October to the end of January. At that point, the US reviewers have made their decisions about finalists and notify everyone on a Friday in late January or early February.

From that point, the finalists are forwarded to the countries of application and an in-country committee reviews those applicants to select the fellows. This can take as little as a month and a half or as long as five months. The waiting game goes on indefinitely for those who are selected as alternates to take the fellowship if a first-choice grantee declines the offer. This seems like a purgatory, because you can't plan for your future with the possibility of going abroad looming over your head.

It's best if you just set aside this tiny bit of hope that you might awarded the grant, neither counting on it nor discounting the possibility. It's much better to go on with your life and pursue your regular activities.

To forget about the Fulbright was the best advice Don had to offer to us. So, in that spirit, but also to increase my chances of getting money go to Senegal, I started searching for other grant opportunities. I maintain that it's always good to create opportunities. You can bet that if you put all your eggs in one basket, you're taking a big risk. Knowing that I would be graduating in the spring and not having any concrete plans, I didn't want to invest all my hopes and dreams in the idea of being in Senegal on Fulbright the following year. If I didn't get it, it would be a whole year for which I had nothing planned.

I remembered that a woman who was a Kiva Fellow with me was doing the Kiva in conjunction with a Rotary scholarship. **I contacted her and asked about her experience with that application.** She kindly provided me with a copy of her final proposal and gave me some details about how Rotary works. I did some searching around, called the national headquarters and asked where I would be eligible to apply. They informed me that my college town of Northampton had an active Rotary Club chapter that sent students abroad almost every year. With a few more informational calls in the area, I got in contact with the woman running the scholarship program. It turned out that Northampton Rotary practically had to beg people to apply for the Ambassadorial Scholarship every year because there were so few people interested. *Perfect!* This was a major discovery for me because it was **low-hanging fruit.** It was not a guaranteed bet to get the Rotary, but my chances were much higher than getting the Fulbright.

My experience with the scholarship outreach person at Rotary was perhaps one of the closest and most nurturing I have had up to this point. I had her personal cell phone number and called her frequently from January until late March of that spring. She wanted me to have a successful application, so she told me what details to include to make it stronger. When I was ready to submit my application, she gave me her home address so I could send it to her directly, and it would be in safe hands. This was the most assistance I've ever received from a granting board.

Ultimately, I was a finalist for the Fulbright the first time I applied, but I didn't get the scholarship. However, I did gain an interview that spring with the Northampton Rotary, who forwarded me to the regional board for another interview.

Reuse your fundamental concept to fit different granting requirements and economize your time. Taking a different angle on your project may even result in an overall improvement. You may never have considered how to incorporate youth into your project, or an environmental stewardship aspect. Maybe you will find a grant that gives money for the type of project you want to implement, but they also require a performance aspect, or a publication. This can help your ideas evolve, but at the same time, you don't want to overcommit or expand the scope to an incredible level.

You may find a grant or scholarship that could fit with your project, but it requires you to have someone dedicated to social media outreach. You hadn't thought of this before, but now you can't imagine your project without that role. Putting together a complete project requires coming up with a few details to supplement what you already have. This goes back to dreaming about what's possible and imagining all the things you could be doing with the skills and resources available to you.

In the dreaming part of project development, you can imagine a wonderful, huge program, but you need to keep in mind that review boards will want to know how you plan on accomplishing everything you set out to do. Sometimes getting the grant is the easiest part of doing your project, and then you actually have to do it! Keep the scope manageable.

All granting bodies are slightly different. Even application reviewers take different approaches. One of my friends, who knew she wanted to be a veterinarian from a young age, applied to multiple vet schools right out of college. She listed equine health as her field of interest, but the reviewer (who had met her in person when she visited one school) called her during the review process and asked if that's what she meant to put down. He told her that her résumé and experience fit better in another field, and she was able to change it after having submitted the official application. She got into the program with her new focus.

Like this lenient reviewer, I had a back-and-forth communication in my application to the Cornell Community Partnership Board (CPB). The CPB had a more flexible approach to applications; they went through the methodology of my project with me and listed their areas of concern. They wanted me to change a couple of details, which then allowed them to grant me the funds. However, some scholarships or programs have so many applicants that they are looking for minor details that can eliminate people and make their job easier.

The Fulbright director for Africa and the Middle East is an exceptionally kind and attentive person. Of all the Fulbright directors, I hear he is the nicest, and based on my correspondence and meeting with him, I believe it. After I didn't get the Fulbright the first time I applied, I resolved to try again. However, I wasn't sure whether my topic was worthy of a Fulbright, and if I'd be wasting my time applying for the same topic that wasn't chosen the first time.

With Don Andrew's help, I crafted a succinct email asking whether I should apply for dance in Senegal again or the other topic I was considering. He responded and explained that while he couldn't tell me exactly what the board thought, *he* thought that pursuing dance in Senegal was a promising topic and somewhat cryptically suggested that I proceed along the same lines. I was touched and amazed that he took the time to remember my topic and to make this suggestion in a very professional way. Don't expect everyone to be this responsive, though. More often than not, reviewers are overworked volunteers and not willing to field inquiry emails.

Once you have done the research and figured out the overall arc of your project, you can get down to the details. Armed with information about the granting body's preferences and past awardees, you can now develop your purpose statement and so-called elevator pitch. You've never heard of an elevator pitch? Don't worry; we'll get into that, too.

CHAPTER EIGHT

ELEVATOR PITCH /
PURPOSE STATEMENT

"Be able to explain what you have to offer in a few sentences. Many people cannot do this. They have never crafted an elevator pitch."

—**Michael Hyatt**, *New York Times* bestselling author

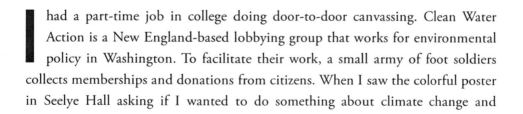

had a part-time job in college doing door-to-door canvassing. Clean Water Action is a New England-based lobbying group that works for environmental policy in Washington. To facilitate their work, a small army of foot soldiers collects memberships and donations from citizens. When I saw the colorful poster in Seelye Hall asking if I wanted to do something about climate change and pollution, I was psyched. Also, it paid a whole two dollars more than any campus job I could find. I immediately signed up.

The first day was the hardest; many people didn't show up for a second day. After arriving in the downtown Northampton office above Thornes Marketplace at 3:30 p.m., we had a fifteen-minute pep talk from our in-office coordinator and then we did some practice canvassing before driving out to the neighborhoods.

Practice consisted of pairing off and rehearsing how to sell people on our issues. The main campaign I canvassed for was raising labeling and regulatory standards for kids' items that contained PCBs. **We had to know key talking points about each of the campaigns.** In pairs, we acted out the scenario of knocking on the door, greeting the person, and giving them a hook line. Our spiel was no more than thirty seconds. If we couldn't get their attention in that timeframe, it was a lost cause, and we checked them off our list. This short introduction was concise, engaging, and articulate: who we were, whom we represented, what we were there to do, and how the person at the door could help us. We were also instructed to never say the word *basically,* because it suggested that we didn't really know what we were talking about.

Learning how to be concise and respectful of people's time and energy was essential for this job. I was not going to waste their time, especially if they didn't have any interest in donating. I got all kinds of responses from doing this work. Some people were really receptive and concerned about helping out the cause. Others were reluctant and just wanted me to get off their doorstep. Then of course, there were those people who were nasty and rude. I don't blame them. It's annoying to be asked for money and be pinned on your doorstep with some nagging social contract to be courteous.

A van dropped us off with maps of the neighborhoods we were to cover that afternoon, sign-up sheets and clipboards, and picked us up at a designated location four hours later. For those four hours, I went door-to-door, each time rallying myself to work up the energy for another sales pitch. If I had a receptive neighborhood, or reached a significant part of my fundraising goal early in the day, I would be optimistic. But if I was having a hard time getting anyone's interest, it would take a lot more self-pep-talking to approach yet another door.

This was hard work. I wouldn't have been nearly as good at it had I not spent the last six months working on fellowship applications. Don Andrew had forced the other applicants and me to state our objectives concisely. Writing a purpose statement over and over again was very good training for knowing how to get people's attention.

**As with any good sales pitch, you need
something to hook your audience.**

One sentence is usually enough to describe your intention. In an application format, your purpose statement becomes the very first sentence of your proposal. Following that, you further explain what you will be doing, why you are doing it, and when and how you are doing it.

The Elevator Pitch

Another good exercise that helped train me to state my ideas concisely was entering Smith's college-wide Elevator Pitch Contest. Although I had been aware of this annual event since my sophomore year, I didn't enter the competition until I was a senior. By that time, I was more emotionally and psychologically prepared.

**An elevator pitch is a ninety-second opportunity for you to sell an
idea to someone, as if you were in an elevator with an executive
and had his/her full attention for the duration of the ride.**

"Have something prepared for the inevitable 'tell us a little bit about yourself' question. This is a good place to use your elevator speech, with a little extra time for some elaboration here and there. You should not only discuss your academic achievement; also touch on your interests, hobbies, or extra-curricular activities. Tell your interviewer what you're passionate about and highlight your abilities and strengths. Don't be

afraid, however, to showcase your weaknesses as well. Contrary to what your intuition might be telling you, acknowledging your weaknesses is a strength. It shows that you know you don't know everything, you still have room to grow, and you're willing to tackle this growth. No matter what the program or position, it will require some growth on your end—nobody expects you to be perfect. Willingness to learn, flexibility, and openness are important components to highlight and continually work on."

—**Gemina Garland-Lewis**, former Thomas J. Watson Fellow and National Geographic Society Young Explorer Grantee

The weekend before the contest, I attended a green energy conference and got an idea for a solar sunshade that generates power while your car is parked. Every afternoon for nearly a week, I went into my room and turned up the music so my nervous voice wouldn't deter me. Again and again, I paced the room, loudly practicing my pitch. Each time, my heart fluttered faster and faster, encouraging me to just drop out. I didn't *have* to do it; I was completely free to liberate myself from the self-imposed obligation, but I kept practicing.

The contest was on a Thursday afternoon, and a small group of students gathered in the sunny, modern student center. Rows of chairs were set up before a small stage, and the panel of four judges sat at the back of the room. It turned out that not all of the people in the audience were going to compete. Only about ten women ultimately signed up. I was the third-to-last contestant—which was terrible, because waiting and watching everyone gave my nerves time to get worked up. Although I've been performing as a dancer my whole life, public speaking terrifies me. As my turn approaches, my heartbeat gets louder and louder until my whole body is shaking and I can't hear anything but blood rushing through my ears.

I was prepared for this pitch, however. I'd practiced and I was a senior, so I was older than about half of the audience. I got up and said my spiel, careful not to use words like *like* or *basically.* I emphasized the benefits of my product and didn't end any sentence with a rising intonation ("My product will be a valuable contribution to *society?*"). By ending each of my sentences on a strong, low note, I projected authority and confidence, and conveyed to the audience that my idea was serious and well thought-out.

TIP: Never use the words *like* and *basically* in a pitch. Also, train yourself to end sentences definitively instead of making them sound like questions.

As the pitches came to a close, I relaxed into my seat, aware that I had done my best and couldn't control anything. For this particular competition, there was a one-hundred-dollar prize for the winner only—no runners up. After a few minutes of deliberation in another room, the judges returned and announced without much ceremony that I had won. They gave me some positive and constructive feedback. They also informed me that I would be competing with this idea at the regional elevator pitch contest the following month, and I would receive coaching.

For the next month, I worked with two professors from the Smith Center for Women and Financial Independence. They sat at a table, while I stood in front of them and recited my pitch over and over again. Each time, they had different criticisms: slow down; don't wave your arms around; don't raise your voice; pause there; maybe try saying this sentence first. They were very helpful, and although I knew it was their job to help me, I felt more and more nervous each time I recited the pitch. My voice got shakier and I made more mistakes. Finally, they asked me why it made me more—not less—nervous to practice in front of people I knew.

"Because you know my pitch and can catch the mistakes more easily than people who don't know my pitch," I reasoned. There was no way around this; I just tried to stay calm and remember to breathe. I was holding my breath, which caused the shakiness in my voice, my increasing speed, and my lack of projection.

Tips for Effective Pitches

- Introduce yourself. Who are you and why should the audience care?
- Start with an attention-getting opening. For example, pick one of the following:
    - ○ Use a quotation
    - ○ Ask a question—participatory or rhetorical
    - ○ Refer to the occasion
    - ○ Paint a visual picture
    - ○ Give statistics
    - ○ Tell a story
    - ○ Use humor
- Organize your pitch logically and simply. Here's an example:
    - ○ Introduce your concept
    - ○ Explain the problem you're solving—what motivates your product/service?
    - ○ Describe how your proposed solution works
    - ○ Identify how your proposed solution is different—and better—than the competition
    - ○ Describe your business model—how will this be an effective business?
    - ○ Recap your concept
- End with a strong closing
    - ○ Emphasize your take-home point
    - ○ Be definite and don't trail off
    - ○ Bookend your pitch with an attention-getting close
- Use precise, concrete words
    - ○ Action verbs
    - ○ Strong modifiers
    - ○ Specific information/numbers
- Project confidence
    - ○ Speak slowly, clearly, and loudly

- ○ Dress formally without flashy clothing
- ○ Keep your hands/body relaxed and don't fidget
- ○ Demonstrate your enthusiasm, but with controlled emotions
- Maintain eye contact
- ○ Find friendly faces
- ○ Look at all areas of the room
- Practice, practice, practice
- ○ Pitch to the mirror
- ○ Pitch to your friends
- ○ Film your pitch and watch yourself

During that month, I also had the benefit of using my physics class as an experimental lab. Solar Power and Sustainability taught us the fundamentals of energy efficiency and photovoltaic technology. I asked my professor what kind of possible electrical output could be expected from a two by three foot photovoltaic array if it were positioned under a car windshield. He said, "Why don't we try it out?" So, during one of our class periods, the whole class went out to the parking lot, where he had his car and a photovoltaic cell waiting.

We took into account the various seasons and different geographical locations that have more or fewer sunny days. This experiment gave me some realistic numbers to cite in my pitch. After doing the experiment, I gave my pitch to the class, working my way up to a larger audience.

On the night of the competition, one of the professors from the Center for Women and Financial Independence drove me to the Connecticut lodge where the event was taking place. A few hundred people, both students and teachers, were in attendance. Before the catered dinner, everyone was encouraged to view student booths set up by entrepreneurship clubs from around the area. We then sat down at designated tables for dinner and listened to a speech from a successful entrepreneurial graduate of UMass Amherst.

Finally it was time for the elevator pitch contestants. All the students had won their school-wide competitions to get to this event. I dreaded the fact that we had to sit in the order in which we would present. Chairs for us lined the back of the stage, practically putting us on the spot the moment the pitches started. Knowing the order of pitches made me more nervous. I had time to work myself into a frenzy, knowing that I was two places away, then one place away.

As the applause subsided for the person before me, I stood up to take my position at the podium, grasping the sides of the slippery, laminate finish tightly to stop my hands from shaking. "Who wants to reduce their electricity bill?" I asked while raising my own hand to prompt the audience as I scanned the twenty packed tables in front of me. "Me too! Well I have a product that can help you with that, the Solar Sun Shade." I continued on with my pitch, **but accidentally started on the third section before the second section of my spiel.**

It's okay, I thought, and continued without a pause. The only people who would know my mistake would be my own professors at the far table in the corner. I remembered to breathe, took pauses, and ended on a strong note. Thanking everyone, I walked back to my table, confident that I had a good chance of winning, especially after hearing all the other pitches. My professors congratulated me and pointed out how smoothly I had covered my mistake.

When the winners were finally announced, a woman from a Connecticut college took third place (her charismatic sell was stronger than her product idea). They read my name second, and my table erupted in shocked applause. I headed up to the stage again to shake hands with Harold Grinspoon, the sponsor of the event. First place went to another woman from a different Connecticut college, which had won first place or runner-up for three years in a row. My recognition came with a $750 cash prize. Not bad. Public speaking and persuasion skills are valuable assets for grant and fellowship applications, and all interviews.

> **Public speaking is valuable for grants, fellowships, and life in general. Success comes from clearly communicating your ideas and presenting yourself as a likeable, trustworthy, and inspiring person.**

This experience helped me later the same year, when I was interviewing with the Rotary Club Scholarship committee. I put together my paper application a few months earlier, but then I had an initial interview with about seven members of the Northampton club. **I was not aware that the interview would be two and a half hours long!** I am grateful to my friend Katherine, a good friend from Santa

Fe and my ride to the office, who waited outside, not knowing when the interview would end. The interviewers came from very different backgrounds. There were a couple of small businessmen who ran a local window installation company. They had never left western Massachusetts. Then there were a couple of women who had traveled more extensively and had international viewpoints. My impression was that the Northampton Rotary Club was on the more conservative side. That meant that I had to successfully address the opinions and concerns this particular group had.

Practice Framing Your Story

"Practice, practice, practice. And then practice some more. Interviews are a nerve-wracking experience for both interviewers and interviewees. Be aware that interviews are a platform for both sides to get to know each other; so don't be afraid to ask questions, or to admit that you don't know something. Honesty always pays off.

Know and rehearse your story. It's your most important ammunition. If you have a boring story, they'll yawn and write you off. Think about how you can tailor your story to make your interviewers relate to it.

Think back to your previous interviews, remember what you did right and what you did wrong, and learn from it. Look up tips online, speak to people, dress appropriately.

Don't be nervous; it's not the end of the world. Whatever happens, happens for a reason. If you don't get this opportunity, you will have others."

—**Vidhee Garg**, Scholarship recipient at
Mumbai University and Cornell University

"Wherever possible, use real-life examples to showcase how you handled a difficult situation, a way you implemented change, achieved a personal goal, or maybe a situation you could have handled better. It's helpful to go into interviews with a few of these scenarios lined up so that you don't have that awkward and hectic rush to run through your entire life to think of something good on the spot."

—**Gemina Garland-Lewis**, former Thomas J. Watson Fellow
and National Geographic Society Young Explorer Grantee

When I interviewed for my college application to Dartmouth, the alumnae asked me what my perfect day would look like. I thought back to a recent day that I felt really great about. "Well, I woke up somewhat early, but well rested. I went to work (it was winter vacation), then I went to the gym, and then to dinner." I paused for a minute, and said aloud, "Wow, that sounds really boring." I was reflecting on how flat the story sounded.

Years later, when I was talking with friends from Brown in Brazil, I told them how badly my interview had gone. "That's not a bad story, you just needed to frame it differently. Preface it by saying, 'I like to have a balanced life of work, health, family time, and friend time. I feel best when I get all of these components into my day,' and then talk about how each of those activities makes you feel." This invaluable advice from Danielle taught me that interviewing is really about telling a story and making it sound interesting.

Interviews require you to think on your feet and come up with a convincing and credible answer on the spot. Having done the door-to-door canvassing allowed me to read the interests of the people I was talking to. During my Rotary interview, after I had explained how other cultures helped to form my opinion in a positive way, one man challenged me, "Well, are you less American now?"

"Of course not!" I defended my patriotism. "Seeing the disparity in economic and social classes in Brazil and the lack of public services in Senegal has made me value and appreciate the great culture and infrastructure we have created in the United States." Another member of the board defended my position as well. Being able to talk to this man's concerns was important to convey a fuller portrait of myself.

Here is an exercise to help you craft a purpose statement. Write down one sentence that you think captures the essence of your project.

_____

_____

_____

Now, referring to the work you did in Chapter Four, revise your sentence based on what you've learned.

_____

_____

_____

Ask yourself the following questions:

Does this sentence tell me who, what, when, and where my project will take place? Y/N

Does the person who wrote this sentence sound confident and competent? Y/N

Does the sentence contain the uncertain words *maybe, could, if,* or does it employ more definite terms, like *will, can, when*? Y/N

Does this sentence make me excited about reading the rest of this proposal? Y/N

You want the purpose statement to catch your reader's attention and generate interest in you.

Rewrite your purpose statement to include the missing information:

_____

_____

_____

_____

CAUTION: Do not include too much field-specific jargon in a purpose statement or objective. These elements require a careful balance to make it sound like you know what you're talking about (convincing language that hints at in-depth knowledge of a particular field), while not alienating your reader. You cannot assume that all readers know Latin names or anthropological categories. List a couple of field-specific terms, but make sure to explain what that term means and how it relates to your project. One sentence usually suffices, because proposals have limited word counts. You don't want your entire proposal to be a vocabulary lesson.

Know Your Audience

By Andy Rotman

When writing a proposal for a grant or fellowship, you should keep in mind your intended audience and craft your proposal so that those readers can easily, efficiently, and enjoyably extract the requisite information from your writing. How does one do this?

As a first step, try to imagine yourself as one of the readers of your proposal. Suppose you are a professor with a busy schedule and you are sitting at your desk feeling tired. Perhaps it's late in the afternoon and you've already had a full day, or maybe it's early in the morning before you've begun your teaching or administrative work. It's hard to find time to read through a large pile of proposals, and now that you've carved out some time, you want to get through the process as expeditiously as possible.

So how does one make it easy for such an individual to read your proposal? First of all, present the material in an organized fashion. Your readers will no doubt be reading your proposal for very specific kinds of information. They may even have a checklist of various categories, such as the quality and viability of (i) topic, (ii) preliminary research, (iii) project goals, and (iv) methodology, and empty check boxes corresponding to poor, good, excellent, or outstanding. What this means is that you'll want to organize your proposal so your data is grouped together cohesively—if possible, in the same categories that your readers will be looking for. This means, for example, that your methodology should not be interspersed throughout your proposal. It should not be spread out across multiple paragraphs so that your readers will have to cherry-pick their way through your proposal to check the appropriate box. You don't want to make your readers do the work of assembling your material into the relevant categories so that they can evaluate your project. You should do that work for them. And don't be afraid to be blunt. If a grant requires that its applicants have advanced language skills in French, then say, "I have advanced language skills in French, having studied the language for three years in college and one year in Geneva."

Here's another thought experiment that might be helpful. Imagine your readers as experienced and knowledgeable consumers. They know what they are looking for, and as experienced consumers, they know where to look for it. If they were in a clothing or convenience store, they could quickly survey the premises, surmise whether the venue was likely to have what they were looking for, and make an educated guess as to where what they were looking for might be. But the training and instincts of those educated consumers would likely fail if they suddenly entered a store that didn't follow the rules of the industry. Their knowledge as consumers would do little for them in a store that arranged clothing according to where it was stitched, rather than by gender, size, or color. What if they shelved the candy, gum, and cigarettes at the back of the store, far away from the registers? Just as a convenience store is supposed to be convenient to navigate, so too is your proposal.

So how can you write a proposal so your readers can easily find and evaluate your data? Start by reading through all the instructions for your proposal very carefully, then identify the topics to be addressed, and use them to organize your material. Remember, you don't gain many points—if any at all—from answering questions you haven't been asked to answer. So if you are asked to explain the relationship between your proposed project and your previous work, make sure you do so. Each word in your proposal is precious. Don't waste any!

Consider these instructions from the National Science Foundation:

In a clear, concise, and original statement, describe research topics you may pursue while on fellowship tenure, and include how you became interested in these topics. Your statement should reflect your own thinking and work, demonstrate your understanding of research principles necessary to pursue these interests, and explain the relationship to your previous research, if any. Present your plan with a clear hypothesis or questions to be asked by the research.

What paragraphs might follow? What should and should not be included? What might the readers of such a proposal be expecting?

Now, in addition to having clear sections in your proposal, make sure you have clear topic sentences, so your readers will know what to expect as they begin each paragraph, and will also be able to scan your proposal for requisite bits of information. For example, consider the following topic sentences: "As an undergraduate at Smith College, I majored in art history, focusing on how images are used to create and contest social identities." Or, "Though my primary research as a social scientist occurred while I was writing my senior thesis, I have also engaged in other research activities that have prepared me for future work in the social sciences." Sentences like these clue the reader in to what kind of information will follow. For readers perusing your proposal for boxes to check, this is very helpful.

TIP: Restate the question(s) in the instructions and formulate concise, bullet-point answers. Readers love having centralized and visually simple text when checking off their reviewing rubrics.

Five men and women sit around a table in a conference room, with a bay window looking out onto a beautiful lawn. The first budding blossoms of spring tease and tempt, feigning a warm glow in the brisk breeze. However, the people are oblivious to the beauty unfolding out the window as they battle over who merits the fellowship.

One woman yells, "Are you telling me that even though I have four ecstatic supporters for my applicant, I have to tell him he doesn't have the fellowship because you don't like one aspect of his methodology?" Personally offended by a colleague's objections, she persists, "I know that we only have twenty grants to give out, even though we have one hundred perfect applicants, but can't you see that this one should be a winner?" Judging from the passion in her voice, you'd think she was advocating for her own child's application.

You may not believe that this scene is realistic, but it is. In the United Way, Gates Foundation, NIH, NSF, Rotary Foundation, and many other funding agency conference rooms, you can find such a forum as the final round of selections are made each year. How did the reviewers become so invested? Because they have come to know the applicants through the multiple rounds leading up to the finale. They have come to love the projects themselves and to gain hope from the possibility of seeing a project through. The best applications win over their readers, who share the applicants' enthusiasm and certainty that the work that will be carried out on fellowship.

The first step to snagging your champion reader is your one-sentence purpose statement that concisely sums up the essence of your project. This is easier said than done. Expect to work on this first, most important sentence for a while, asking as many people as possible to read it and give you comments. Not only must it encompass your intention; it must also speak to what the reviewer wants to see. What do they care about? What does the fellowship ask for? Know whom you are trying to convince and tell them what they want to hear. Intrigue them by asking interesting and important questions, and follow them with meaningful and compelling answers. Your job is to demonstrate that your project will do these things, and that you have some special skills and knowledge that make you well suited to carry it out.

"Don't be tentative," says Andy Rotman. "Use the first-person, active voice (e.g., I will study…; I will interview…; I will complete my fieldwork by…). Show them that you have the ability, wisdom, passion, and patience to produce—and finish—an intriguing project."

"I wasn't sure that I could email the grantor(s) and ask questions. I always pictured it as if a faceless person or group of persons would read my application. I failed to realize that it would be a bunch of real people with real emotions, feelings, and thoughts."

—**Vidhee Garg**, Scholarship recipient at
Mumbai University and Cornell University

I volunteered to review the initial applications for the Mandela Washington Fellowship in Fall 2014. It was tough ranking all the applications. Besides just determining whether all the materials had been submitted, I had to rank people's dreams and aspirations. I will tell you that I ranked highest those people who made me understand their passions. When people love their jobs, it comes through in their writing. It's yet another reason to pursue the things you love, because it will be easier to persuade others to support your worthy cause.

CHAPTER NINE

LINE UP YOUR CONTACTS

"The best advice to me was to get a strong and detailed letter of support from my host institution."

—**Jere Gilles**, Associate Professor, University of Missouri

Why is it important to have professionals vouch for you? First, social endorsements reassure your reader that you aren't just all talk and no action. Think about how you are much likelier to connect with an acquaintance if you have a friend in common than if that person is a complete stranger. Professional recommendations act in a similar way to legitimize your project. In addition, having a contact shows that you have already invested time and energy into your project.

A network of professional contacts adds invaluable support to your application.

Since I traveled to Senegal twice before applying to study there, I already knew people who would write recommendations for me. I had been studying with the same tradition-holding family for years and they were well known. When I needed letters of support for my application, I was easily able to get one from the member of the family living in the United States.

The second contact I needed to get was from an institution. This one was much harder. I had attended a presentation by a Senegalese professor during the spring of my sophomore year. The professor was visiting multiple colleges from l'Université Cheikh Anta Diop in Dakar, and I enthusiastically approached her after her presentation. It turned out that she wanted to help me, but it was very hard to get in touch with her once she went back to Senegal. I didn't know until the last minute whether I was going to get a letter of support from her, but days before the application was due, she came through.

Lining up contacts for your project can be difficult. It can take months to find a contact and then, once you have one, working out the terms of your association. In some cases, research institutes will host foreign students and researchers for a fee. Other contacts may not require anything from you, but they want to know about you before vouching for your project. Especially if you plan on working in a foreign country, there can be obstacles to communication and coordination. Perhaps a reliable Internet connection is still an issue in the country. Or it could be difficult to navigate the administrative structure of the organization to find out whom to talk to. Talking to a teacher at a university may not secure you any privileges, whereas a dean might have the authority to grant you permission to use the library, for example.

Systems are different in every country. My friend who studied in Italy said that books there were categorized by size, not by author name. In Brazil, the class materials for each course were photocopied in various unorganized copy shacks around campus. There can also be a language barrier. Depending on your level of fluency, you may have trouble getting information from a host institution.

Peter Cohen explains

[I]f the invite is from the dean (or local equivalent) of the faculty within which you wish to work, even better, as in almost all nations, a faculty member will need the dean's (and provost's) approval for any invite, anyway. But this is tricky. You don't want to write to the dean directly, as in most developing nations, as well as Europe, that is considered pushy, unseemly, and possibly undue influence. What you really want to do is to impress your putative faculty host to such a degree that he or she contacts their dean, on their own initiative, on your behalf as a prospective Fulbright Fellow at that foreign institution. It worked for me, anyway (I was still careful to follow British-style Commonwealth protocols and cultural norms).

Misunderstandings with my contacts have been my greatest downfall and my greatest challenge. I struggle to this day to have clearer communication at the outset, to eliminate these challenges down the line. I started out partnering with people by believing that I had to shield the difficult issues from them to get their support. I thought that, somehow, the harder business details would work themselves out later. This is absolutely the wrong way to go about being a good partner. Although you don't want to emphasize the harsher realities of working together, it's best to lay them out on the table.

When I was working with the artists in Senegal, learning about the traditional dance form, we discussed how many times a week they would be teaching. I did not want to talk about how much money they would get, because I didn't know how many people would be interested in the classes yet. We were all excited about the prospect of having regular dance classes, so I left the discussion on a high note. Only later did the issue of money come up. I could subsidize the classes, but only to a certain extent, so the teachers were getting less than they expected while the class was building popularity. You might want to be buddy-buddy and not talk about money or deadlines or expectations, but it gets harder and harder when responsibilities go unstated.

The biggest example of this is dealing with money. If there is payment involved with your partner, outline at the beginning what they can expect to be paid, in what intervals, and in return for what products. Laying out payment details as early in the relationship as possible will clarify expectations. Warning: this does not always completely eliminate arguments down the line, but at least you can point back to a document that was agreed upon.

When I did my first Cornell Community Partnership Board grant, I was working with two drummers in Ithaca. I had proposed to pay them each twenty dollars per class when I first contacted them, months before the kids' dance class even started. But then we had a verbal contract when the classes started, which stated that I would pay them every four classes, to keep the receipts for the grant to a minimum.

A few months later, after a rocky start to the class, the drummers wanted to be paid at every class. I accepted, understanding that with the uncertain nature of the schedule, they may go a couple of months before completing four classes. This worked fine for a few more months, but one spring day, the community center where we held the class closed for the day without letting me know. I arrived at the center, only to see the drummers' truck speeding away down the street. I went up to the front door to find that the center was closed and went home.

Later that day, the drummers called me and told me that it was not working for them to drum anymore. They said they weren't getting paid enough and that I had dropped the ball somewhere, which had led to that day's missed connection. I reminded them that we had agreed upon that price months before and if that was a problem they should have let me know beforehand. I think the drummers were just looking for an excuse and there were other things they were dealing with that had nothing to do with me, but it left me in a bind for completing the grant. I ended up teaching a body-percussion class for the remainder of the spring term, feeling upset and disappointed with the way the partnership had worked out.

Partner to Supplement Your Skills

My instinct tells me that sometimes having partners can make your life easier when you're trying to get a grant or scholarship. Nobody is perfect at everything, so it makes sense to supplement your own knowledge with other peoples' expertise. The trick to this is delegating tasks and being a good manager with good communication skills. If you don't trust anyone else to take responsibility for part of the project, you're not going to benefit from what they can contribute. Working out tasks and making clear deadlines in the beginning of a partnership is essential to making the relationship work.

The second Cornell Community Partnership Board grant that I got was to fund a facilitation workshop for teachers and youth workers. The curriculum and program were already developed and had been in use for more than a decade. I was trying to move into a phase of collaboration instead of solo project execution. I partnered with a woman who had been a teacher in Santa Fe for many years and who had taken part in this training in the past.

Unfortunately, neither of us had experience with bringing a pre-made program into the city before. We started out trying to coordinate dates that would work. Initially we wanted to do the program during the summer so that teachers would have more time to attend. But then we didn't have everything together in time to do a summer program and we hadn't even been in clear contact with the people from the organization bringing the program. It took until the end of the summer to finally get in contact with the right people, but we still were not sure about whom to send the facilitation payment to and who was organizing plane tickets for the facilitator's flight. I ended up buying a plane ticket and organizing a place to hold the training in mid-September, only to find out that that date was not going to work because of conflicting public school and community arts festival calendars. The ticket was non-refundable.

First major lesson.

We rescheduled for the second time to hold the event in early December. This time, we knew we would just pay the organization for the facilitator's daily fee and his plane ticket. They would take care of scheduling his flight, while we would take care of his accommodations and pay for the workshop space.

The date of the rescheduled workshop was approaching quickly and the only thing we needed to do was to recruit people. I got the grant with the intention of making the training free for all teachers and participants. I figured that teachers are so poorly paid and strapped for time that they should get some free perks every once in a while. If this training was going to give them tools to inspire youth and to reinvigorate the teaching experience (it has become dreary and repressive), I was going to make it as available as possible.

Unfortunately, the parent organization thought they needed to charge for the training, and insisted up until the very last few days that people would have to pay. A week and a half before the training, there were four people signed up, including myself and the other organizer. We wanted to bail. I wanted to offer a no-fee option, and the former teacher wanted to postpone the event again. I knew that postponing was not an option, so I just informally let people know that if they couldn't afford the high price, we could work something else out.

In the final week leading up to the training weekend, we managed to get twenty-eight people signed up, almost all of whom had some special financial arrangement. We asked some people to bring food for snacks, others to bring art supplies, others we just told they could come, because it would be better if more people contributed. It was all about filling the seats, because the facilitator was booked and there was no turning back. **It all ended up working out well, but it taught me that, even when it seems like partnerships are going to be a great fit, there is still a learning curve each time you work with someone new.**

Lining up your contacts proves that you have support for your project. A granting body wants to know that other people believe in you enough to give their time, money, or energy to the cause. I see a parallel in how people meet new friends. Very few people make honest and trusting connections with people they've met at a bar. More often, I find that I have made friends with a new person whom I met through a mutual friend. This assurance that someone I trust approves of the new person allows me to be more open with that person and begin to form a connection. The same goes for people giving you money. They want to have some kind of assurance that you're not a complete liar who is going to take their money and run. A trusted contact or another granting body vouching for you provides this kind of security.

In Chapter Six, I explained that having a couple of smaller fellowships or grants under your belt acts in the same way to show that you are a capable scholar. Grants and fellowships build off of one another. Since I've been quilting frequently, I see the connection with building upon a basic foundation. I started by learning to cut very even, four-inch squares. Sixty-four of these squares are enough to piece together a simple quilt, but from there, I could also use the squares to make different patterns, like half-square triangles, and from there, I could make pinwheels. Without the foundational basis of a square, I wouldn't have been able to make the more complex or intricate patterns. Building up your repertoire of grants, fellowships, and contacts is essential to move up to the next level.

My friend Vidhee Garg advises

You have to be persistent, and then some more. But there's a fine line between being persistent and being a pain in the butt. Don't cross it. Sometimes, people will not reply, and if they do, they may not seem friendly. Don't be discouraged; keep trying. Cast your net widely and catch as many people as you can. Know the right questions to ask and the right things to say. Research the people you are going to meet and know everything you can find out online or through other means.

Networking has always served me well. Undoubtedly, you already know some someone (or someone who knows someone) who can help you with fellowships; it's just a matter of seeking them out. Once I started getting fellowships, I started asking other fellows how they had come to their situations. I found that many of my colleagues had a history of grants leading up to the current one. Asking them about these other opportunities sometimes led to me applying for those same positions myself. For example, one of the Kiva Fellows with whom I was working was doing a Rotary scholarship as well, so I ended up applying for it, too. Once I was a Rotary Scholar, I was talking to another person who was also an EPA Fellow. I did apply for the EPA Fellowship, but only got to the first round of selections. That was okay, I still wouldn't have even known to apply for that had I not asked my fellow Rotarian about it. People who are knowledgeable about grants and fellowships are usually in the know about more possibilities. It's kind of like a club that once you enter, you have increased access.

Advice from LinkedIn

You'll find that connecting with groups will help you along the application process. I'm part of the LinkedIn Fulbright group, and I asked them, "What's the best piece of advice you got when applying for the Fulbright?" This is what they said:

Two pieces of advice helped:

One was to make sure you demonstrate how the project you are proposing will make an impact in the place you are planning to serve. The program is about cultural exchange and building bridges. That should be your underlying guide.

For countries that require local institutional support, take the time to do most of the legwork before submitting your application. It might help when you are compared to someone else who did not take the time to find a local organization.

And one thing I learned: when seeking references, find one who will take the time to write a mind-blowing letter for you. When I went to my Fulbright orientation, two committee members commented that they were convinced after reading just one of my reference letters. So ask people who know you and what you have to contribute. Good luck!"

—**Tavon Cooke**, World Dreamer and former Fulbrighter

"I concur with Tavon Cooke's advice. Having been a reviewer for Fulbright, what we look for is a strong proposal with clear goals and feasible outcomes. The better you summarize that in the introduction, the clear research or teaching goals, showing how your proposal will impact work with other scholars, contribute to an ongoing area of research, or help with developing approaches to certain types of scientific, educational, economic, cultural, political, or environmental issues, the more likely your proposal will be considered to move forward. Provide some background academic references or past work that supports your proposal, but be succinct.

I know that many people write proposals with long, detailed pros about why they are drawn to a particular country. Have a real reason that your research must take place in the country you are proposing, such as facilities, the groups you are working with are only in this country, you have a relationship built with colleagues and you need to spend a significant time working with them in person, or that your research subject is in-country. Please do not include that it's your life dream because you saw a movie or read a book. I hope this is helpful and good luck!"

—**Kathleen Fritz**, CEO/Founder at CREATOMbuilder

"The best advice was to be yourself and they will love you for who you are. So I tried to speak with my heart, and it worked. Also, don't be afraid to be creative. Fulbright is not only about academics; I think it's more than that!"

—**Bénédicte Nègre Vermongen**, Professeur de FLE et de Lettres Modernes and former Fulbrighter

"Work the application from both ends. In other words, get a foreign university to be interested in you and, in the best of all possible worlds, obtain a letter from that institution in which they express their interest in you and your field of expertise. And then submit their letter of interest to the CIES. Good luck."

—**Craig Beles**, JD, LLM, MCIArb, experienced Independent Arbitrator & Mediator, Fulbright Specialist in International ADR, former litigator

"The best advice I received when applying for the Fulbright was to combine my scientific and analytical skills and research experiences with my ambition to serve as a future US cultural ambassador to Thailand. Currently, my Fulbright research is about the life-cycle environmental impacts of implementing electric motorcycles in Thailand as a strategy to meet energy reduction targets for the country's transportation sector."

—**Piya Kerdlap**, Fulbright Research Fellow

"The best advice I received came from a staff member of the Turkish Fulbright Committee at the very first social gathering where they introduced the program. She told us to work on the essays very hard and make them sound personal and real. That was very helpful for me because, even though I was a sociology graduate and had written many essays by that time, I was stressed about those two essays. I chose to write with an open, honest, and passionate tone of voice. I underlined the vitality of the scholarship and the program I wanted to be educated in for my future goals. And it worked! Good luck."

—**Nazlihan Eda Erçin**, Performer/Researcher, PhD Candidate in Performance Practice at University of Exeter

"Your level of commitment to give back to society or your sponsor institution when you return to your home country. State that loud and clear."

—**Daniel R. Castellón Alvarado**, International Account Manager, Telefónica Group at GBM Corp. (An IBM alliance company)

"To not spell Fulbright *Fullbright*. Just kidding, but that was one of the suggestions. The best thing was that there was a Fulbright advisor (she was the one with the spelling suggestion, among others) on campus that briefed all the candidates at a meeting and was subsequently available for consultation. She was a big help and it's something I recommend for any campus."

—**Jeffrey Diamond**, Founder and Director of VerbMatrix, Director of the English Center at Tecnun, the Engineering School of the University of Navarra

"If you are applying for a teaching Fulbright, do not overemphasize what you can do for them. Instead, balance this with some of the many things you'll learn while you're there and what this will enable you to do for others upon your return."

—**Ann Garry**, Professor of Philosophy, California State University, Los Angeles

"Work both ends of the process. I am convinced my application was accepted over others because I already had a promise from the Australian National University that I would be given admin support (an office, computer, copying and library privileges).

On the home end of the process, follow the rules. The Fulbright selection committee, like any major fellowship committee, is going to go through a lot of applications, and once you get down to it, they are all going to be good. The committee needs a reason to separate lots of good applications, so if your essay is too long or doesn't fit in the document box, it's an easy dump. Don't make the assumption that your application is *that good* and the committee will see that. The application next to yours is also *that good*, and that person followed the rules."

—**Eric Shibuya**, Associate Professor at
USMC Command and Staff College

"Some advice only from my own experience as a Fulbrighter. 1) Letters of support from institutions that historically have had good Fulbright participation and/or representation from respective countries is a big help, and 2) I formed my own review team with a very good writer to review both the technical attributes of my proposed research, but equally important, had them really 'peer review' the quality of the application, proposed research, and materials in total. I believe these two features were very helpful in my application process."

—**James Austin**, Global Product Development Manager, BASF Corp.

Although these LinkedIn comments particularly address the Fulbright process, they can be applied to any application. And, nearly all applications will require you to have strong contacts. Gemina Garland-Lewis advises:

I've sent a lot of cold-contact emails in my life, and almost all of them have come back with a positive response. At the end of the day, we're all human and we've all been there—people are able to look back on the times in their own lives when they were looking for help and are often willing to help out someone who is now in that place. As long as you are professional and show how your interests are relevant to the person you're contacting, you'll likely get a response.

Make sure that you don't mass email people with a generic letter. You *won't* get a response to this. Do your research and find a few key players that you think could really help you, and then make an effort to tailor your approach to each one individually. If it's clear you put care into it, you'll likely get that back. As with many things in life, you get back what you put in!

Katherine Noble, PhD student at University of Utah Department of Biology, offers this advice for the challenge of finding good contacts:

The most important contact for me was made through email—I looked up a professor at a local natural history museum, asked to visit the lab, volunteered my time/services, and ended up making a great future contact. I made a positive impression by being super friendly and hardworking, even though I was totally embarrassed by my language skills. My abroad program offered connections and setups with local organizations—I can't believe I never took them up on this. Network at your abroad program; they are used to helping American students find places to volunteer their time, and if you ever want to come back, they will remember you and help you out. Create your own auspices for making contacts at universities. I have two friends who set up little research projects while abroad, and have since gone back to get master's degrees on these same projects. They learned to use the libraries, connected with professors, and interviewed people while they were there. Generally, people are excited if you show an interest in their interests, and will later serve as important contacts.

List everyone you know who works in your field of interest:

_____

_____

_____

List everyone you know who may be in or from your country of interest:

_____

_____

_____

List everyone you have heard of who has won your scholarship of interest before:

_____

_____

_____

List all the universities in the geographical area you're interested in (universities are a great resource and will usually give you referrals to faculty or community members who can help you):

_____

_____

_____

If you're having trouble listing these individuals, contact your mentor and ask for suggestions.

SECTION THREE

JUST DO IT! WRITE AND REWRITE

The next three chapters get down to the nitty-gritty of cranking out an application. You've done the research and soul-searching, now it's time to put it on paper. Don't be daunted; you've already constructed the key points throughout the exercises in the previous chapters. All you have to do now is mold them together into a proposal and personal statement.

CHAPTER TEN

THE CHEAT CHAPTER, OR WHO, WHAT, WHEN, WHERE, HOW, WHY, AND RESULTS

"To be a Fulbrighter requires a lot of hard work, but it's worth it. I would suggest you make serious preparation, especially with the statement letter and study objectives. Ask people (more than one) to review your statement letter and study objectives. Keep them precise and interesting. Remember, there are thousands of people who dream of being a Fulbrighter, so don't beat around the bush. Convince the selection committee that you are unique and special."

—**Itha Priyastiti**, Lecturer at Sekolah Tinggi
Ilmu Ekonomi Kristen Wira Wacana Sumba

I f you want to skip the rest of this book and get to the basic, how-to nuts and bolts, this is the chapter for you. There is a basic format for all applications, you just need to include **who, what, when, where, how, why, and results** of your project. Review the worksheet you filled out in Chapter Four, revise the aspects you have changed after reading the last few chapters, and then build upon that foundational document. During my time at Smith College, I learned that it works well to format applications in the following sequence:

1. Objective
2. Rationale
3. Methodology

Who, What, When, Where, How, Why, and Results

You can assume that any application will want to know the basic who, what, when, where, how, why, and the expected results. Even if the grantor doesn't state these objectives clearly, you want to have the answers to all of these questions prepared when you are thinking about your project. The goal of dreaming is to come up with the what and where. The other aspects can be worked out further down the line. After you have done your imagining about what your perfect project would look like (what you could imagine yourself doing in the future), then start to imagine more of the details.

- What would the arc of your project be (the scope)?
- What would be the auxiliary tasks involved in completing your project?

Thinking about whom you will need to help you will start the process of approaching contacts for your project, as Chapter Nine explains. Asking yourself these questions also forces you to clarify what you're planning on doing.

STATEMENT OF GRANT PURPOSE
Lucy Gent, Senegal, Dance 2009
Sabar: From Cultural Tradition to National Treasure.

OBJECTIVE:

I propose to study the extant instruction and transmission of Sabar, the traditional dance of Senegal, and how aspiring performers can prepare to become viable professional artists or academics within modern Senegal. Sabar dancers have become internationally recognized for their talent, spurring demand for these artists abroad who are unable to achieve the same success in their home country. After seeing the reception of their national ballet in Europe, the Guinean government decided to nationalize the ballet in 1958 to promote their national culture, ideology, and sovereignty. The Ministry of Culture continues to support Guinean dance and brings foreigners to study what has become the most widely transmitted form of West African dance and music. The uniqueness of Sabar lends itself to the same promotion within its own country and expansion into others. As a future dance teacher and community leader, I aim to understand what types of support and promotion are necessary to accomplish the evolution of the Senegalese artist into a prosperous professional and to promote Sabar internationally.

I look forward to the opportunity to immerse myself for ten months in the traditional transmission of Sabar dance with the Sing Sing family, effectively becoming a case study myself. Having studied with the Sing Sing family on two previous short trips to Senegal, I already have a relationship on which to build my research. By establishing a comfortable familiarity with the dancers, I plan to begin the process of connecting the Université Cheikh Anta Diop and the artists themselves to the Senegalese Ministry of Arts for future collaboration. During the course of my Fulbright, I will lay the foundation for a program to promote Sabar between griot (tradition-holding) families and all other interested individuals. The program will offer Sabar instruction to students of any age and experience level from within and without Senegal. Websites and association with the Ministry of Arts will bring international attention to the program to expand beyond what I am able to initiate during 2011. The cross-cultural collaboration of the program will thereafter evolve according to the interests of the stakeholders.

RATIONALE:

Culture is like oxygen: it surrounds us, often without our awareness of its crucial function to our lives. Senegal has a rich dance and drum tradition, which uniquely defines it from the rest of West Africa. Unlike the Guinean government, which has fostered the development of its artistic industry for domestic and international marketability, Senegalese artists have developed individual careers, but mostly only after leaving Senegal. I have seen from the United States that touring artists sponsor entire families back in Senegal. Sabar is what defines Senegal for me as a foreigner, but young Senegalese are eager to study more lucrative professions than their traditional art forms. Sabar dancers who have not been able to succeed financially within Senegal have captured devoted students and audiences in the United States and Europe, creating a demand for classes and performances that Senegal could now provide as a commodity. I want to encourage partnership between the government and the griots by presenting my findings to the Ministry of Arts and to university boards, both in Senegal and abroad. My work can also provide information about how artists can create revenue for themselves and for their government as a niche industry for research and professional development. My earlier study of Sabar in Senegal and my ability to communicate in Wolof have prepared me for this research. My academic studies of foreign languages and economics, my intensive African and Sabar experience, and my immersion in

Brazilian and African cultures, together with my affiliates, ensure that I will successfully undertake and communicate this research. I possess the background, passion, and diligence to carry out this project and create more venues for future studies in Sabar.

METHODOLOGY:

I foresee implementation of my research over the grant period following distinct, yet overlapping phases.

Phase One: In the first three months of the grant, I will conduct individual research on the transmission of Sabar, while also recording professional biographical interviews. Through previously established personal contacts, I will work and live with the Sing Sing, Faye, Ngom, and Mbaye families, taking dance classes and learning the griot traditions. Aziz Faye, internationally renowned performer, dance teacher, and drummer, has sent me a letter of support to sponsor my proposed Fulbright research. Concurrently in phase one, I'll be identifying and interviewing other institutional stakeholders in the Sabar community. When I arrive in December 2010, I will build the foundation of my research working with the West African Research Center (WARC) to gather academically archived information about the griot culture. I will also access resources at the Université Cheikh Anta Diop (UCAD) with Professor Penda Mbow, who has also provided a letter of support.

Phase Two: During month four of my grant period, I will facilitate conversation and collaboration between the various individual and institutional stakeholders. By joining in academic discussions with the UCAD through Professor Mbow, I aim to begin increasing recognition for traditional art forms. As an experienced performer and student, I will help both the university and the artists themselves gain a student following for the new dance program. The focus of working with UCAD will be to create a prototypical program for young people to study dance and music.

Phase Three: By the fifth month, I intend to be working with identified resources (locations, pre-existing classes, WARC outreach) and teachers on beginning a program for young students to learn Sabar in Dakar.

Through pamphlets and local dance competitions, the Guinea model of dance promotion will begin to take hold in Senegal. I will volunteer in Senegalese schools by bringing Sabar into an increasingly diverse arts curriculum, as well as initiating an Internet presence.

Phase Four: In the last months of my grant, I will research the program's viability and sustainability. I want to see this program promote the financial and institutional support of Sabar artists by stimulating cultural and academic partnerships. My documentation will contribute to the body of knowledge about Senegalese arts, and I will also present at a number of American dance and cultural venues upon my return to the United States. Presenting lectures and video footage will expand transnational understanding between living history and living culture in Senegal, and will inspire future scholars. The exchange of ideas between Western and Senegalese peoples will enhance a worldly understanding on both sides of the Atlantic.

Clear Writing Comes from an Outline

I will be forever grateful for Donald Andrew's tutelage in formulating a three-part proposal: objective, rationale, and methodology. His system of breaking a proposal up into these parts clearly delineates all the information required by grantors and evaluators, visually easing the content while also bookmarking check-off items so readers know exactly where to look for each of the required responses. This format has become my default outline for all applications unless the directions specify a different structure. Like any piece of good, legible, and interesting writing, you want your proposal to be well written. Some part of this comes from editing drafts, but it helps a lot if the initial draft is well structured. An outline can help you do this.

In each subsection (objective, rationale, methodology), start to bullet-point the main elements you want your reader to come away with. Don't worry at first about the order of your points, just make sure the major groupings make sense and that you have them in the correct sections of the application. You may realize that you want to start telling the reader about how you want to accomplish your project in the objective section, when that point should really be put under the methodology section. Having a good outline helps you organize your thoughts so that when you start writing, you can just focus on explaining yourself clearly.

The **objective** should begin with your purpose statement. Remember in Chapters Four and Eight, when you crafted a single sentence that explained exactly what you wanted to do? Start your objective section with that sentence. From there, expand into a few more of the details about what your project entails:

- What will you do?
- Where do you plan on working?
- Whom will it serve?
- When will it take place (generally)?

These should all be about one-sentence explanations, or perhaps two sentences if you need to explain a field of research or a term. The objective should be short and sweet; something that hooks a reader and gives them just a taste of what's to come later in your proposal.

The **rationale** explains a little more about why you are doing your project. This could also be described as the Problem.

- What is the need for your work?
- What is the background of the area you chose?
- Why is it essential that you go there?
- How will your work be effective in addressing this problem?

This is where the research behind your proposal comes in. It helps to give some statistics (properly cited, of course). Basing your statements in fact helps convince reviewers, because numbers stand out more than general statements. Also, giving the history of the problem provides context:

- When did the problem start?
- Is this the pinnacle or is the problem getting worse?
- What other efforts have been made to address the issue?
- How is your effort different?

- Why is it essential to take action right now?
- What are possible ramifications of non-action or delayed action?

Convincing the grant review board that your topic deserves immediate attention brings it forward from the stack of other applicants.

The **methodology** works best as a timeline. You could start the methodology by saying what actions you plan on taking and/or the overall approach you have to solving the problem. After that, breaking down the larger actions into smaller tasks or goals according to a logical and chronological sequence helps you and your reviewer envision what the end product will look like. Try to include a sequence of progressive steps that lead to a culminating project. The methodology could also include organizing the myriad components of setting up a class or an event.

Within the methodology, I have found that reviewers also like to see that you give yourself time for reflection and possible redirection. They realize that things don't always work out as you plan. If you take the time to correct or improve what you're doing midway through your project, then the end product will be better. This also demonstrates your maturity. You don't assume everything you do will be perfect and that unexpected things won't happen in life. These are realistic expectations that show you have experience with working on projects in the past.

The outline should follow the funder's questions, guidelines, or selection criteria for the proposal. As I mentioned before, if the funder does not specifically give questions to answer, then fall back on the objective-rationale-methodology format. Sometimes, even when I am provided with questions to answer, I initially use the objective-rationale-methodology format to organize my thoughts for myself, and then I fill them into the application. If the funder has bulleted questions they want answered, use those questions as your format so the reviewer doesn't have to sift through long paragraphs to find what they need. You want the reviewer's job to be as easy as possible.

You can also combine the funder's guidelines with the objective-rationale-methodology format. For one grant, I was asked to explain my project in 500 words. To clarify the different parts of my project, I inserted my basic formula into that first question.

Cornell Community Partnership Board 2012 Application

1) Abstract: In 500 words, describe your project.

Objective:

I propose to teach a weekly West African Dance class to high school students from New Roots Charter School during the academic year 2012–13. Utilizing knowledge from over fifteen years of West African Dance experience, I will transmit what I have learned to enrich the academic and cultural experience to students in downtown Ithaca. Unlike many other dance classes, this project will be accompanied by live instrumental support from three local musicians. The combined historical context, exercise component, and culmination in a student-led final production will ensure a well-rounded initiation into the world of African dance and music.

Rationale:

Culture is like oxygen: it surrounds us, often without our awareness of its crucial function to our lives. West Africa has a rich dance and drum tradition, which uniquely defines it from the rest of the world. Much of the traditional dance and music that has come from West Africa permeates modern arts in the United States through the roots of the slave trade and the increasing availability of world music online. High school students find rap and R&B culture appealing with little knowledge of its origins. Bringing the raw dance and drum from West Africa into a classroom illuminates the fundamental connections underlying our cultures, while fostering a respect for traditional art forms.

As a returning Fulbright Fellow, I want to enhance cross-cultural understanding among nations and generations. My documentation of dance and cultural events from Senegal will contribute to the knowledge of my students about Senegalese arts. Presenting lectures and video footage as part of the class will expand American understanding of living history and living culture in Senegal to inspire future scholars. The exchange of ideas between Western and Senegalese peoples will enhance a worldly understanding on both sides of the Atlantic.

Methodology:

Three Cornell students will undertake the instruction of these classes. I am a graduate student in the City and Regional Planning Department (2013), Teal Arcadi (2014) is an undergraduate in the history department, and Kia Albertson-Rogers (2013) is an undergraduate in CALS studying communication. Teal partakes in the College Scholar program and will help with the historical component of the class, along with helping coordinate the final production. Kia was the worldwide president of Key Club International and currently works through the Youth Advocate Program as a creative advisor and sound engineer. He has years of hip-hop experience and will engage the students with the evolution from West African to pop music.

Weekly dance classes during the school year will allow for an hour and fifteen minutes of dance and a short period for learning about the origins of the dance. As we develop rapport in the class, students can take initiative to direct the studies and influence the exploration into the historical or modern context of the art form. Finally, the students will decide upon a venue and theme for a final production, which will be choreographed, in part, by the students themselves.

2) Philosophy Statement: Explain how your project meets each of the following components of our philosophy statement

Part of understanding the privilege that comes with the ability to attend an Ivy League university like Cornell is taking into account that opportunities to travel only extend to a limited demographic of

America. Only a small number of citizens in the United States have the financial ability to travel and most of those that travel internationally do so for pleasure, not cultural tourism. Having had the great fortune to travel abroad and benefit from the resources and carbon impact that travel requires makes us responsible for forwarding the learning on to those less able to travel. Native Ithacans are exposed to the vast privilege of Cornell faculty and students, without the benefit of enjoying these luxuries themselves. By spreading the knowledge that we, as Cornell students, have gathered, we are balancing the injustices of monetary wealth differentials. By providing a chance to share what we have learned, we are not only bridging the gap of experience, we are also united a community that can otherwise be divided by resentment and misunderstanding.

As the lucky recipient of a Fulbright research fellowship, I have taken on the challenge and committed myself to disseminating the traditions I learned. The mission of the Fulbright fellowship is to "increase mutual understanding between the people of the United States and the people of other countries" and to contribute to finding solutions to shared international concerns. Having traveled extensively myself, I know that learning from other cultures has changed the way I see the world and opened new possible ways of thinking. Teaching a dance class to high school students would help expand the way these younger Americans think and learn. This, in my view, is a way to help raise the awareness of the next generation of Americans so they are thinking as global citizens whose future is interrelated and inseparable from their peers across the world. From the patience and joy of sharing I benefitted from in West Africa, I've learned that teaching is one of the best ways to form community and bridge cultural divides.

Like travel, education is a certain privilege as well. Cornell has many areas of study to explore because of our vast funding, but small public schools like New Roots lack such diversity. By funding an African dance class, we are addressing root social problems of access to varied dance and art forms. African dance classes in the community cost fifteen dollars, which is prohibitively costly for many interested students. Families struggling to feed themselves can't afford to "try out" new arts for the sake of expanding their children's education. Integrating the dance class into a school curriculum shows parents the value and support of arts in education, as well as offers a chance to try something new without personal costs.

From working with children in the past, and having learned new and interesting art forms as a child myself, I know that these experiences have a lasting effect on a child's life. Not only will the unique dance moves and lessons about African history contribute to these kids' expanded world-view, they may also discover a new passion. This dance class will provide an outlet for creative expression that was previously lacking in their educational framework.

From the beginning stages of this course, students will take the lead on directing the trajectory of instruction. Based on feedback and interactive student leadership, the teenagers will be able to use their creativity to design what they desire to achieve out of this class. As trained facilitators, the Cornell students have experience working in a democratic decision-making process, whereby students review their learning goals and augment the course materials to match their objectives. The students will also plan and decide upon the final presentation, which could take the form of a performance, a video installation, a workshop for their peers, or something else they come up with. This final production will represent what most appeals to the students. Knowing that they are in charge of the final project will engage students throughout the course to build upon a foundation of knowledge they will eventually exhibit and share.

A feedback process will be built into the class from the very beginning. As Cornell students, we are aware of the frustration students can feel if they start to disengage or feel distant from the material they are learning. Both the pace of the course and the material covered will be determined by the feedback given by students. If they feel bored by the repetition of dances, we can move faster onto new rhythms, if they want more history of a culture, we can spend more class time on a lecture-style learning environment or student reports. We are not forcing a set of knowledge upon students without their stated interest; therefore the development of the class will be an iterative process.

This project will include both graduate and undergraduate Cornell students, along with members of the community. Not only will the New Roots students benefit from this exposure to Cornell students of different backgrounds, the Cornell students will also benefit from a stronger relationship with the youth of Ithaca. The New Roots students will see that Cornell University is comprised of very diverse individuals, much like themselves. This understanding will hopefully expand the realm of perceived opportunities in the minds of New Roots students. Bridging the gap between adults in the Ithaca community with students at Cornell will also prove valuable. The musicians and teachers at New Roots will experience the expanded benefits of programs offered by Cornell.

The Cornell students could not undertake this project without the help of the musicians. Endeavoring to teach this dance class is truly a partnership that encourages people to work with each other, especially students and community members. The New Roots school would not otherwise be able to make this project happen if Cornell was not willing to initiate programs in the community. At the same time, we are benefitting hugely from the opportunity to practice teaching and working on community projects. While many other student groups fly off to distant poor countries to work with the non-Americans, our dance class addresses a social inequality right in our neighborhood. Fostering a good relationship with our own neighbors may be the best investment to make because, whether or not we like to admit it, we depend on each other. This project will help Cornell students better understand and improve conditions of the historically disadvantaged in our own town. Through greater exposure to the needs of the community, the Cornell students can direct other services, programs and peers into Ithaca's local scene.

A dance class addresses a need amongst the teenage community in Ithaca to experience new and different cultures. Teenagers often suffer from troubled years of identity crises and self-exploration, and this will give some students a connection to historical and perhaps genealogical ties to the past. African dance is a less commonly available art form that, if available at all, can be too expensive, especially for working families. As part of a rounded curriculum, African dance presents a unique lens into an art form that embraces all body types and social backgrounds.

The history that accompanies African dance traditions also gives new alternatives to problem solving that may not enter a typical classroom. Through democratic decision-making and self-evaluation, the students will direct the course of study. The students will also delve into the modern expression of African traditions and see how music is a social and political tool to raise awareness, gain support, and transmit tradition. Depending on whether the students want to integrate their studies of West African dance and music into their academic projects, the Cornell students can help facilitate extended research into this field. All three of the Cornell students are trained in Action Research, which can be used to help students understand their objectives for the course and proceed in the direction they desire. These skills of self-direction and self-evaluation are good tools to help students in their generation studies and life experiences. Each of the three Cornell students has individual fields that contribute to the wealth of knowledge provided in the class. City and regional planning contributes skills in facilitation; communications studies give students tools in how to best express themselves; and history will enhance the background information for the course.

As stated before, evaluation of the course will be ongoing and iterative. The students will give verbal feedback at the end of each class, but periodically during the semester, there will be an evaluation and discussion on the direction the course is taking. All of these comments will be documented, and the progression of the course will reflect the feedback gathered weekly. The input and comments from the teachers at New Roots and the musicians accompanying the class will also be taken into consideration and documented for evaluation purposes. The desired outcome is a harmonious learning and working environment for all participants.

The reflection tools utilized will be a "whip" time where every student says daily how they're feeling about the class and how they're feeling in general. The larger feedback tools will be an analysis of Strengths, Weaknesses, Opportunities, and Threats (SWOT), which will be diagramed on a large notepad. This will allow a visual and consensual agreement on the progression of the course by all members. There will also be time taken twice during each semester for students to write short reflection pieces to communicate their personal accomplishments and struggles within the group that they may not feel able to voice openly. All evaluations will be kept for the final report. After the final presentation, the class will meet again and do a "course evaluation" in which they describe what they liked, didn't like, or could do better in the future. This reflection time will give the most benefit to the students who can carry on similar projects in the future. Some of the students many accompany the Cornell students at the April reception to give testimony and appreciation to the grant board. All gathered materials (written, photographed, and videotaped) will be presented in the final grant report.

3) Participants: List ALL participants in this project other than the main contacts

Lucy Gent Foma, MRP Candidate 2013

_____, BA 2013

_____, BA 2014

_____, Local drummer and carpenter

_____, Local drummer and vendor

_____, Local drummer and teacher at New Roots School

4) Budget: Prepare an Itemized budget detailing how the funds from this grant will be used

Category	Amount Required	Notes	Source
Live Accompaniment	$1200 = $40 per student per semester Assuming ~ 15 students = $40 x 15 students x 2 semesters	Live accompaniment is the most crucial component and cost of this project. A dance class like this cannot exist without live drumming. Cornell dance classes require $40/student/ semester for live accompaniment	http://registrar.sas. cornell.edu/courses/ roster/SP12/DANCE/
Studio Rental	$712.50 = $25/hr x 1.5 hr/class x 19 classes/year	Southside Community Center gym rental	http://sscc-ithaca. org/
Costumes and Final Demo	$87.50 = $5.80/yard x 15 students	African fabric available by yard	http://www.online fabricstore.net/ specialty-stores/world -store/african-fabrics/ african-cotton-print- fabrics. htm?N=11931 &gclid=CO2whPW1w a4CFUHf4AodsgrLmA

5) Time Line: Create a timeline that outlines both the planning and implementation stages of the project.

Wednesday, September 5, 2012	Start of classes
Monday, September 10, 2012	Start of dance classes (weekly classes on Mondays will continue throughout the semester)
Monday, October 15, 2012	First evaluation and mini student demonstration
Monday, November 12, 2012	Second evaluation and mini student demonstration
Monday, December 10, 2012	Last class of fall semester
Monday, January 27, 2013	Start of classes for spring semester
Monday, February 18, 2013	February Recess
Monday, February 26, 2013	Class decision on final presentation format
Monday, March 11, 2013	Spring Break
Monday, March 18, 2013	Classes resume
Monday, March 25, 2013	Class choreography or presentation of material outlined
Monday, April 1, 2013	Costuming and theatrical preparations finalized
Monday, April 15, 2013	Final presentation
Monday, April 22, 2013	Class evaluation and conclusions
Monday, May 6, 2014	Final grant report

6) Please tell us how your project will continue once you have used your funds

The project will continue once the school receives and recognizes the benefit of having a West African Dance class for its students. Student fundraisers may be a way to raise money for future classes, or the school may decide to reallocate current funding to continue the program.

Please tell us how you heard about the Community Partnerships Board.

Jennifer

Cornell Community Partnership Board 2013 Application

1) Abstract: in 500 words, describe your project.

Objective:

I propose to coordinate an introductory *charette* to the Power of Hope camp in Santa Fe, New Mexico during the summer of 2013. A charette is a technique for consulting with many stakeholders that promotes joint ownership of solutions during an intensive work weekend or period of days. For the past 17 years, the organization Power of Hope has been empowering youth through arts summer camps, bringing together teenagers from wealthy and extremely poor families alike. Launching a New Mexico branch of the program will take $100,000, but in the interest in starting to build the momentum to develop the program, I will be working with youth groups in Santa Fe during a training charette for three days this summer.

Rationale:

New Mexico is the worst state for children, according to the Foundation for Child Development's latest Child and Youth Wellbeing Index.[8] The Foundation grouped 28 indicators on children under age 18, including family economic wellbeing, health, safe/risky behavior, educational attainment, community engagement, social relationships, and emotional/spiritual wellbeing. New Mexico scored -0.96, the closest to the worst possible ranking of -1 on a scale of -1 to 1. New Mexico has the fourth-worst score for reading proficiency and the second-worst ranking for young adult education in the country. It is also the fourth-worst state in the nation for health insurance coverage

8   http://fcd-us.org/our-work/child-well-being-index-cwi/national-cwi.

among children. This dismal environment results in one of the worst high school graduation rates in the country, 63 percent for 2010–11. Santa Fe's graduation rate jumped in 2012 from 56.5 percent to 61.8 percent, a coup for the new Governor.

As a native New Mexican, my goal since coming to graduate school at Cornell has been to cultivate skills and resources to take back to my home state. Although my academic focus is city planning, I have always reserved time to work with local youths. In the past, I have developed my own programming, first with Go Green Africa in Cameroon, which was funded by Smith College's Ruth Dietrich Tuttle Prize, and currently with my Southside Community Center kids' African Dance class, funded by the Cornell Community Partnership Board. Now that I will finally get to return to New Mexico, I am initiating my community involvement by building momentum to bring the Power of Hope program to Santa Fe.

Methodology:

Two outstanding people, Charlie Murphy and Peggy Taylor, who believed that young people are an untapped resource for community renewal and social change, started the Power of Hope program in 1996.[9] Instead of treating teenagers as a problem to be solved, this program facilitates inner transformation for these young people, who can then feel free to express themselves. This program is unique because although youths come from all different backgrounds, many of them are invited because they have experienced homelessness, anger, and self-destruction. The program is made available to all socio-economic groups, regardless of ability to pay, which produces a truly diverse environment. This interface between disparate backgrounds lends to cultural understanding that would not happen in daily life. By the end of the summer program, the young people transform into leaders, able to inspire hope and empowerment in their peers.

---

9   http://www.powerofhope.org/about-us/history.

2) Philosophy Statement: Explain how your project meets each of the following components of our philosophy statement

STUDENT MANAGEMENT, SOCIAL RESPONSIBILITY & EDUCATION:

In the early stages of planning to implement this program, I have engaged numerous public school teachers in Santa Fe, as well as several well-known youth programs that achieve slightly different missions. Warehouse 21 has been the locus of teenage arts and culture in downtown Santa Fe for over 20 years.[10] They provide music venues for teen bands to perform and regularly host local and traveling bands ranging in genre from heavy metal to emo. The blasting music on Saturday nights and continually changing graffiti mural walls that surround the facility provide a liberating but safe space for teenagers to hang out.

_____ is a program run through _____, which fosters a cohort of about 15 teenagers from all the public high schools during the academic year, engaging them in activism covering environmental and social issues.[11] _____ school has a program called _____, which brings under-served youth in Santa Fe into a thriving academic curriculum to supplement an otherwise lacking educational environment, pushing a college preparatory agenda.[12] As a former employee of _____, former intern with _____, and _____ alumna, I have maintained relationships and built trust with all these partners, which will enable a successful collaboration. These groups will come together for the three-day charette to brainstorm and begin training to raise funds for the $100,000 needed to initiate the program. The CPB grant will pay for a student ambassador and facilitator ambassador to bring back educational and fundraising tactics to recruit donors and participants for the camp in 2014.

---

10 http://www._____.org/.
11 http://www._____.org/.
12 http://www._____.org/.

PARTNERSHIP & EVALUATION:

    In addition to these partner groups, who could contribute to training and recommending students for the Power of Hope program, the _____ has offered to be an umbrella organization to sponsor the summer program once the fundraising gets under way for the actual summer camp.[13] Other local restaurants have also offered to provide food for the youths and the location has been scouted: a campground set up for Boy Scouts in northern New Mexico. Once the ambassadors return to New Mexico and we conclude the charette, we will conduct an evaluation to reflect on which tactics are most important to include in the camp and which fundraising tools we will use in the year to come.

3) Participants: List ALL participants in this project other than the main contacts

Lucy Gent Foma, MRP Candidate 2013

_____, Public School Teacher and Activist, Santa Fe, New Mexico

_____, _____ Director, Santa Fe, New Mexico

Others yet to be determined

4) Budget:

$600—Flight for Power of Hope trainer to come facilitate the charette[14]

$250—Three nights of accommodation[15]

$300—Payment for facilitator[16] ($100/day)

$200—Rental space to hold the charette[17]

$150—Food for charette participants

$200—Promotional materials (flyers, posters, etc.) for facilitators to distribute when they return to Santa Fe

$300—Seed money for the first fundraising event

---

13   http://www._____.edu/.
14   http://www.cheapflights.ca/book-flights-online/?source=intl-CFUS-search.
15   http://www.thesantafesuites.com/.
16   http://www.powerofhope.org/about-us/facilitators-teaching-artists.
17   http://www.railyardperformancecenter.com/.

5) Timeline:

March 16—Meeting in Santa Fe with _____, director of _____

March 21—Meeting in Santa Fe with _____, teacher in SF Public Schools

March 22—Meeting in Santa Fe with _____ of Warehouse 21

April 12—Phone conversation with _____

April 13—Phone conversation with _____

April 15—Set dates for summer charette

April 30—Receive confirmation from participating trainees

May 15—Finish curriculum/Agenda for charette

Mid-June—Conduct three-day charette

Mid-July—Follow up with evaluation and first phase of fundraising for summer program 2014

September—Begin fundraising, coordinating with Santa Fe public schools to begin recruiting students

December—Secure funding to reserve the campground, gain in-kind donations for volunteers and food for students

March 2014—Coordinate training for summer facilitators

May 2014—Finalize student participants

June 2014—Review training for summer facilitators

July 2014—First Power of Hope summer camp

6) Please tell us how your project will continue once you have used your funds

The Community Partnership Board grant is only the first part of the process to implement this camp. We have also applied for funds from the Robinson Appel Humanitarian Award at Cornell to fund the charette itself and fundraising will really start once I return to Santa Fe and coordinate events to gain awareness and support for the program.

7) Please tell us how you heard about the Community Partnership Board

Jenny

Organize Your Research

While writing your outline, you have the chance to organize the research and supporting materials that bolster your case. That includes information about what you have done in the past (other projects, grants, program descriptions) and historical or contextual data. As I mentioned in the CPB grant above for the New Mexico program, New Mexico has very poor conditions for raising children. I knew this before writing the grant, but I needed to find the data to support my statements. While I was writing the outline for the rationale, I looked up the data and provided the citations for this information. You can also include budgeting information in your outline, although sometimes the fellowship you're applying for gives a base amount. Nonetheless, if you are describing a program that you plan on implementing, it helps to show that you have thought through the logistics. These details help the reviewers see that you have done your research and are fully invested in making your project a reality.

Lucy Gent
Northampton Rotary Club
Rotary Ambassadorial Scholarship 2010–11
Statement of Intent

Economic Opportunity through Environmental Protection

On January 30, 1991, the Pan-African Conference on Environmental and Sustainable Development in Bamako, Mali adopted what has come to be known as the Bamako Convention, or "The Ban of the

Import into Africa and the Control of Trans-Boundary Movement of Hazardous Wastes within Africa." For decades, developing countries have been dumping grounds for dirty industries and toxic products that are banned in first-world countries. Despite opposition from the United States, this convention raised awareness and regulations to stop harming populations and ecosystems in Africa. It is not just a metaphor to think of the relationship between human beings and the environment in terms of war and peace because in a way, we are waging all-out war against our own planet. By coming into harmony with our environment, we can ensure peace for future generations. Unfortunately, African countries still suffer from high rates of air pollution and water pollution because creating regulations and enforcing them inevitably prove difficult.

In the United States, strong citizen support is leading our country in a greener direction. By contrast, Africa's populations and governments barely address precautionary measures to stop environmental degradation and its effect on citizens. Mali has the second largest airborne particle pollution (PM10) in all of Africa, with 165.2 micrograms per cubic meter. Major concerns for human health from exposure to PM10 include: effects on breathing and respiratory systems, damage to lung tissue, cancer, and premature death. The World Health Organization guideline for an acceptable maximum is PM10 of 50 micrograms per cubic meter or lower. Gambia ranks 8th, Burkina Faso 9th, Ivory Coast 36th, and Ghana 38th in Africa's highest rates of PM10, all of which are above 50 micrograms per cubic meter. I am keenly interested in how microfinance, the business of lending money to poor people, can act as a grassroots solution to eradicating poverty and initiating greener industries. Therefore, I am excited to study development in West Africa through a Rotary Foundation Ambassadorial Scholarship. The great opportunity extended through the scholarship will expand my knowledge of microfinance and sustainable, community-based economic development through study, research, and community service in a developing country.

I will graduate this May from Smith College with a double major in Economics and Portuguese. Economics fascinated me when my high school social activism professors passionately described the negative impacts of the World Bank and the IMF on developing countries. Economics provides solutions to problems resulting from imbalanced development in West Africa—we just need to think creatively. Following my interest in alternative ways to help people out of poverty, I started making small loans out of my allowance to entrepreneurs through Kiva. org, and then became a Kiva Fellow in the summer of 2008, working in Cameroon with a microfinance institute. This work experience in financial services complemented my academic background in economics, making me a qualified candidate to enter the microfinance and development industry. The Ambassadorial Scholarship's combination of study, research, community service, and cultural immersion will enhance my credentials even further.

Promotion of microfinance and green energy furthers the Rotary Foundation's mission to advance world understanding and peace. Majora Carter, of the Sustainable South Bronx project, states, "You can actually link environmental remediation to poverty remediation." By renovating communities with increased employment opportunities, I propose a community project that fulfills all of Rotary International's goals. Just as Rotary International devotes itself to helping communities through service projects, so will families benefit from increased income and more sustainable economies.

Living and learning in a West African community is the next step to my career of environmental remediation and poverty alleviation. I want to connect microfinance and green jobs to enhance economies, while increasing energy efficiency and reducing the impacts of climate change. Van Jones, the author of *The Green Collar Economy*, said, "Dr. King didn't get famous giving a speech that said, 'I have a complaint.' It's time for us to start dreaming again and invite the country to dream with us. We don't have any 'throw away' species, nations, or children. We must birth a global, green economy strong enough to lift people out of poverty." Jones indicates a solution for both the United

States and the rest of the world to combat global warming and high unemployment. This model for an economy empowers people to use resources for their own success while improving conditions for many generations to come.

On my previous trips to Africa, I lived and worked with ambitious citizens who utilize microfinance and traditional arts to support their families in the absence of government infrastructure. The solution to natural resource exploitation in developing countries lies in the hands of the people. Africans have organized systems of cooperative financing to deal with strains of disease, war, and exploitation without government help. Entrepreneurs abound in Africa because the only way to persevere is through communal support, and individuals I met demonstrated rapid adaptability to new strategies. There are a few companies that are doing more than microfinance in Africa at the moment. One of them is E+Co, which takes viable business proposals from African entrepreneurs who want to introduce alternative energy industries, and coaches them sternly along the path to running successful and competitive businesses. Respect and serious economic feasibility considerations are cornerstones for microfinance firms because they emphasize that giving aid to poorer countries is a degrading and patronizing practice. E+Co recognized the potential for environmentally friendly business expansion by and for African communities and extended financing to those entrepreneurs who were ambitious enough to confront traditional energy industries. Inspiration for my ambassadorial focus comes from Van Jones' motivational words and the work of companies like E+Co, who have begun the task of greening Africa.

I have proposed five universities, located in Abidjan, Côte d'Ivoire; Bamako, Mali; Serrekunda, Gambia; Accra, Ghana; and Ouagadougou, Burkina Faso. * Through much research, I verified that all of these universities match my geographic and educational criteria. All five countries are considered third world—or developing—countries, where over 40 percent of the population lives in poverty or absolute poverty, and all have high pollution rates. Therefore, any of these countries would be good case studies for microfinance. All of these countries host Rotary International clubs and all partook in the Pan-African Conference on Environment and Sustainable Development in Bamako, Mali.

As I mentioned, all these countries also suffer among the highest rates of all pollution in Africa. With their nominal support of environmental protection stated during the Pan-African Conference and need for economic development, I think they demonstrate ideal circumstances to adopt a green-jobs-training microfinance center.

I attempted to select large universities in urban areas, while still fulfilling the geographic requirements proposed by the Rotary Foundation. However, all of these urban areas have poor, rural villages on the outskirts of the cities. This geographic combination will allow me to study the poor population on the city's borders, while still having access to the microfinance resources and organizations available within the cities. Having studied a semester of French while doing Junior Year Abroad in Brazil, followed by an accelerated class in beginning and intermediate French during my senior year at Smith, I will continue to take summer and post-baccalaureate classes to be completely proficient by the time my scholarship starts.

All five identified programs are broad enough that they offer the potential to support my career goals by helping me understand the economic situation of developing countries. Each program will also uniquely reflect its respective local situation in a region that has continually struggled with economic development and growth.

In the table below, I list the five universities, their respective locations, and the proposed course of study at each university.

In order of preference:

University	Location	Field of Study
Université d'Abobo-Adjamé	Abidjan, Côte d'Ivoire	Environmental Management
Université de Bamako	Bamako, Mali	Law and Political Science
University of the Gambia	Serrekunda, Gambia	Economics and Management Sciences, Public and Environmental Health
University of Ghana	Accra, Ghana	Social Studies, Business School
Université de Ouagadougou	Ouagadougou, Burkina Faso	Economics and Management Sciences

Having volunteered in Brazil and Cameroon over the past year, I plan to continue being an active community volunteer while being an ambassador of goodwill. One specific project that stood out to me was the West African Project Fair (WAPF Abidjan 2008). This project, launched in Côte d'Ivoire in 2008, obtains capital through the Rotary Foundation and other sponsors. The fund is then used to support Rotarian community service programs to develop and execute efficient projects that address challenging issues of development and lack of water and natural resources, while tackling problems of renewable energies and environmental protection. Contingent on my assigned location, I would either like to get directly involved with this Rotary-run project in Côte d'Ivoire, or similar projects involving economic development in neighboring countries. The opportunity to participate in these Rotary projects will serve as an excellent vehicle to further enhance my study and research objectives. Other community service opportunities would be possible through well-known organizations such as UNICEF, Foundation for Sustainable Development (FSD), Save the Children, or Freedom From Hunger—organizations that all have active operations in the West African region.

A green Africa is possible, maybe even more so than in the United States, because infrastructure isn't as developed yet in West Africa. In the beginning stages of building a public utility, for example, governments have the opportunity to *start* with clean energy instead of retrofitting systems, as is the case in the United States. It is possible to bring Africa up from amongst the lowest environmental ratings in the world to a model of sustainability. I would be greatly honored to be endorsed by the Rotary Foundation, and be given the opportunity to spend a year in West Africa as an Ambassador and advocate for equality and a greener world. The Ambassadorial Scholarship will help realize my lifelong goal for a career in sustainable development, addressing the humanitarian need to reduce poverty and work towards a more peaceful world. As has been established, the link between poverty, the environment, and peace is clear.

*As you may have deduced from my life story, I ended up going to Senegal for my Rotary scholarship. After I received the confirmation that I was selected as the winner, I wrote them another rationale for why Senegal was actually the best place for my course of study. Keep in mind that you can sometimes change your desired location of study or work if you provide a good reason for the change. See the section on Placeholders and Milestones in Chapter Four for more about this.

Timeline

Including a timeline in your project description helps both you and the granting body to break down your specific tasks. In a way, by doing this, you are helping yourself more than you are helping the foundation. As a friend of mine put it, applying for grants for her project—regardless of whether they were successful—is a helpful exercise in and of itself.

In fact, I often think of it as a challenge or a tool to clarify my thinking around an idea even further, and to think of it in a different framework. So for me, the process of it always feels like progress, even if I don't ultimately get the grant, if that makes sense. Of course it is more fun when I *do* get it, and a little external validation now and then is certainly helpful.

Thinking through what could be possible in a given time frame adjusts your expectations and forces you to be a little more realistic about your ambitions.

Proposals are generally optimistic in nature, but at least having goals keeps you focused and gives you a sense of achievement.

Budget

No matter what, you don't want to be over budget (because the money will come out of your own pocket). One thing I've had to learn is that I should always overestimate my budget. Things inevitably cost more than you expect, and there can be setbacks that you don't expect. When I was doing the Cornell Community Partnership Board grant in New Mexico, we bought a ticket for the facilitator that was non-transferable and non-refundable, only to reschedule the event and thus lose that money. I had budgeted for a higher-priced ticket in my grant application so I was covered, but otherwise I would have had to pay hundreds of dollars out of pocket (in addition to all the unpaid time I invested in making the project happen).

Over budgeting means buffering the expenses within reason. I would not double the cost of things, but I would add about thirty to forty percent of the expected cost. Whenever I have thought I was going to get by with the minimum amount possible, I have been sorely disappointed. If I were reviewing grant applications, I would want to see that the applicant planned on spending wisely, but would be skeptical of very low prices. Granting bodies are not looking for the cheapest bid, they are looking for an effective program.

Aligning Your Objectives

You have to be thinking about both your own objectives and those of the grantor. Ideally, they align, which will make you a good candidate to receive the grant. If they don't exactly align, you have to think about how your objectives fit into the grantor's objectives. You will know your grantor's objectives from the research you did back in Chapter Seven. Reading every piece of information about the grant or fellowship usually gives you a good idea about their mission. Once you have your own objectives stated in your proposal, you should state how those objectives fit into the grantor's objectives. I have been so blunt as to insert the grantor's own wording. When I have reworded their phrasing, I make sure that I've hidden their objective in plain sight. Again, you don't want the reviewers to sift through your application and make more work for them. Make it easy for them to understand why your proposal will meet their guidelines.

Reviewing past grantees helps to determine your chances of winning. Sometimes granters have slight biases that are not outwardly stated, but can be revealed by their funding history. For example, the Fulbright makes it very clear that their mission is to foster cross-cultural understanding. They want students to represent the United States positively in the world, while also bringing traditions from other regions back to our own culture. This is the overall mission of the Institute for International Education, which funds Fulbright. However, hundreds of Fulbright fellowships and scholarships are awarded every year to dozens of countries. While the American committee reviews and selects the finalists, the country that will host the scholar chooses the awardees. Each country has a different preference for the type of studies that will take place. While it is never a good idea to make your objectives political or clearly agenda based, some countries shy away from even economic research. Fulbright has a database of the projects in each country that dates back about a decade. I saw that Senegal had a history of funding the arts and culture, but they had never awarded a dance scholarship before. This gave me a clue as to their preference for fields of study and my chances for applying in a related but unprecedented way. When I looked at Cameroon's past scholars, I could clearly see that they preferred scholarships in the hard sciences: chemistry and biology at that time. This gives an idea about the unstated preferences of the granting body that can help you understand the objectives they hope to meet.

Quantify Your Outcome

If you can quantify the outcome of your project, you will add tangible bang for the funder's buck. For example, if the funder aims to improve school attendance in grades 9–12, you can estimate how many teens your program will reach and provide that number. These are not hard promises, but rather a glimpse at what's possible if you are given a chance. Giving an idea of what the result will look like gives your project more substance.

OBJECTIVE:

Use your revised sentences from Chapter Four and Chapter Eight to begin your objective section. Follow this statement with sentences explaining what genre of work you will be doing, where you will be doing it, and whom it will serve. Don't get into *why* this work needs to be done until the rationale section. Instead, use this first paragraph to succinctly state *what* you will be doing.

_____

_____

_____

RATIONALE:

Why is this work essential for your target audience and the world? This section is your elevator pitch; use your most convincing arguments to win the reader over. Begin with a problem statement (i.e., *New Mexico is the worst state for children, according to the Foundation for Child Development's latest Child and Youth Wellbeing Index.*[18]). Follow this with your background in the given field and why you are the best person to address this problem with your program and skill set.

_____

_____

_____

---

18 "National CWI," Foundation for Child Development, accessed June 1, 2015, http://fcd-us. org/our-work/child-well-being-index-cwi/national-cwi.

METHODOLOGY:

Write down the timeline, starting from before you are awarded the fellowship, and include events that will take place to ensure you successfully complete your project. Break up segments of the project into periods (i.e., before project begins, first three months, second half of year, etc.). Make visual breaks between these segments to make the timeline easy to digest for the reader.

_____

_____

_____

Your proposal is the nuts and bolts of your project. It shows the research you've done in your field and demonstrates your knowledge about the funders' preferences. Reflect on what impact the funding agency wants to make and respond to their questions about how you will undertake the project. Make sure that you don't leave their specific questions unanswered. If you were in an interview, the proposal would be like reviewing the job description. Next, you will work on the personal statement, which is like asking about your family and your passions. The personal statement is like getting to know you over a casual lunch or coffee date. Separate your personality from your work capacity, and add the special details about who you are in your personal statement.

CHAPTER ELEVEN

THE PERSONAL STATEMENT

"I think this is the most important part of any application. Your story should have a clear narrative arc and the main character—you!—should overcome some adversity by the end. Humans love stories; give the people reviewing your application something good to read."

—Artis Henderson, former Rotary Ambassadorial Scholar

"Your essays and personal statements are really your time to shine and show why you're unique and an excellent fit for the scholarship, fellowship, or study abroad program you're applying to. Of course the requisites will vary with each application and program, so it's

important to cater applications individually to exemplify what they're looking for."

—Gemina Garland-Lewis, former Thomas J. Watson Fellow and National Geographic Society Young Explorer Grantee

At the tail end of our year in Senegal, we decided to spend a month in the Gambia (a short, seven-hour drive from Dakar), where my sister-in-law was finishing her MD. We were staying in a compound of hotel-style rooms with an open-air patio where all the residents could share meals or converse. Among the tenants were a couple of students like my sister-in-law, a few foreigners who were staying for a couple months of volunteer work or vacation, and then there were a couple of prostitutes.

The prostitutes were normal, young, attractive people who were trying to make ends meet for their families. One was a young woman from South Africa, who had a toddler back home to support through her night work. Another was a young, attractive, Gambian man, whose elderly, Dutch girlfriend paid his rent and his school fees and would come down to visit him for a month at a time throughout the year. One of the short-term residents was a woman in her early twenties from Alabama named Leslie. This young woman stuck out because of her incredible self-knowledge and almost reckless forward motion into her life's purpose.

Leslie was one of the foreign volunteers. She was spending the final summer of her graduate degree in Public Health working for the United Nations office in Gambia. I'd never met anyone from Alabama before and upon first meeting her, I thought she must be older because of the life experience that showed on her face. We ended up spending lots of time with her. She was having a more difficult time with her experience in Gambia than most of the others. Not only had her idealized view of the United Nations been shattered by her work in the country; she was also suffering from stomach problems and a facing a likely breakup with her boyfriend. Nonetheless, she was able to view the world through an optimistic lens. The stories of her life were incredible; sometimes I thought they must have been made up.

Leslie came from a family with many health problems. I'd never heard of a more cursed situation. For example, her aunt had been diagnosed with colon cancer, and the doctors cut out more than half of her intestinal tract, only to find out after the fact that they had misdiagnosed the illness. Leslie had already come through a kind of cancer by the time she was twenty-three. Despite—or maybe because of—this reminder of fatality, Leslie lived a very full life. As a young teenager, she bought a small airplane and said she would regularly phone home for dinner to tell her parents she'd be late because she was a state or two away.

Later in life, when she was spending time in Europe, an NGO was looking for a pilot to drop off donated provisions in Somalia. She volunteered and flew an aircraft from Europe down to East Africa, where rebel fighters shot her down. Another craft from a nearby NGO was able to come rescue her. She told us this as the three of us were walking down an endless dirt road in search of an eco village we'd heard about. I told her that she should write a memoir some day.

"About my stupidity?" she asked mockingly. At least she could decipher less logical decisions and the danger she had put herself in. Her master's in public health came from her desire to bring medical assistance to people around the world. As a part-time volunteer at the Gambian hospital, she gave me an insight into Africa that I would have never gained in any other way.

Over dinner one evening, she mentioned her experience from that day, clearly still shocked and processing the trauma. She said that a young woman had come into the hospital with a severe asthma attack. Her hospital did not have any way to help the woman since medications were short. There were no inhalers. They took the young woman to another hospital that had a defibrillator but the electricity at that hospital was out. **The woman vomited as she gasped for air and wilted next to the unplugged nebulizer that could have saved her.** Leslie said that she vomited too as she watched the woman expire. As I listened to this story, I couldn't for the life of me understand where someone would find the internal resources to put themselves through this kind of experience.

Making sacrifices was not new to Leslie. She had taken time off from school in February of that year to help a marathoner run 100 miles to raise money for cancer research. She spent that month driving in a rental car about ten miles per hour behind the man as he ran from Washington, DC to Montreal, Canada. To help pay for school, she had been a grant writer for organizations throughout her college career and also worked finding homes for foster kids. She said that the way she knew whether a home would be good for foster kid was by checking to see whether the family had a kitchen table to eat breakfast at. During her time working with homeless people in Alabama, she said she learned so much from them. If she were ever homeless, she said she knew how to survive: where to get food, where to sleep so she'd be safe and warm, and where to use the bathroom. Leslie didn't share all these details about her life upon first meeting her, she wasn't the type of person who introduces herself with her life story. Instead, the stories leaked out, gradually explaining that aging I could see in her eyes the very first night I met her. Knowing where she came from and the things that weighed on her seemed to drive her forward. Incredibly, these experiences propelled her instead of jaded her.

I'm sure that these remarkable women have recounted these stories about themselves countless times in personal statements. The way they talk about themselves, they are not bragging, but rather just telling their stories as they happened, which makes it much more impressive.

Confidence vs. Arrogance

When you are writing your proposal, it can be hard to walk the fine line between impressing your audience by outlining the novel ways in which your project will achieve your project goals, and overselling yourself. You want to sound confident and competent without exaggerating. This is a very hard thing to do. If you are humble, you don't get noticed; but if you are arrogant, readers get turned off and can detect falseness.

I remember when I was writing my first Fulbright application, I wrote, "After my Fulbright year, I will be the premier American scholar on Senegalese Sabar dance."

Don Andrew said, **"I doubt that you will be the best."**

I knew that there would definitely be people with more experience than me after my year abroad, but I was trying to sound confident and sell the reviewing committee on what a good investment I would make. I came away from the Fulbright application experience realizing that even with my more modest, winning application, I was still being optimistic about what I would accomplish. I think the reviewers realize this, but it was a good insight into grant writing. You need to aim for the stars (in a realistic way), while staying grounded. That balance is very hard to strike.

Professor Marguerite Harrison's advice:

"First off, a word about the personal statement. The way I see it, it should be an honest assessment of yourself, positive but not arrogant. A personal statement demands that you focus on what you do well in relation to the research proposal or position you are requesting. It's your opportunity to show off your best qualifications. I think a personal statement should be specific and to the point, allowing you to articulate how well you fit the profile of the position/proposal. You must define yourself within those terms, tailoring your statement to the specific qualifications required. You should strike a balance between being humble (meaning someone who has a lot to give, but also still has a lot to learn from the experience) and demonstrating that you are perfectly suited for the position. A personal statement that allows you to give concrete examples of why you would be suited for the position is better than one that might simply list qualifications and experiences."

Professor Pike Oliver's advice:

"How to brag about yourself without sounding arrogant?

My general advice on this topic is to get someone whom you know has a high regard for you tell you briefly (orally or in writing) why they do. Then take their words and make them your own. I did this for a former student and I told him, 'preserve that tape.'

In your case (meaning Lucy) I would say something like, 'You have the willingness and ability to figure things out. You listen well and present clearly with enthusiasm. While respectful, you are not easily intimidated. And you have one of the better smiles that God gave anyone. All wonderful gifts that you use well in pursuit of the greater good.'

So, if I were coaching you, I would ask you to take that statement and play it back to me in your own words (assuming you roughly agreed with it.) One way to do this, if someone is a bit shy about tooting their own horn, is to use the introductory phrase, 'I've been told that…,' or 'My graduate school advisor told me that…'"

Don Andrew's advice:

"How to brag yourself without sounding arrogant:

You should never brag about yourself directly. Most applications have an essay component and then another component where you list stuff. Say you won a prize and if it doesn't fit into essay, you just have to leave in the résumé or list of past awards and hope it gets noticed. Always put best first, don't do it chronologically.

You never like to talk about yourself directly with superlatives or adjectives ('I excel at…')—just say what you did. If you were awarded something, say so. But you'll have a lot of achievements that won't fit into the flow, because the essay is like a story. Just tell it like it is: what happened, what you did. And if it came with a prize, say that. Never make a self-judgment."

Professor Mike Manville's advice:

"As for bragging, you're right that it's a fine balance. My suggestion is to make everything as plain as possible, don't dwell too much on things, and convey the information. So instead of 'I was greatly honored when this work won the prestigious blabbity-blabbity award,' just write, 'this work won the blabbity-blabbity award.' And then make sure your references, in their letters, do the main bragging for you."

Put It on Paper

Remember all that work you did in Chapter Two? Take that soul-searching and put it into your personal statement. Much like how you mold and frame your project to fit the funder's goals, you also want to know what kind of personal traits the funder is looking for. Based on the type of scholar or leader they are looking for, you will pick and choose examples from your past that demonstrate these skills.

The personal statement often gives you a chance to be poetic and ambitious. While the proposal should be cut and dry, maybe even leaving out *I* statements, **the personal statement provides a taste of you**.

The reviewers want to know who you are and what you're like. Descriptive language and examples bring the personal statement to life in a way that makes you a real person, not just an automaton who robotically completes tasks. Especially when you are applying for a student fellowship, the reviewing board likes to imagine the person they're investing in, dreaming about all the things you're capable of doing. I think the reviewers take on the dull task of reviewing all these proposals because they get to hear about you and what you can do. Take this opportunity to inspire their dreams for you.

When I got the Kiva fellowship in Cameroon, we went to San Francisco for the training before departing to the heart of Africa. I met one of the women who had interviewed me for the program, and she confided in me how envious she was of my upcoming adventure. While she was stuck working in the San Francisco office, all of the Fellows would be traveling to different countries and having adventures that she would only hear about through our journals. In a way, she was able to live vicariously through us, but I imagine that when she was interviewing me, she was envisioning how well I could take on the task of working in a foreign and unfamiliar field office. It was my job when I applied to let her know I was capable of that based on my past experience and my attitude in life.

Tell stories about what you've experienced and how it has changed you. How have you been formed by the unique things that have happened in your life? When I was a microfinance fellow in Cameroon, blog posts were part of my job, but I am glad that I was forced to do it because I captured events happening in real time that have stayed with me over the years. I think this was a defining moment in my experience.

Death of a Client: Kiva Journal August 4, 2008

On Friday, three members of the GHAPE office went to the funeral of one of our members, Bih Josopha. She was forty-eight years old and left eight children behind, four of whom are under the age of fourteen. The daughter had come to the office to inform us of her passing on Thursday, immediately after it occurred, and we decided which office members would go and pay respect. For GHAPE members, attendance at a fellow member's funeral is compulsory, punishable by a fine. Some of the members were a little disconcerted, but most wanted to show their respect for a friend. Many of the women made food to feed the GHAPE members during the funeral and also to contribute to the grieving family. A lot of work went into the funeral to make it happen only a day after the death, but it seemed that everyone pulled their strengths together, understanding the need for the effort.

When we were doing the training to become Kiva Fellows, one section of the training was about being sensitive to social interactions among office members. For example, maybe, as Americans, we would find ourselves wanting to be more physically affectionate than locals would feel comfortable being. It was a good lesson to take into the field, to be very observant of the way my colleagues acted before asserting my own personality. After all, it's better to come off as a little cold in the beginning, than to make everyone around me feel uncomfortable with the way I'm acting.

It turned out that the GHAPE office members are just as physically affectionate as I am, but I took a couple of weeks before I let myself be that open with them. I wanted to make sure that it was okay to joke around and play.

Going to a funeral was a challenge of a different kind for me. Not only did I have little observation time beforehand, I was there as a detached member of the company to which Josopha owed money, and the only white person in attendance. (The loan was forgiven, as happens upon deaths within GHAPE.) I did my best to imitate an appropriately somber demeanor, but not be weepy. I didn't know Josopha, but I was really sad to see her young children so overwhelmed with grief. Part of the Cameroonian burial ritual includes music and dance, however, which lifts people's spirits and brings some light into the ceremony. In this way, friends and family leave the funeral having grieved for the loss, paid respect, rejoiced in the life of the person, and praised God for what they have remaining in their own lives.

I had been wanting for some time to go to what Cameroonians call a "Cry Die," which is the commemoration of a person's death. I heard that many of the tribes come to support the family and dance and play music in honor of the deceased. As a student of African dance, I am very interested in seeing how the Cameroonian tribes dance and drum and a Cry Die has been recommended to me for this particular display of tribal culture. I hadn't understood that a funeral service would include dancing and drumming as well, but now I've seen that it does.

Upon arrival at the funeral, Mercybertha, Fointama, and I were led inside to see Bih Josopha's corpse before she was placed in her coffin. I wasn't extremely comfortable with seeing her, let alone photographing her, but my boss at GHAPE said I had to take pictures to make a good journal for the Kiva lenders. Fointama had a camera of his own and was unabashedly documenting the entire event. Somehow I felt a little more self-conscious wielding the camera in light of the fact that I was a foreigner. Later in the process of the burial, there was dancing around the newly packed grave, and as a GHAPE member, I was asked to come into the dancing circle and sing with the other GHAPE members. I tried to look around and determine whether I should be animated, or sad and somber, but I really got no definitive answer from those I saw around me. Some were smiling and singing whole-heartedly, while others were doing more of an obligatory march around the grave, not singing at all. I didn't want to be too animated, for fear of disrespecting the death, so I did a side-to-side step behind the others and didn't sing. I hope that I didn't offend anyone by not participating as much.

From what I've experienced, death carries a different tone in Cameroon. The family that I live with has nine children: four of their own and five orphans who are cousins or friends of the family. The orphans all lost their parents at young ages. Three of the five are siblings and they lost their father first to an unknown disease and then a few years later, lost their mother to brain cancer. They said they never expected to lose their father *and* their mother, but it just happened that way. Medical care is not very good here, and for something as delicate as brain cancer, there's really no hope of being cured. I've heard the women here talk angrily and disdainfully about doctors' inaction for hopeless cases. Usually these decisions are made upon little more than a basic inspection of the patient. The orphans who I live with are very sympathetic and wonderful people, but they have expressed how death no longer affects them like it used to. They say they can hear of a death or go to a funeral and feel little more than pity. Death is so common here, and unnecessary, preventable deaths are part of everyday life. It seems to me that people try to celebrate the person's life and incorporate a hopeful element into the ceremony, so that the event isn't so bleak.

Bih Josopha died six weeks of complaining of chest pain. Her brother explained to me that he had taken her to get an x-ray but, not being a doctor, had been unable to diagnose her from what he saw in the results. Josopha had been taking care of her eight children alone, after her husband left her, and the four young children now have to find somewhere to live. The brother has seven children of his own and is already stretching his resources. Maybe Josopha's older children will be able to take care of the younger ones, suggested her brother. The family is not as fortunate as those orphans living in my house, with more affluent relatives to provide a home, an education, and affection for them. I hope that the outpouring of support I saw during the funeral service will carry on to help the family afterwards.

A funeral is not something I can say I was happy to have the chance to experience. A death is always going to be a sad thing for me. I would like to say, rather, that I felt grateful to the family for allowing me to attend the ceremony. I'm trying to be sensitive to where my presence is welcome and where it is not, with the understanding that perhaps not all things should be made accessible to foreigners. With this, I extend to the Kiva lender what I hope is a respectful little glimpse into what happened here on Friday and what happens here in Cameroon every day.

Cut the Adjectives

One of the best pieces of writing advice I ever got was to "Show, not tell." It came from one of my best friends, Aurielle, when she was reviewing a cover letter I wrote in college. I was telling the manager of the business how I was a diligent, intelligent, and adaptable worker. I used adjectives, which quickly bored the reader. Adjectives alone mean nothing; they have no substance, and they get lost in a chunk of words. Instead, I rewrote those adjectives into concrete examples that demonstrated those traits. Showing instead of telling works well for drawing readers in, hooking them to read the rest of your story. Another benefit is that you also can be more efficient in portraying multiple aspects of your personality and background, rather than making a list of achievements.

Jenny started her Fulbright personal statement by describing what is was like to sit in the back of a hot bus in Gambia, where she had been a Peace Corps volunteer. The sticky seats and hot air, waiting long hours with no bathroom or food breaks, and finally encountering some street vendors who would hand street food through the top of the bus window, perfectly demonstrated a moment in time for her. **She was not only viscerally describing what it was like to have to wait in a crowded, hot bus** (which spoke to her adaptability, patience, and experience living for extended periods abroad); she also opened a story about how food is a recurring theme throughout her life. The Fulbright was to study at culinary institutes in Italy, so she followed the thread of food from her childhood to the present day, integrating details about her foreign experience.

Since the Fulbright personal statement must be 500 words or less, my friend had to be concise. Combining examples of her experience that substantiated personal qualities as well as her background was the best way to do this.

Jennifer Marotto Lutter
Fulbright Personal Statement
2013

Chicken never tasted so good. By bargaining from the back of a hot, crowded van, screaming out a sliver of open window, I finally had my hands on a Farafenni chicken sandwich. Full of bones, dripping with oil, and stuffed into a crispy roll, this sandwich was my afternoon euphoria. I ate cheerfully as the van pulled away from the stand and towards my village.

Food went from being an everyday enjoyment to a shimmering pedestal during my two years as a Peace Corps Volunteer in West Africa. Suddenly, I was living in a place where food was scarce and often a source of stress. Something as small as a chicken sandwich brought rapture to me. Thoughts of my grandmother's kitchen in Ohio, of afternoons shared together over food and pleasant conversation, were always with me. Like many children, I spent countless hours in my grandma's kitchen with cookie dough on my fingers and flour unintentionally dusted over me. I took for granted the warm bread from the oven, the homemade pasta drying on the counter, and the endless ceremony surrounding mealtimes. I sat in awe as my grandparents told stories of their involvement in the "old community," requiring meals each Sunday at the Italian Center and never-ending debates over who made the perfect cannoli. Whatever their stories held, food was always at the center. While my memories of cooking at home were accurate, most of what I remembered about my community was a comforting illusion.

My dreams from home were of country foods full of flavor and richness, especially the thick dairy products and baked goods lacking in Gambia. I kept a list of foods I longed for in the back of my journal, and it soon overflowed into a second notebook. Returning home was difficult for many reasons, but maybe the most painful was that the place I returned to fell far short of what my mind had created while in Gambia. I could not find the "real country food" of my nostalgic fantasies, nor the real country itself. Most of the farms near me had been converted to produce mass quantities of soybeans or corn, and urban sprawl had begun to seep into the open spaces of my childhood. This place looked like so many others in America, and it tasted that way as well. I had been homesick for an Ohio that was fading.

My disappointment at the state of Ohio's land use and food culture sent my mind reeling. I searched for a career path that would involve me in reviving the soul of places. I needed to understand how a community could maintain its identity and why some have failed while others thrived. My investigation led me to City and Regional Planning, a field that will allow me to work as a placemaker, modernizing communities while preserving their heritage. Since beginning my studies, the significance of food in all aspects of city planning has become evident. Transportation of goods, conservation of farmlands, access to healthy ingredients, sharing of local heritage and knowledge; food issues saturate the field. As a planner, I want to bring back the Ohio of my memories by fostering quality food production and inculcating respect for local food traditions, but also influencing the physical environment.

My vision of ideal communities has roots in my undergraduate experience in Italy: narrow, pedestrian-filled streets, beautiful public spaces, and an incredible food culture based on seasonal, regional ingredients. The food and scenery of Italy is the setting of so many dreams for my fellow Ohioans, yet drawing on the coveted aspects of Italian cities and culture for our own communities is rarely the case. We think of it as a dream too good to realize.

If I have the opportunity to study Food, Place, and Identity at the University of Gastronomic Sciences I can add to my toolkit of community development skills and assist residents in building the places they envision. Academic knowledge and the experience of living in the envied Italian culture will make me a resource for communities wishing to build places as grand and distinct as those in Italy. Stories about the "old community" can be followed by tales of the new great places we have created, starting at the kitchen table.

When I was accepted into the Smith program to apply for a Fulbright, I was given access to past, winning proposals from Smith students. Reading proposal after proposal, I started to see some trends. Particularly in the personal statement, I could tell that the winning individuals had done a great job at capturing the reader's imagination. I read about childhoods in foreign lands, precious moments of realization in coffee shops, and musty and claustrophobic nights spent in libraries that these women had attributed to their passion for scholastic pursuit. These statements made me feel like I knew the women who wrote them and made it clear to me that their whole lives led up to the logical and inevitable event of getting a Fulbright.

Reading a great example is easier than describing a great example, but that's why there are real winning essays in this book for you to get a sense of what works. Once you know your story, you can weave an enchanting tale with your own anecdotes you have uncovered. **This takes time.** Really consider what you want to portray about yourself and think about a moment in your life that relays that.

Write Your Short Story

Writing a Personal Statement could be seen as writing a short story about yourself. As one of my writing teachers, Candace Walsh, advises, you want to include in your story elements of sensationalism, specificity, and universality. Sensationalism is what draws the reader in, making them want to know more about you. What is the unique element about you that could be shocking or intriguing? Obviously, with a personal statement you are making the case that you are more unique than the next applicant. **You need to convince your reader that you have special abilities that prepare you to undertake your proposed project in a way that nobody else would be capable of**. That specific information that makes you different will be the main body of your statement. Sometimes it's hard to make the specific information about yourself sound special. You do not always have to try so hard. Trying hard to talk about your abilities can come off sounding arrogant and off-putting.

I remember one application essay in which I tried to explain my rebel nature, which resists being categorized. In high school, I started ninth grade in a new prep school where I wasn't sure of my place or status. It was perhaps a chance to reinvent myself, although I had no problem with who I had been up until that point. Somehow my persona was not unique enough in my new environment, so I searched for a more compelling, attention-getting character. The new me didn't care enough about grades to work long into the night or do homework during lunchtime. I wore band t-shirts from groups touring at the local teen center in a size too small and Dickies black work pants low on my hips with a studded belt. A year later, I added dreadlocks, which were followed by a braided weave. **I wanted to explain in this personal statement that, although I was**

grungy, I also got my nails done and ate organic food religiously. In my effort to highlight what you might expect from me (only to be dispelled by my other attributes), I alienated the reader. I started to insult the reader by assuming they were shallow enough to make assumptions. That same writing teacher once told me never to be a mean girl or obnoxious.

While I was studying in Brazil, I visited a good, old friend who was studying in Argentina. We were out shopping in Buenos Aires with another student who was attending my friend's program: a brown-haired, fast-talking Manhattanite. As we were in the dressing room of a large boutique that evening, I attempted to get to know the brash young woman a little better as we waited for our mutual friend. "Where are you from?" I asked.

"I study at Columbia University," the girl replied, in a practiced voice that intoned a careful and measured non-commitment and demanded a gasp of awe from the listener.

"Oh, cool, what do you study there?" I asked, having practiced how to not gratify Ivy Leaguers with fawning amazement about their assumed superiority.

"I know you don't really care—you're just being polite—but I study English," she added, with a burnished, habitual tone intended to grab attention. I was taken aback, as she hoped I'd be, but my friend butted in.

"Lucy is sincerely interested in people; she doesn't just ask polite questions." I was glad my friend stood up for me, because I was blindsided by this ploy for attention. This girl was trying to be intriguing and unique with a rote conversation that all of us had had hundreds of times over our college careers. While it did get my attention and shocked me, it also assumed something about me that I didn't like and made me disinterested in her.

Like her attempt to seem witty, I had done something similar in the essay about my idiosyncrasies. I was assuming something about my reader that put them off. Luckily, I had a writer friend review this essay and she gave me her honest feedback. She had been reading multiple essays I was preparing for a scholarship and she told me over coffee that she didn't like this person as much. She encouraged me to try again with another essay. I had tried and failed to demonstrate a part of myself that was hard to illustrate. Perhaps if I had sought out an example of how my idiosyncrasies play out harmoniously in my character, I would have been more successful.

Humility is a very hard thing to achieve. It doesn't mean underplaying your achievements or not mentioning them, but you will never get noticed if people have no idea about your capabilities.

- Make sure that you talk (or write) about yourself, but don't make the story all about you.
- Talk about who helped you get to your current position; acknowledge those who have influenced and inspired you.
- Mention how lucky you have been to have the opportunities you've had and state how grateful you are for all you have.

I've also written into my proposals how I would feel honored to be given the chance to represent Fulbright and Rotary. You are, in some ways, playing with the reader because you've led them to believe that you deserve this chance, but you also want to make it clear that you don't take these things for granted.

In addition to making your personal statement sensational and specific, you also want to make your statement universal. **You want to connect with the reader on a level where they feel like they know you and could envision being in your shoes.** As I mentioned before, you want to transport the reviewer into a world of possibilities. For them to feel a connection with you, you need to show them that, in some ways, you are just like them. This is where you can weave in seemingly mundane elements of life that most people can relate to. Maybe you could include a sentiment about feeling afraid when you went away to college, or alienated when your parents separated. If there was a turning point in your life that shifted how you saw the world, find that universal element—how you felt—and share that with your reader so they can identify with you. From here, your reader can imagine being in your shoes, which will help you when you're describing the excitement and passion you would feel as a fellow, or scholar, or grantee.

When I was writing my graduate school application essays, I told a story about becoming intimately aware of city planning policies when our family business was possibly in jeopardy at the whim of park developers.

In 1996, my parents started managing the Railyard Performance Center, located in the historic Railyard District of Santa Fe, and later bought and renovated the arts studio. Contention over this piece of real estate played a central role in planning the newly developed Railyard District. For over ten years, my father attended city council meetings, spoke publicly for the rights of small business owners, and endlessly negotiated for my parents' hard-won investment. Ultimately, our building was declared city property and was seized in exchange for a fifty-year lease. I understood from this experience that activism is a norm for those who are vested in a community's future, and that planning a city is complex because of limited space and many competing interests. Only by following and participating in that process can I help direct the inevitable change equitably and creatively.

Although not everyone has parents who have to negotiate for years to keep their family business, I was adding a universal element by appealing to a reader's ability to imagine what it's like to be personally threatened by other people's decisions.

The Challenges that Define You

As adults, we can sometimes feel like we have not had significant struggles to talk about. I agree that people who complain about first-world problems are narrow-minded and largely ignorant of just how good most of us have it. **On the other hand, we can't deny that certain events in our lives have formed who we have become.** For me, the period of my life when my parents were struggling to keep our family business was a defining moment. Although we didn't lose our house or lack for food, the anxiety of that time greatly impacted my consciousness about the roles my parents and I had in the world.

One of my in-laws overcame much bigger struggles in her life, and when I occasionally hear her talk about them, my respect for her grows. As a child, her home environment was shaky. For multiple years, her mom raised her and her two brothers alone, telling them at Christmastime that Santa Claus wasn't real so they didn't feel unloved when they didn't get any presents. When she was still young, her stepbrothers were teenagers with raucous, partying lives. One night at a party in their house, someone fired a gun. On Sundays, her parents dropped her off at church while they went off and did drugs or other unmentionable things. Church was her place of solace and safety, something she held onto tightly until she met my family. **She doesn't bring up her past regularly, or in a way that excuses her to play the victim.** She tells some people about her childhood, but anyone who knows her can tell that she has intentionally chosen *not* to be a victim of these things over which she had no control. She has chosen to focus on other paths in her life, but if she ever chose to write grant or fellowship proposals, she could point to these experiences to explain her knowledge of these problems and they would make her a credible candidate to carry out relevant work.

Your Story

The personal statement is a chance for you to outline your story as it relates to the work you intend to do. What have been the moments in your life that led you to applying for this fellowship or grant? **Where did this passion stem from?** These are the things that intrigue the reader and tell them a story about you. In most cases, you want to include some kind of emotional attachment to your cause. Combine that with your technical and professional preparation and you have a great case for winning that award.

I've written multiple proposals where the personal statement and the proposal were combined. In these cases, the emotional and technical preparation are cut short and have to be seamlessly integrated into the rest of the writing. You don't have a dedicated, 500-word essay to explain who you are, so there is even more pressure to find a core explanation or to describe a key moment in your life that led you on your path.

When I was writing grant applications for the Go Green Africa project I did in Cameroon after graduating from college, I often had to combine my personal statement with my proposal. I had to relay why I was so passionate about environmental issues in Africa, so I described the very first day I ever spent in Africa.

For the trip my family took to Nigeria in 1997, my parents prepared their wills in advance, not knowing whether we would all make it back alive. Although we had a caring and well-connected host, there were many unknowns about what we would encounter. When we arrived at the Lagos airport late on a July night, the terminal was damp and vacant. I remember looking for a bathroom and finding a water closet that had no lights, no door, and no toilet seat. **The toilet bowl was empty, but the dripping faucet in the sink led me to believe that I couldn't flush even toilet paper (which was fine, because toilet paper was nowhere to be found).**

As we walked out into the dimly lit parking lot, it felt like we were the only people who had disembarked from the plane. We were certainly some of the very few white people who had landed in Nigeria that night. Taxi drivers, money converters, and hawkers strained to see us, leaning over rusted parking balustrades. We didn't dare merge with the crowd before we knew where we were going. Watching over our luggage was the last thing we had on our minds.

Two police officers presented themselves and told us in the most un-reassuring way, "We're here to pick you up; you can trust us." Not knowing whether these two men were leading us to safety or away to be shot in a dark underpass, we followed them past the crowd into a parking lot. The tiny, four-door 1980s Toyota was supposed to hold my parents, my brother, my grandma, our good friend Jodi, and me. Sitting on each other's laps, with bags filling the last bit of space between our bodies and the low roof, I craned my neck out of the window to see Nigeria for the first time. Even after flying for nearly thirty hours, I was alert and curious to smell the damp night air and see the differences between this land and my own. I was ten years old, and the Nigerian highway made the contrast blatantly obvious, even without much traffic at this hour.

The first thing I noticed was how few streetlights there were. When the plane had circled the city in preparation for landing, the dwellings below us were specked here and there by what appeared to be bare light bulbs. From the lack of electric lights, I would have guessed we were landing in a village, not one of the biggest cities in West Africa. On the highway, potholes and garbage in the streets forced the driver to swerve erratically. **People crossed the highway at odd intervals, clearly aware of the danger in not being seen, but fearless in their persistence.** The initial hot, sweet, humid smell of ocean air was quickly replaced by a black, chemical waft that I instinctively covered my nose against. As we drove down the highway, I saw the source: piles of burning trash that produced more light than the sparse streetlights. It seemed like this was how the city dealt with garbage. My American child-brain registered the dangers of this practice immediately. I knew that breathing these black fumes would be harmful to my lungs, not to mention my brain. **A small part of me also began to grasp how the infrastructure underlying our American lifestyle neatly took care of these problems.** This was the beginning of a greater understanding of and appreciation for public investment and well-functioning governments.

Obviously, this practice of burning trash also alerted me to the fact that humans were damaging our environment. It wasn't until years later that the short film *The Story of Stuff* presented the concept that there is no way to "throw away" things, they all still existed far beyond the point when we put them in the trash. This idea was planted in me back on that night in 1997, when I saw the way this African country had to handle the problem.

As a twenty-one year old, I went to Cameroon for the first time. I was not familiar with the food from this culture, but I was surprised to find that they had some foods that were similar to those from New Mexico. There were meat-filled cornmeal pockets cooked traditionally in banana leaves, which were like the tamales cooked in cornhusks that I grew up eating. What a wonderful thing—I loved this food and was familiar with it. Also, the banana leaves added an element of excitement because banana leaves are rarely seen in American fare.

Slowly, however, I started to notice that some people substituted plastic baggies for banana leaves. Boiling plastic releases toxins, and that made me reluctant to ingest the food inside. I started to ask people why they were changing from biodegradable banana leaves to plastic. "It's modern," was the most common response. Not only was the plastic a non-biodegradable waste product that would have to be burned with the other piles of trash in Cameroon, but the Pidgin word for the baggie was "paper," indicating the lack of awareness of the fundamental difference between the two products. I asked people if they knew that plastic baggies were a petroleum product made with chemicals and non-organic materials. Most people did not. I decided this would be the very first lesson in my kids' summer camp. If this myth could be dispelled, then maybe it would increase awareness in future generations and perhaps even in adults.

In my application materials to fund this project, I couldn't tell the whole story about this problem. Instead, I had to condense the essence of my original inspiration and put it concisely to explain why I was passionate and what the problem was. This is what I ended up saying:

> I distinctly remember the nighttime drive away from the airport and seeing frequent and evenly spaced piles of burning trash where there would otherwise be street lamps. Even at age ten, I knew that burning plastic was very bad for humans and for the environment, although it didn't seem like any of the people there understood that. When looking at first-world countries, I see that there is plenty that needs to be done to change our habits, but when I look at third-world countries, I see that there is not even a basic understanding that plastic disposal is different than organic disposal; plastic bags are called "papers" and everything is burned.

I called upon this same experience to recount a different aspect of my personal development years later when I applied to be a Presidential Management Fellow. Although I was unsuccessful in winning the fellowship, I enjoyed telling my story in a new way to highlight how I appreciated the role of government and would welcome the opportunity to be part of the relatively well-functioning federal system.

1) What has been your journey, the key experiences and decisions that have brought you to this point? (3000 characters, 200–300 words)

I grew up as a child of two parents who engaged in community development as small business owners. My mother created and, for over twenty-five years, has maintained an artistic community with enormous vitality. As small business owners in a downtown redevelopment district, my father attended city council meetings and spoke publicly for the rights of small business owners like him. I understood from this experience that city planning and governance is complex because of limited space and many competing interests. Only by following and participating in that type of process can I help direct the inevitable change equitably and creatively.

In 1997, our family traveled to Nigeria, which at a young age juxtaposed my American identity to the more complex existence of being non-American. I learned that America is the most supportive and organized government in the world, and therefore I am accountable for my own success because I have had every privilege imaginable. As a young witness to worldwide disparity, this period of my life defined my life-long motivation to serve others.

After graduating with my Economics degree in college, I was very fortunate to get a Fulbright Fellowship and Rotary Scholarship to Senegal, where I went to study dance and environmental issues. While there, I saw once again the contrast between American city planning and the lack thereof in Dakar, where livelihoods are threatened as the result of poor planning in the floodplain areas. My graduate degree in City and Regional Planning at Cornell will enable me to continue the strong tradition in America of considering human, economic, and environmental components of building our future.

In my view, there is no more direct way to serve people than by working for the federal government. The structures that support our country, both social and physical, come in large part from federal agencies. I am grateful for the investment our government makes in transportation, education, and safety. We all benefit from the diligence and thoughtfulness of civil servants working across the broad network of federal agencies. In order to contribute to society in a meaningful way, I want to become part of the workforce that ensures the ever-improving quality of our country.

Your personal statement can follow a formula, in which you start with an anecdote about yourself. I prefer to start with a moment in time that defines what I want to illustrate. When I was helping my sister-in-law Nicole write her personal statement to get into an herbalist training program, I asked her to think of a moment in her life when she knew that she wanted to be an herbalist.

- What did that moment look like?
- Where was she?
- What was she doing?
- Could she describe both her environment and what she was feeling?

This moment in time set the stage for the rest of the personal essay.

Next, it works well to give some kind of explanation about your background in the given subject area.

- When did you first start studying or practicing that thing?
- What was the chronological series of events and how were they linked together?

Describing succinct events that are tied to each other and helped you progress along the in pursuing your passion provides a sense of durability. You want to demonstrate how you have committed yourself to this field and what you have undertaken to promote yourself.

The next segment of the personal statement describes your future, or where you want to go next. In this section, you tie in how working on the project you're proposing leads you to that specific future. You want to line up the next phase of your life so that the scholarship or grant becomes an essential stepping-stone to your final goal. If you outline this personal statement, it could look something like PRESENT > PAST > FUTURE.

Nicole's essay for the herbalist program:

The best gift I could think of giving this holiday season was a healing remedy. While looking through Rosemary Gladstar's recipe book, I found a nice cough syrup formula that I altered slightly according to what was available locally. Osha, one of our many native herbs, was the addition that I felt was necessary for our New Mexican immune systems. The dialogue I develop with the herbs when I'm handling them inspires me to become a vessel of the healing properties they offer. I want to spend my life working with the herbs to help keep my community strong and full of vitality.

Since I was a young girl, I have always loved music, but most of all I loved to dance. Like most dancers, I began with traditional ballet and jazz until anorexia blinded me to the world around me. In order to heal from this disease, I knew I had to stop dancing. My mother began to miss watching me dance and the joy it inspired, so she brought me to a West African/Haitian dance class. She wanted me to see real woman with real bodies dancing and being joyful. It was love at first sight in more than one way; I was home. Seven years later, nothing feels better or more freeing than dance. This dance community, along with nutrition and herbs, is what enabled me to recover from anorexia. These components in my life gave me the desire to be as healthy and strong as I possibly could be to do what I love.

My dance community is a microcosm of the Santa Fe culture in which I was raised. I am grateful to have grown up surrounded by the multitude of healing arts. My mother, a midwife, treated me exclusively with homeopathy, herbs, and acupuncture during my childhood. With my growing appreciation of the healing art forms, I have increasingly sought out information to educate myself. My mom's midwifery partner Seva is also a homoeopathist and has willingly shared her knowledge with me through the years. I have also benefited from the mentorship with my acupuncturist Harijot Khalsa, who has expressed his wish to have me follow in his footsteps. I feel blessed to have grown up in such a nourishing community that appreciates nature. I can't help but feel that the proximity of the mountains and high desert remind us daily of our intertwined relationship with the Earth.

Growing up in the mountains has always provided a magical sanctuary to which I can escape. Breathing the crisp air and feeling the soft earth under my feet centers me. I am able to find harmony up there, where I can listen to the plants around me as they speak in the quiet breeze. This land is rich with Native American culture, which was a strong influence on my family's history and is the reason they came here. For three generations, my family has cultivated a partnership with Native artists, learned their traditions, and traded their crafts. The treasured morsels of knowledge that have been passed on to us from these Native cultures enriches our familiarity with the local herbs around us. I look forward to having the ability to use this knowledge to keep the culture alive with future training.

My desire to work in this profession led me to apply for a competitive position at our local store, Herbs Etc. Over eight other qualified applicants, I was given this opportunity because the owner, Medical Herbalist Daniel Ganon, believed in me and in my aspirations. Working in this environment has exposed me to the wealth of knowledge I could attain if I had the good fortune to attend your program. I'd be honored carry on the mission of meeting the health needs of my community through educating people about the healing properties of herbs.

One of the great things about Nicole's essay is that it begins by demonstrating her knowledge of the topic at hand: herbs. She didn't *say*, "I know about herbs and how to use them." Instead, she *showed* this fact with an anecdote about her thinking process and the actions she followed according to that knowledge. She also makes a point of including her accomplishments in a quantifiable way ("Over eight other qualified applicants, I was given this opportunity because…"), while also sounding humble and grateful for what that meant to her. As I mentioned before, it's good to end on a humble note, acknowledging that you would greatly appreciate having the opportunity to be part of the program to which you're applying.

Describe a story, scene, or event that illustrates who you are today or how you came to be the person you are.

_____
_____
_____
_____

Does this anecdote about your life have the element of sensationalism? Does it make you sound like the unique person you are?

_____
_____
_____
_____

Does it highlight a specific quality that you will use in conducting your project?

_____
_____
_____
_____

What about universality? Is there something in this story that relates to most people? Ask someone else to read it and tell you whether they want to know more about you from this short introduction.

This will become the beginning of your personal essay.

From here, describe three key moments from your life that have brought you to this point of applying for a fellowship.

Event 1:

Event 2:

Event 3:

Connect these events or decisions together to make a logical transition to the present. How have each of these events tied together to make this fellowship/scholarship/grant the most logical next move in your career, and how will you tie your past experience together to successfully complete your project?

Each of these sections should be about a paragraph in length (think the five-paragraph essay structure).

Finally, describe how completing this fellowship/scholarship/ grant opportunity will naturally launch you into your future position/ job/place in the world, where you have always aspired to be. Take your experience and make a meta-picture that serves humanity. Don't be afraid to sound cheesy; a final sentence on moving society towards peace and justice is not uncommon in the grant-writing arena. Make the reader believe that you can make a difference on Earth.

Here are some additional examples of how I began essays with anecdotes that I proceeded to explain.

2012
Presidential Management Fellowship

How do you know you are well suited to manage the realities and challenges of working in the federal government?

During my year in Senegal as a Rotary Scholar and Fulbright Fellow I learned the truth in the Wolof proverb, "Slowly, slowly, is how you catch the monkey." Patience always served me in my journey as a foreigner adapting to this new culture. Navigating bureaucratic obstacles within the American Embassy and the Senegalese government taught me perseverance and compromise. I realized that in order to work successfully in Senegal, I would need to find common goals with my counterparts and work towards them together.

Although I have never worked in the federal government, I know that I have developed the personal skills needed to manage a federal job. Watching my parents create and sustain an evolving community helped form my personal capacity for compassionate leadership. Music, languages, and participating in public forums developed my skills as an effective team member and thoughtful listener, able to facilitate a vision that is grander than my own individual idea.

Having traveled and lived abroad extensively, I am practiced in the art of adaptation. Despite never having been to a South American country before spending my junior year of college in Brazil, I was able to adjust to my new environment with relative ease. Upon disembarking the plane, my senses became alert to highlighting the cornerstones of a new system with parallels to others I knew: ATM machines, public transit, common courtesy, and safety measures, among others. I have learned to first observe before acting when I confront a new situation.

Keeping both my eyes and ears open led me to study three languages in college so I could comprehend and converse with people of different backgrounds. Speaking French enabled me to facilitate discussions about cross-cultural interpretations of sustainability in my Masters of Development Practice class in Dakar. Thus, my fellow students understood my respect for their culture and background, which enhanced our intellectual exchanges and resulted in more nuanced and diverse conclusions. Communication and adaptation would serve me as an employee as well. I have learned to listen, which is the foundation of problem solving and efficient teamwork in any language.

2013
National Park Foundation Transportation Scholars Program
Bandelier National Monument

Streets were created in response to the physical challenges of land use, accessibility and activity patterns, but can unfortunately present new constraints on human interaction and a sustainable environment. As a native New Mexican, I appreciate the roads that allow me to visit the state's natural and cultural sites. Roads also make urban development possible in New Mexico, which supports regional sustainability. I studied transportation in order to contribute to the advancement of mobility options in New Mexico. At Cornell University, I was awarded one of five university-wide, federally funded Foreign Language and Area Studies Fellowships to research transportation systems in Portugal. I have been studying how Portugal maintains ancestral layouts while finding new ways to accommodate larger vehicles and multi-modal transportation. My research aims to bring new ways of planning to my beloved New Mexico, where I have a vested interest in ensuring its natural beauty remains accessible, with or without a car. As a child visiting Bandelier on school field trips, I vividly recall climbing inside cavates and the resulting amazement at experiencing a completely different form of habitation. Everyone should get to use parks, and I want my own future children to have the chance to learn from nature and history the same way I did.

Since May 2012, I have been working with the Santa Fe Metropolitan Planning Organization (MPO), first as a paid intern and now as a pro-bono researcher on the future Santa Fe Bike Share. In response to growing concerns over climate change, American public health, and attracting tourism, the Santa Fe Bicycle and Trails Advisory Committee has expressed the desire to explore the feasibility and best practices of bike sharing. A number of recent developments in Santa Fe indicate its readiness to implement a bike share. For example, the New Mexico Rail Runner Express carries approximately 4,500 passengers between Santa Fe and Albuquerque daily and between 2,000 and 4,000 bikes come aboard the train monthly, demonstrating an existing bicycling population. In the transportation demand analysis, I am conducting research on employment and tourist clusters, taking into account favorable zoning, proximity to bike lanes, land use regulations, preservation codes and signage, and way-finding options that would best establish a bike share network of stations. My experience with the Santa Fe Bike Share research equips me to fulfill the duties of the Bandelier Scholar position because of my familiarity with transportation planning and with the Northern New Mexican communities.

During my time as a graduate student at Cornell, I have focused my studies on transportation planning. Currently, I am working with a team of ten graduate students looking at transportation issues for the new Cornell NYC Tech Campus on Roosevelt Island. The phased build-out of the campus will start in 2018, bringing thousands of students and faculty, but more importantly, facilitating the growing tech "ecosystem" between New York City's boroughs. Roosevelt Island has a long history of isolation, mostly due to its murky history, which includes a smallpox hospital; proper transportation planning will ensure connectivity to transit options and the success of this multi-billion dollar investment. Our client, the Director of Capital Projects, has employed our student research group to discover the best options for expanding inter-borough transportation. Although NYC is vastly different from Bandelier National Monument, I see transferable work experience and skills in alternative transportation planning coming from the project.

As a college student interested in environmental issues, I traveled to Brazil, Senegal, and Cameroon. In Cameroon, the lack of awareness around trash disposal inspired me to secure funding from Smith College and private donors to implement a summer program. For six weeks, 100 middle-school students learned about environmental policy and wrote letters to the Federal Environment Department about plastic disposal. Setting up programs and seeing them through is gratifying, but not always easy. As a graduate student, I am a grant recipient from the Cornell Community Partnership Board to teach underprivileged, inner-city youth about dance. Despite a tight academic schedule and logistical obstacles, I remain invested in serving the local community because of my commitment to giving back. I find that I can make a lasting impact not only through volunteering extra-curricular time, but also through projects related to my graduate work.

I would be the ideal candidate for the National Park Foundation Transportation Scholar Program in Bandelier National Monument because of my dedication to New Mexico and my experience in transportation planning. I have experience working with New Mexico transportation agencies, specifically in the field of bicycle planning and alternative transportation. I also have an intimate knowledge of northern New Mexico as a Santa Fe native who spent camping visits and school trips in the surrounding wilderness. I would be able to bring my New Mexico registered car to the site and I have a valid New Mexico driver's license. As specified in the position description, the lodging would suit me well and I would be available to attend the pre-project orientation at the beginning of June, immediately before starting the scholarship. Becoming a Transportation Scholar would fit the natural evolution of my career and passion for public service. I cannot imagine a better way to begin serving northern New Mexico and my country than by helping to expand visitor access and exposure to Bandelier National Monument. I look forward to being part of making parks more available and easier to use for present and future generations.

2011
Sustainable Global Enterprise Immersion Application

My parents are small business owners in Santa Fe, New Mexico. They instilled in me both a strong environmental conscience and a value for entrepreneurial ventures. I have grown up participating in city council meetings and community forums, and on the weekends, I would help clean up events at our performance center until 1:00 a.m. or later. Working in our family business in our small, high-desert mountain town gave me the sense that the sustainability of our community depends upon active citizen participation. We are all responsible for what becomes of our home.

Since financial sustainability is a key concern for a small business, I decided to major in Economics in college. At Smith, I was fortunate to be exposed to people and ideas from around the world, which led me to study in Brazil for my junior year, and subsequently to apply for the Kiva fellowship in microfinance. As the only undergraduate selected, I apprehensively took my assigned post in Cameroon as an internal auditor and office liaison to the San Francisco Kiva headquarters. Even though the challenge was great, I stepped up and came out of that amazing experience with a strong desire to work in international sustainability.

I dove head first into my senior year at Smith by taking advantage of every opportunity offered by the institution. I was awarded first prize and one hundred dollars for the Smith College Elevator Pitch Contest, where I presented my idea to make an individual car sun-shield with PV cells that could charge small electronic appliances. I went on to a second-place prize and $750 at the Harold Grinspoon Regional Elevator Pitch Contest. I was also awarded the Ruth Dietrich Tuttle Prize (consisting of $2,500) from Smith for a program I pioneered in Cameroon to teach middle-school students about climate change. My Fulbright Research Fellowship and Rotary Ambassadorial Scholarship to Senegal this last year would not have been possible without learning how to market myself and use the resources available to me.

What I've learned about going into the world is that the biggest difference in global sustainability I can make is at the city and regional level. Logically, I decided to come into Cornell's CRP program to learn how regional systems work. Even without this training, I feel like I could have easily stepped into co-owning my family business. Two years ago, for example, we installed low-flow toilets upon my finding and figuring the feasibility of a city tax credit. These choices make a big difference in the desert, but I think for environmental sustainability to become the norm, I need to learn how to partner with bigger businesses and work on a larger scale.

I see the Sustainable Global Enterprise Immersion program as the perfect way for me to complement my CRP courses about the physical technicalities of sustainability with the ability to leverage corporate systems to adopt sustainable practices. Merging environmental management and corporate responsibility can lead to the best outcomes for both worlds and I see myself being able to facilitate these liaisons if only I had the business IQ. Being part of this immersion program would afford me the opportunity to learn how to make the money of corporations work for the world.

Northampton Rotary Club
Rotary Ambassadorial Scholarship 2010–11
Brief Autobiography

"Now that's primitive!" exclaimed my grandmother over an elegantly set table in a café where we awaited our coffees. The description of life in Cameroon during my microfinance fellowship the previous summer shocked my grandmother, bringing into question anyone's possible attraction to living standards far below our own. I recounted how my younger Cameroonian friends, Sheila and Nadej, had mastered the art of cooking, a skill I have yet to acquire in my transition to adulthood. Describing their process of butchering, cleaning, and searing off feathers over a floor-fire to prepare chicken astounded my grandma. Arduous daily chores are not so wondrous to African women who feed and provide for their families. My grandmother's reaction didn't surprise me; instead it took me back to a thought I often have: What can we learn from a different way of life?

My double major in Economics and Portuguese from Smith College propelled me to study abroad in Brazil for junior year and interact with people from around the world. At Smith, I studied Wolof, the national language of Senegal. I also studied comparative economic systems and economic development, but I'm striving to find out more than what I learned in those theory-based classes. Upon entering college, I didn't know that studying economics consisted mainly of neoclassical models, leaving the more interesting aspects of economics, those pertaining to human rights and environmental protection, untouched.

Concepts like the Triple Bottom Line (people, planet, and profit) are never mentioned in undergraduate economics, but my independent interest in the field opened the door to becoming a microfinance fellow in Cameroon during the summer of 2008. The challenges I confronted during my fellowship pushed me to find a source of confidence and determination in myself. As the only undergraduate selected by the program among seasoned finance professionals, the organization expected me to successfully overcome all possible situations in the field. The responsibility I took on enhanced skills I had merely discussed in college and emboldened me to seek more community development challenges. Microfinance tackles poverty form the ground up, using economic principles of loans and interest payments to finance small-scale entrepreneurship.

Working with community projects and entrepreneurs has been my focus for many years. While spending my Junior Year Abroad at the Pontifícia Universidade Católico in Rio de Janeiro, I grasped every opportunity to involve myself with fellow students and organizations. Interning at the Brazil Foundation and volunteering to teach English to underprivileged high school students from the favelas of Rio extended my time and abilities to my new community. Preparation for studying abroad started in my first semester at Smith, beginning the two-year process of learning Portuguese to study economics courses while in Rio. Living and learning in another country was not merely a matter of learning the language, because I also discovered a different pace of life that forever changed how I understand other people with a global perspective.

Going to Brazil was not my first solo trip outside of the country. Being a dancer, I studied in Senegal during summer 2006, where I tuned my senses to a new language, culture, and place. Not knowing a single word of French or Wolof at the time, I listed for cues to quickly understand my surroundings. I was the only foreigner staying with the Faye family of tradition-holding storytellers. The family became dear to me and I felt honored to share household responsibilities, doing my part. Along with immersing myself in the Senegalese language and dance, I had my first chance to live without running water or personal space, and limited electricity. In the middle of Dakar, I saw an incarnation of a sustainable, self-contained community, even with the challenges of dense populations and limited resources.

Most Americans have barely read about life in West Africa. Media only covers refugee camps in Darfur, pirates in Somalia, and political unrest in Zimbabwe. Upon my return, people did not inquire about the serenity of Senegal, with its close family relations, communal living, and deep cultural traditions. Even with all the positive qualities I saw in Senegalese society, I was saddened by the scarcity of money despite people's efforts to improve their situation. By the age of 22, my Senegalese friend Fili Mbaye had completed two associate degrees and still found employment impossible. I do not pity Africans, because that would offend them immensely. Instead, I want to learn how Africans can finance themselves. Some creative strategies have evolved in West Africa to enable entrepreneurs to survive.

I mastered my economics classes, only to find they didn't prepare me for what I encountered in Brazil and Africa. Economic models describing trade relations and commerce with the Heckscher-Ohlin model, based on identical tastes and economic situations across countries, ignores the reality I found in Africa. Senegalese families operate according to different initiatives than Americans and share almost none of the same preferences. When westerners refer to "climbing the economic ladder" to support African economic development, I realized that many Africans do not climb alone. As their income increases, they demonstrate symbols of status and success by sharing the wealth, not hoarding it.

From my very first experience in Africa, I knew that my college skills would prepare me for any venture I undertook, but that I would find more of my education outside rather than inside the classroom. I needed to learn neoclassical economic theory to understand where the system is broken so that, from there, I could tackle underlying problems.

One way to confront negative systemic behavior is by teaching young students how to act differently. After spending time in Cameroon for my microfinance fellowship, I initiated an environmental education summer camp for high school students to learn about ecology, climate change, and responsible waste disposal. My first venture is called Go Green Africa, and it contributes to a new subject for Cameroonian students. It incorporates hands-on art and service activities that enhance the educational process and get kids to educate their peers and elders about sustainability. I continually challenge myself to involve communities in reinvigorating their economies. Ultimately, I would like to work in development economics and sustainable development for emerging economies. Researching alternative energy production with microfinance became an interest because I believe that within these fields, we can find solutions to poverty. With this knowledge, I intend to pursue a career in microfinance that directly advances sustainable economic development, prosperity, and peace.

For my graduate degree, I want to pursue a Masters in Public Policy and/or Resource Management with a focus on economic development. Although I will spend next year developing the Go Green Africa project, the opportunity to fulfill an Ambassadorial Scholarship through the Rotary Foundation would be an ideal stepping-stone in my career.

Don't worry if your first attempt at a personal essay feels inadequate. This is a 500-word document that you will edit, rewrite, and review dozens of times. The first step is making an effort and writing a crappy draft. The mentors and network of support you have been building will help you refine this story to meet the needs of the application. If you feel disenchanted with your personal essay, start again from scratch. There is no great writing; there is only great rewriting, which is what you'll learn to do in the next chapter.

CHAPTER TWELVE

REWRITE, REWRITE, REWRITE (AND ATTENTION TO DETAIL)

"Start early, don't wait, and get feedback. Good luck!"
—**Lindsay Van Dyke**, Digital Media & Video Strategist, former Fulbrighter

J ames, two years since receiving his BA and six months since returning from development work in Uganda, got encouraged by a mentor to apply for a Fulbright Fellowship. He coaxed his close friend Marcus, an engineering undergraduate, to join forces with him and also apply for a Fulbright Fellowship.

Their shared mentor encouraged them every step of the way, but it was up to them to follow through with this high ambition. Despite full loads already on their plates with work and school, James and Marcus made the time to write and revise their applications together.

"The library just didn't fit with our style of work so we ended up spending our nighttime work sessions at a variety of large hotels in the city."

Starting at 10:00 p.m., they'd sit in the lobby and write, then discuss, then write again, taking a break every few hours to discuss something else and share a funny YouTube video or two. "James would read what I had just written," Marcus said, "and he would tell me 'I see what you are *trying* to say, but sorry, you're not saying it.' 'Fine, yours is crap too,' I'd counter, and we would go back to the drawing board." They'd often stay there late enough to catch the early morning continental breakfast and coffee, a much-needed wake-me-up for the duo to get ready for their normal lives after a long night of work. Marcus ended up going to Spain for his Fulbright and James went to Uruguay. Nearly a decade since their midnight marathons, they fondly recall the long hours they spent on their applications and still to this day support each other's respective goals. James summarizes,

> We learned so much through that experience! We learned to be better writers, to be stronger supporters of each other, but probably the best lesson we took away was this: There is tremendous power when people work vigorously together on something that initially seems only like a distant, lofty idea. The idea becomes a dream, the dream becomes a goal, the goal gets etched into a timeline, and shortly thereafter, what is only an image in our minds becomes a wonderful reality! I hope others understand the great powers of writing and collaboration!"

It feels great to just get your ideas down—this is half the battle—but then comes the hard work of refining what you have written. I have heard that there is no great writing; there is only great rewriting. I find comfort in this when I confront a brand new project, because it takes the pressure off of doing something perfectly the first time. You should give yourself ample time to rework the format of your proposal and personal statement. Having a reliable group of reviewers, or even a writing partner, helps a lot when you approach the editing stage.

I have always found it helpful to get other people's ideas about what I have written. After spending weeks or months on the concept of your proposal and personal story, the cohesive picture is very clear to you. This doesn't always come across in writing, however. Perhaps you've forgotten an important link in describing your purpose, or you've skipped a step in your methodology. **Having a second (and third, fourth, and fifth) pair of eyes is invaluable to make sure you've answered every question and been clear in your writing.**

Expect to write at least five drafts of an application. After you've written a first draft, go back and spell-check. Read it aloud to listen to the flow of the language. After you've gone over the draft once or twice yourself, send it to a reviewer. You don't want them to be correcting spelling, although they may have suggestions for cleaning up sentences. Don Andrew was one of the best editors I've ever had. He would look at a sentence, then take one segment of it and move it around in the line or into another sentence and all of a sudden it was like the words had been set in their perfect place.

TIP: Don Andrew gave me the great advice of not ever using *et cetera* or *etc.* in an application. In one of the first drafts of my first Fulbright application, I said that I wanted to study the "dance, culture, etc." What a terribly vague statement! He first asked me what else I meant to study, and when I didn't really have an answer he said to just say "dance and culture." *Et cetera* makes you sound un-knowledgeable about the topic at hand and demonstrates ignorance.

When you are in the rewriting stage, you may want to revisit the grant or fellowship guidelines. Make sure that you answer all the questions asked of you. The worst thing you could do is to submit an application with blank spots. Rereading the guidelines can also give you a more nuanced view of what the granting body is looking for. Now that you've finished writing your proposal, does it sound like you are the perfect person for this opportunity? If not, how can you tweak it? Perhaps you can reframe your mission to more perfectly address the application.

At this point in the application, it all comes down to details. Most applications are only about 500–1000 words so you can rework these words until they are nearly perfect. With only 500 words, every word counts and you want to make sure that every word, punctuation mark, and paragraph break is in the correct space. You can refer back to basic, good writing principals to guide you.

The Writing Journey
James Gutierrez, Fulbright Scholar

Writing is the easiest activity in the world, said no one ever! I surely am not an expert writer. Though I am not sure I have ever met one either. I have, however, interacted with many skillful *rewriters*! My writing journey has taught me the lessons of rewriting and other key practices we can use to greatly improve written work, and hopefully help us enjoy the process.

These tips can help whether we are writing something as seemingly ordinary as an email, as creative as a poem, or as weighty as a fellowship application. In short, here are James' Top 10 Tips for Effective Writing, with brief examples from my experience writing my application to be a Fulbright Scholar in Uruguay:

1. **Get Comfy**
   We must always know how and when we do our best work. For me, it is usually at night in a lightly trafficked place. Most of my Fulbright

application was written in various cafés and hotel lounges, typing away until sunrise.

2. **Set Goals**

Take time to consider the audience and what major and minor points you want the readers to take away. First, I hypothesized the various types of individuals who might be on my selection committee (e.g., federal government officials, professors, former Fulbright Scholars) and then wrote down what I wanted them to know (e.g., *Unequivocally who am I? Why is this opportunity perfect for me? What will my contributions be?*).

3. **Outline**

This may be the most important step in the process! Often most people just start by typing their stream of consciousness and sometime thereafter wake up wondering why most of their work is disjointed, redundant, or irrelevant. Some of my major goals, which I turned into headings on my outline, were: *Tell them the arc of my unique story from rural New Mexico through the African savannah to a Beijing stadium and beyond. Why is this opportunity particularly significant amongst many? What will I contribute as a scholar while in Uruguay and in the United States upon my return? What will I gain personally and professionally?* Then, I wrote down subordinate ideas under each major objective, such as *Gain fluency in Spanish, Be a bridge to both cultures,* and *State clear research objectives.*

4. **Know the Flow**

After the outline is filled in, map out a logical flow, connecting and rearranging ideas as appropriate. This revised outline helps us see where our ideas dovetail and intersect. At this point, a coherent storyline begins to emerge.

5. Ideas > Sentences > Paragraphs

The most difficult aspect of writing is coming up with good ideas. With the outline already formed and reshaped, the writer is already over this biggest hump. Each of the outlined ideas can fairly easily be turned into complete sentences. These sentences will flow into comprehensive paragraphs that can stand alone.

6 Step Back

As a recovering procrastinator, I know one of the biggest luxuries is stepping away to let my ideas and words sit—often because I am pressed by an imminent deadline. Thus, it is most prudent to start the writing process as early as possible. For my Fulbright application I started the ideation and writing process about three months in advance of the deadline. This alleviated the unnecessary stress I had often previously experienced. Since months of advance work is not always feasible, I recommend that writers give themselves whatever amount of time they can to step away from their writing. Even just getting up from our chairs for a fifteen-minute walk will add incredible insight to what has previously been written and will spring forth new inspiration for the words and ideas to come.

7. Introduction and Conclusion

It is scientifically proven that people remember best what they hear or read at the beginning and end of any oral or written communication. Therefore, it is important to take special care for what the introduction and conclusion will be. I usually save this step until I have a fairly well constructed piece of writing. By this time, these sections are much easier to write because they simply foreshadow or reiterate a summary of what has already been composed, hopefully in a creative and thought-provoking way.

8. Seek Detailed Feedback

There is only so much fresh perspective we can glean from our own writing. It is an excellent idea to get detailed feedback from others. In order to prevent any inherent biases, it is best to seek viewpoints from people both familiar and unfamiliar to us and to the subject matter. There will be immense value added from the variety of perspectives! Also, this will help us find typos and understand what intricacies the various readers are taking away. A good friend of mine, Marcus, decided to also apply for a Fulbright Scholarship at the same time as me and we served as primary writing partners. We continually encouraged each other through the arduous moments and gave each other specific advice on areas we could improve.

9. Tweak, Tweak, Tweak

We have to continually assess if our written work fittingly matches the ideas we wish to convey. Continue stepping away, looking back, and revising. However, it's good to recognize that perfect writing does not exist. As we are constantly evolving with new ideas, our views on our writing will also evolve. For example, though I was fortunate my fellowship application was received favorably and I spent an incredible year based in Uruguay as Fulbright Scholar, I have on occasion looked back at my application essays and felt a visceral need to still refine many things. That's okay. I recognize that the words on this page may too someday prove to be cringe-worthy for my future self—but I take heart knowing this would be a sign of my growth.

10. Have Fun

Finally, we should allow ourselves to enjoy every step of the journey we take writing. As frustrating as it can sometimes be, writing is a privilege and it should be fun. It is a privilege to paint pictures from the disparate ideas in our minds that one day might rouse others to think deeply, connect thoughts, and paint new pictures through writing of their own.

Keep your draft as a Word (or similar) document until you are completely finished with your edits. A lot of application websites will have online forms to fill out. Become familiar with these forms at the beginning of your application process (so that you don't miss a category or pertinent information), but don't fill it out until everything is complete. This will save you the hassle of trying to remember which draft is most updated. You also don't want to make the mistake of accidentally submitting your application while you're fooling around with the content. Once you submit an application, you can't get it back.

When we were working on the Fulbright applications with Don Andrew, he would make us **send back drafts with a header that stated the date of the latest version.** When corresponding with people via email it can quickly get confusing which draft they're working on versus which draft you're on. Especially if you have a number of different reviewers, people will get back edits to you at different times so if you wrote the last edit date on the top of the draft, you won't confuse yourself or your reviewer with versions. Listing the version with the date instead of something like "Draft 5" also clarifies the process. These are the techniques I've learned, and they've been helpful to me, especially when I'm juggling multiple projects.

Hopefully you'll finish your edits and be prepared to submit materials a couple of days in advance of the final deadline. You don't want to be putting all the materials together a few hours (or minutes) before the deadline and have something go wrong! At the very final stage of the editing process, print out your materials and read through them to make sure you have everything checked off the list. At this stage, you are ready to either fill out the online form or print your final submission materials. If you are submitting materials online, fill out all the categories **(if possible, just copy and paste from your final document so you don't make spelling mistakes when retyping)** and then print out the filled-out application. Make sure that text doesn't disappear beyond the box limits or that the formatting isn't skewed. The most important thing is to make sure that all your answers are legible and nicely spaced in the area provided. Look over it yourself and then have another person look over the printed version as well. Do all of this before the final submittal so you can change things around if need be. Proofread everything out loud, as always, and slow down your eye. This is not the time to rush. You've spent months working on this project and it would be a shame if, in your haste, you misspelled or omitted some sentence that you'd been working on for months.

Years ago, before I was applying for scholarships and fellowships, my mother confided in me that when she's sending an important piece of mail, she always says,

"Abracadabra!" over the package before handing it over. At first I thought it was silly, but then I started practicing this superstition as well. "Make sure you wave your hand over the mail while you're saying it," my mother implored. For years now, every time I mail a package of information or even while I press the submit button on an application, I say, "Abracadabra," and wave my hand over the mail or the computer screen. I even shared this practice with another friend who has won many scholarships and fellowships. She told me years later that she still does this, even though we're not in college anymore.

Rewriting is a challenge for me. I find that after I've written something, I cringe when I first reread it. I tend to think that my writing is crappy and not worthy of anyone else's eyes or time. I've had to come to terms with the fact that I feel this way and just tell myself to *do it*. Just go back and start from the beginning. Usually I find that the first draft was not quite as bad as I thought and a lot of the material is usable. The key is just sucking it up and sitting my butt down to accomplish the task.

Like any type of writing, you can't wait for inspiration to hit you. Sometimes I've had to sit in front of my computer for a couple of hours before I could bring myself to look at a piece of my writing. Once I finally get into the zone, I can focus and really craft the sentences and paragraphs. **If I'm fighting against myself particularly hard, I think it helps to focus on the little things first. Just start with grammar**. This is rote editing; I don't have to think too hard. Then I can move on to cutting down unnecessary words and switching passive verbs to active verbs. From there, I can start to look at the actual vocabulary and pick more appropriate adjectives and nouns than I chose the first time. From there, I look at the paragraphs as whole units and check to see if they have topic sentences and flow smoothly from one to the next. Again, I have come to appreciate the short-essay format of most grant applications because usually the whole piece of writing fits on one page and is quite manageable. It's like a five-paragraph essay: easy to outline and easy to manipulate in a shorter amount of time.

It helps if I give myself a break from the writing before I go back and review it. If I've just finished the first draft, starting back at the beginning to edit immediately feels too fresh. I don't have distance from my writing and I'm still too emotionally attached (i.e., feeling like all of my writing is bad). If I take a day or two before revisiting the writing, I can kind of trick my mind into thinking that

I'm reviewing someone else's writing and become more objective. I really enjoy reviewing other peoples' writing, so if I can switch into editor's brain instead of self-criticizing brain, I'm good to go.

Another good way to start the editing process is to make myself accountable to someone else. I will sometimes approach a faculty member or a friend to review my writing and tell them exactly when I will get the draft to them. This motivates me to have the writing prepared for them because I don't want to waste their time. I also realize that if someone is kind enough to take the time for me, I want to respect the window of time they've cleared for me. For example, if I ask a friend when they might have time to review my work and they tell me they have a window of time on Thursday afternoon, I'll be sure to get them my draft before then. If they've offered to review another draft, I'll try to make the turnaround quick enough that they will still be able to accommodate me. **Don't take weeks to get your drafts back to your reviewers.** They'll forget that they offered to help you and you don't know what their schedule will be like by then.

I have come to rely heavily on productive procrastination to get my initial and final drafts done. What I mean by "productive procrastination" is that **I find another task that I would like to do less than editing or working on a proposal.** There's always something less appealing than applying for money to pursue my dreams, whether that's cleaning the bathroom, or working on another project for school, or exercising. I'm good at making myself feel like I need to be doing something at all times, so if I can think of something I should be doing that I don't want to do, then the prospect of working on editing a draft seems much more appealing. I think this is why I got so many grant proposals finished in my senior year of college. I was experiencing major senioritis in some ways, just sick of the classes I was taking and anxious to move on to the next phase of my life. I had figured out how to manage college with less effort, I had a strategy so I didn't stress out or spend unnecessary time studying. This gave me a lot of time to pursue grants. When I didn't want to work on tedious Portuguese or French translations, I would procrastinate by searching online for scholarships and grants or editing a proposal I was working on. This felt like I was being productive, even when I wasn't doing what I was supposed to be doing.

I'm not sure this is a great thing to rely on, but it works if you're having motivation issues. Sometimes I think the worst time to get writing or editing done is when I've cleared a whole afternoon or day to complete that task. I have found that I just spend hours messing around, cleaning the house, or taking forever to get to the library or somewhere where I can finally work. I'm sure that some writer's retreats work because there is nothing else to take one's attention away, but if I were to go away to a cabin to write for a week, I think that I would waste a lot of that time. I work better when I fit writing, editing, and researching into the hour or two that I have between other things that are more pressing. You may work differently than me, but this is what I've found for myself.

"[Motivation] has to come from within. External forces can be inspiring, but you'll only recognize the inspiration if you're looking for it. Otherwise, you might have the most inspiring person in the world standing right in front of you, and you won't feel a thing."

—**Vidhee Garg**, Scholarship recipient at
Mumbai University and Cornell University

End on a High Note

After eighty minutes of high-energy dancing and motivational yelling to a group of fifty or more people, you would think that my mom would just count down the minutes until the ninety-minute dance class came to a close. You may have experienced other classes where the teacher ends abruptly on the dot, regardless of where that left the group in the process of learning. Not so with Elise Smith Gent. As she's explained to me, "We can't end until we are on a high note." What she means is that class can't end until the energy in the room is upbeat. We can't be lagging, tired, and frowning at the end of class. The drumming needs to be energetic, and the dancers need to be feeling happy and good about what they've learned. Most of all, my mom needs to feel like she has done a good job for the day.

I adopted her motto when I was writing this book. I reserved twenty minutes or 500 words (whichever came first) each day for six months, but even if I had already completed my 500 words, I didn't stop until I felt like I'd ended on a high note. What that meant in writing terms was that I left the page on a topic or sentence that I knew I would eagerly greet the next day. Otherwise it would be too hard to return and maintain enthusiasm in the process. Although writing and editing are not everyone's piece of cake, I challenge you to find the joy in what you're doing. End on a high note every time you put down your application, anticipating with excitement the next time you get to work on it. This will show through in the writing, especially if the final sentence of your application is upbeat and conveys that the world is your oyster.

MOTIVATION FOR YOUR PROCESS

These final two chapters will help you emotionally prepare for the waiting periods and inevitable rejections that come once in a while. Resilience is key, and having realistic expectations will set you up for success.

CHAPTER THIRTEEN

BE OPTIMISTIC, BUT NOT NAÏVE

"When I went into the Fulbright office in Colombia to get the forms, the woman behind the desk said, 'Why are you bothering? It's too hard.' That comment ensured that I prepared for all aspects of the process."

—**Leila Cobo**, Executive Director, Latin Content & Programming, *Billboard*; journalist, novelist, TV host, Latin music expert, former Fulbrighter

"Rejection is just part of the game, and at some point or another it will happen to you. It will happen to you no matter how well qualified you are and it will happen for reasons outside of your control.

How you deal with rejection, even though it always hurts, is up to you. Accepting rejection is not usually something that comes easily, especially the first few times, but over time I've come to really trust that if something doesn't work out it's because there's something better waiting for me. I know that it's hard to trust this sometimes (and believe me, I've had some tough times following my own advice), but in the end it always comes back around to this for me.

Give yourself some time to mourn the loss of something you care about, but don't let this consume you or assume that rejection is a statement about your abilities, your character, your passion, or your future."

—**Gemina Garland-Lewis**, former Thomas J. Watson Fellow
and National Geographic Society Young Explorer Grantee

During my senior year of college I started doing Bikram yoga. Yoga had never really been my thing; I've always been a dancer and the stagnant overstretching never felt very good in my body. I was overweight from my year in Brazil (pão de queijo and açaí are very caloric foods) and I had a new love in my life who inspired me to get my body back. In addition, my new little sister at college, Aurielle, told me that she had been doing Bikram regularly before arriving at Smith that fall. I offered to go with her to get her back in the rhythm of balancing exercise with school, but it soon became my thing more than her thing. I would go on Saturday and Sunday mornings, starting my weekend at 9:00 a.m. with a hot yoga class. The one redeeming quality about hot yoga is that it makes me sweat and get to the point in my head where I can't worry about anything else because I'm so absorbed in not passing out. So far at college, I hadn't found anything that made me sweat and forget my worries like African dance, so I was relieved to have finally found Bikram (albeit in my last year).

Over the winter months, I would bundle up in an unrecognizable blob of sweaters, sweatshirts, sweatpants, jacket, hat, scarf, stained and fake UGGs, and sunglasses to protect my eyes from the snowy glare. I didn't mind how I looked, because I took the backstreets between my campus house and the studio. Starting out at 8:30 a.m., I trundled along, weighed down also by a shiny, pink bag stuffed with towel, yoga mat, a gallon of water, and a change of clothes. The fast clip got my spirits up and motivated me to make it through that class and my work. I also took this time to give myself little pep talks and envision success.

By winter, I had submitted my Fulbright application and a couple of small project grants. I was also mentally preparing my project for the Rotary Ambassadorial Scholarship. This was my alone time to see my future as the bright oyster that it was. **Sometimes, I even went so far as to say aloud, "I'm going to get it!"** I would think about what it would be like to be in Senegal the following year, dancing my heart out and meeting with artists to discuss their own visions for the future. I imagined opening the mailbox and seeing the acceptance envelope, opening it and reading my congratulatory letter, how I would feel and what a wonderful moment that would be. These thoughts propelled me through the snow and cold on my way to yoga. It also helped me to keep applying for other grants and scholarships because it cemented my conviction that I could win a scholarship, even if it wasn't the Fulbright. What became apparent was that I needed to create options and opportunities for myself, not just sit around and wait for someone to recognize me.

I've found that I can stimulate my enthusiasm for continuing the funding process by taking rejection as correction. Some grant applications are really great and provide you with feedback about your proposal. This is gold. If they can tell you what to correct, then you can improve your application for another grant (or maybe for the same grant in the following year). For example, I applied for the Environmental Protection Agency's Science To Achieve Results (EPA STAR) program for graduate school funding. I didn't get it, but the amazing thing was that they sent all of my reviewers' comments back to me with the rejection. There were three faculty members in different departments throughout the country and each was required to fill out an evaluation of my proposal. They commented particularly on elements of my methodology, scope, background, and supporting documentation. They gave me three pages of commentary from each of the three reviewers, which was a wealth of information for me in my quest for funding. I did not apply for the EPA STAR program again, but I could not have been more appreciative for this review of my proposal. Part of the reason I didn't reapply was because my focus for graduate school shifted, but had I been pursuing a PhD in the field for which I initially applied, this feedback would have honed my doctoral research objectives and strengthened my academic focus.

Even when I don't get intricate comments back from reviewers automatically, I don't let it stop me from investigating the reasons for rejection. Especially if I've made it to a finalist round of applicants, I make a point of trying to ask some key questions about why I wasn't selected. As happened with the Fulbright African and Asian Field Director, when I didn't want to waste his precious time by just asking an open-ended question about whether I should reapply for Senegal and dance or for Ivory Coast and environmental studies. Instead, I asked a select few questions that Don Andrew had reviewed that targeted the most important information I needed to proceed. I would never just write to a funding body or call them and ask, "Why didn't I get this?" Instead, I would look back over my proposal and at the funding guidelines once again (maybe even looking at those people's proposals who did win) and pick out what I thought were my weakest points. Then I would think about how I could improve those points and ask the funding body whether those improvements would give me a better chance of winning the grant.

Another way to get feedback is to try to contact the people who won and ask them for advice about your project. Often people are helpful and eager to share their insights. **This is why networks are important.** Once you start to apply for grants and fellowships, you'll find that you learn about more opportunities. I've discovered a fair number of fellowships (like the EPA STAR) through talking to fellow scholars about their past experience. Reach out to and talk with people as much as possible, especially once you start to enter the grant-seeking realm.

Here are the realities of applying for grants. For every ten or twenty grants I investigate, there are maybe two that apply to my project. Then, for every three to five applications I submit, I can expect maybe one grant. With these odds, you can see why I need a lot of optimism. Knowing this, however, I can have a healthy expectation of results.

Grant writing has never been my main focus in work. I've been a student, a teacher, a transportation planner, but not a grant writer as a full-time position. This has saved me from burning out. I need to get really excited about a project to keep up the stamina that I need to go through dozens of revisions and rejections. It's best for me to apply for a couple of grants per year, when I've found something that can sustain my interest and enthusiasm. As I've stated before, I also think it helps me a lot to work on my own fellowships and grants because the reward comes to me and not to someone else. I can hold this goal in my mind and really concentrate on attaining it.

For me, being optimistic means tapping into my source of power, for lack of a better word. **I just have to become an invincible person, resilient to rejection and hard work.** This is the part of me that knows I can do anything if I work hard enough at it. Anything worth recognition requires work, and I just have to get through my self-doubt and criticism. I also have to overcome my lazy side. I have a very big lazy side that I succumb to after I've accomplished something. This is the part of me that cuts corners and watches whole seasons of TV shows in a couple of days. After working for months on a project, be that writing a grant/application, learning how to quilt, writing intensively, or cleaning out years' worth of junk from the closet, I allow myself to just relax. I don't know how anyone can go, go, go all the time. I don't think they do. Everyone must have something that they do to regenerate, but maybe they don't completely shut down like me. For example, when I was still a student, I reserved the first two weeks of summer or winter vacation for doing nothing. I would sit around and eat tons of food and watch movies. No books, no appointments, no obligations. I tend to wear myself out so completely finishing up projects that I just need to take time for nothingness. This is not the most sustainable pattern, but it's how I seem to operate and get through the final hurdles of school, or work, or applications. Even when I don't need to get through something quickly (like quilting), I tend to get a little manic about finishing a project instead of letting it drag on forever.

One of my writing mentors, Tanya Taylor Rubinstein, says to her students, **"Allow yourself the gift of completion."** Completing a project is the only thing that gets me through sometimes. It just feels so great to have done my best, finished off all the edges nicely, and trimmed the stray threads. Then I can rest easily, not having the nagging feeling that I could have done better or if I had just persisted a little longer. The finished product is enough of a reward in and of itself that it motivates me to get through.

I remember reading the testimonials on the fellowships office website for Smith College. Many of the comments said that the process of preparing and revising the application was a reward in and of itself, besides whether the fellowship was ultimately awarded. I completely agree with this sentiment, even though the gratification of winning is really nice too. The fellowships program was optional at Smith and, although there were information sessions each spring about the office, the fellowships advisor did not recruit people to apply, as they did at Amherst College. Amherst's fellowship office contacted a friend of mine who fit the profile of a successful applicant. She hadn't considered applying before, but they talked her into it. She didn't end up getting the grant, I think partly because she had not initiated the process, but also because it's not all about having the highest grade point average or what you've done before; it's about having the passion and the vision to complete the application and the drive to complete a fellowship project.

I knew a senior in college who had applied for the Fulbright in Theater Arts in Burkina Faso. She was a talented dancer, yet cerebral enough to write a thesis about dance as well. She had a keen ability to describe the importance of arts and she had done enough research to find a niche market. There was a performance company doing groundbreaking productions that combined traditional dance from Burkina Faso with modern dance. These productions were beginning to be recognized by the western dance world and had that exciting, new, and exotic element that would pique an academic's interest. With her background and this research topic, the woman was a very good candidate and actually won the Fulbright.

When I talked to her immediately after winning, she was excited, but not in the way you'd expect from someone who got a Fulbright. There are people who go through the whole process of applying and being admitted to these prestigious programs, only to decline the offer because, in this case, she didn't want to spend the year in a country to which she did not feel connected. I think it's better to save yourself the time and the internal grief of having to choose what's really right at the beginning rather than at the end.

Find something that really piques your own interest. Applying for scholarships takes resolve that can't come from an external source; you need to really want that prize. Otherwise it will be too easy to quit after the first rejection.

Rejection is part of the experience of applying for scholarship and grant money. Having this expectation is good because then you'll have an easier time recovering. There are a couple of things that you can do to buffer the rejection and get back on your feet to start the process again. I always think the best thing to boost my chances is to have multiple applications in the works at one time. When you're doing research on grants, you should keep track of a couple of possible options. Hopefully these grants will be similar enough that you don't have to completely reinvent the supporting documents.

Trying again is the hardest part of fellowships. Especially if I've put a lot of effort into something, I feel very disappointed when I don't succeed. With the Go Green Africa project, I had a huge setback after I didn't get the Power in Numbers grant from Mountain Dew. **This was partly because it was one of the first rejections I got, but also because the grant required me to put so much time into getting votes after I was nominated.**

With this particular grant, I found out that I was a finalist on the first day of my spring break during my senior year. I had just arrived in New York City for the week and I got a phone call from Mountain Dew saying I would need to get a form signed, notarized, and sent back to them within twenty-four hours to secure my place. I was on the bus arriving into the city when I got this call and, between the hectic transition of getting into Port Authority and the noise coming from overworked bus engines and the city soundscape, on top of picking up my bag and getting to the subway I needed to take uptown, I was completely overwhelmed.

I went into overdrive. I needed to find a place to print the form, then sign it and have my partner sign it (she had gone to Portland for break), then I needed to find a notary and a FedEx to send off this form with a short twenty-four hours counting down. Luckily I was in New York City, where I could find a copy center and notary within walking distance. I found a FedEx that had a notary, but the person saw my finicky, New Mexico, fake-looking ID and had to get a second opinion. Leave it to New Mexico to put clouds and funny imitation Native American colors and designs on our drivers' licenses. Waiting impatiently, I held back from snapping at the notary as they made a couple of phone calls and had someone else come check the ID for validity. Finally, they did stamp the form, and I was able to send it with a couple of hours to spare.

Immediately after I secured my finalist place, I was told that to actually win, I had to get the most votes within a two week time period. The voting rules were that people could vote up to once per day for two whole weeks, totaling a possible fourteen votes per person whom you recruited. **I was star struck by having my project photos on the front page of the Mountain Dew community grants page. It was shiny and professional looking, with intricate graphic design and**

rotating project features. Those were my own words published online on a major corporation's page. It was intoxicating.

I didn't know how I was going to get people to vote for me every day for two weeks. That seemed like an impossible obligation to ask people to make. What I did, which my mom thought was questionable, was to make up a sheet that had a check box next to each date, so people could put it by their computer as a reminder. If they brought me back the sheet with every day checked off, I'd give them a small bag of candy. "Isn't this bribery?" my mom asked. I figured there were people giving out favors to get people to vote, so this wasn't that much different. Only one girl in my French class cashed in on the candy bribe.

The other thing I did (in all my free time as a senior) was to print out little instructions for voting and tape them to lollipops. I went through all the school libraries and passed them out to study groups, asking them to please vote for me. I don't think this was a particularly effective use of time, in hindsight. I didn't win the grant and was so upset. I inwardly felt betrayed by my friends and classmates, thinking that they didn't care enough about me to make this tiny effort. They probably did vote for me, so this was an unfounded sentiment. I don't know how the winning projects did it. I have this picture in my mind of pretty cheerleaders setting up an information booth in front of a campus center with an army of foot soldiers soliciting votes with shiny brochures and flashy project materials.

I think a part of finding the perseverance comes from the conviction that you deserve to be awarded money for your project. You've put work into this effort and you owe it to yourself to see it through. Rejection just means that the grant you had applied for wasn't the right one. There's a reason why you got rejected and it was probably only because you weren't the right fit. Don't despair. There is a right fit out there for you, just keep searching.

"Don't think about things you cannot control: number of other applicants, quality of other applications, or the results. Think about things that you **can** *control, and do that to the best of your ability. Don't lie to yourself. Know that you are entirely responsible for your application, no excuses will do, and if you put in your 100%, you will still be happy even if you don't end up getting the grant. But if you put in a half-hearted effort, you have only yourself to blame."*

—**Vidhee Garg**, Scholarship recipient at
Mumbai University and Cornell University

If you are getting rejection after rejection, try taking another approach. Rejection calls for renewed perseverance, but other times, it's a sign that you're on the wrong path. This is what happened when I applied for the Presidential Management Fellowship. I applied for it because it was a popular thing to do in my graduate program. Friends of mine in many different fields were applying for this opportunity to rise up the federal government ranks quickly. The exam and application are notoriously tough, so I knew my chances were slim to begin with; but also, when I looked into the possible offices I could enter, I didn't see many in New Mexico. I knew that I wanted to return to New Mexico after graduating, but the main federal office there is the Bureau of Land Management. The Presidential Management Fellowship is much more beneficial to people who want to work in Washington, DC, not New Mexico. When I didn't get through the first round of selections, I took it as verification that that path was not the right one for me. Had I gotten into the program, I may have felt like I couldn't turn down the position because it was so prestigious and ended up forcing myself to live on the East Coast for another two years. I was partly relieved that I didn't have to make this decision. They made the decision for me; rejection was a relief.

CHAPTER FOURTEEN

TRY, TRY AGAIN

Elise laughs when she falls.
—My mother's college dance advisor

A s the fortieth US president took his oath of office in Washington, DC, my mother was in the middle of her college career in a small town in Vermont. The liberal arts college extended the bubble from reality for the young artists who trained there. My mother's college advisor was more of a friend. He insisted on including the line "Elise laughs when she falls" in the letter of recommendation she asked from him.

"Did you fall down often?" I asked her jokingly one day.

"No, but when I did, I guess I would laugh." And she still laughs when she falls.

This is a good metaphor for her approach to life. What can you do but laugh and get back up again? We all fall sometimes. Taking a tumble can even make us stronger. So take it in stride when you get the inevitable rejection. Don't take it too personally, because it happens to everyone.

Trying and Failing: It's Just Practice

In 2011, while I was studying in Senegal, I wrote the following essay as part of an application for a fellowship at Cornell. I had been accepted to Cornell and instantly started agonizing about how to manage taking on that much debt. I searched around for a couple of weeks and finally found a scholarship to live in a student house for two years and participate in the student government of the house. **The scholarship was amazing: tuition plus room and board for two years.**

Unfortunately, I found out about the scholarship a week before it was due, which meant not having nearly enough time to complete the three essays and one writing sample, plus get a recommendation letter. This went against all the rules I have about applying for scholarships (allow months of preparation time to research and revise the application materials). Despite this, I made a desperate dash to write the essays and this was the first and best of those three:

My knocking knees tried to bring some blood back into my numb fingertips and lips as I sat in the ninety-degree heat. *Oh god oh god oh god,* I thought, *what am I doing here? This is great. No, this is terrifying, but exciting!* The buzzing in my ears was not from the piercing thwack of an orchestra of sticks slapping goatskin drumheads nearby, but from the blood zipping around my body. A single line of lights, precariously twisted onto a live wire, drooped across the cleared street to end on an Acacia tree branch. I cowered in the half-light at the edge of the circle of bystanders, guests, and drummers, trying in vain to wipe sweat from my forehead with my sequin-embellished silk gown. Barely a half-minute passed without a new dancer leaping into the circle to show off her Sabar moves to a rapt and voracious crowd. Some had attitude, some were shy, but everyone was caught in the adrenaline rush of the party. I've practiced this dance a million times with my teacher; why am I nervous? I tried to calm myself down. If I didn't jump in soon, the rhythm would change and I'd have to think of a whole different set of steps. Suddenly, I leaped up, unsure whether my legs were really my own, and ran in front of the drummers to dance. They called the break, I changed steps; they called the break again, and I jumped to land in a pose at the exact moment the drummers ended in a collective *thwack!* The crowd roared, "Lucy! Lucy! Lucy!" and ran to give me hugs.

Long before I went to Senegal for the first time in 2006, I took African dance classes with teachers all around the United States. My mother has been teaching an African dance class for over twenty-four years in Santa Fe, New Mexico. Dancing in this forum has always been a relaxing and joyous event for me—a place where, three times a week, I get to have fun with some of my closest and oldest friends. We start in a circle, whether there be fifteen of us or ninety, as is often the case during summer months. The circle makes us look at each other and recognize that we are here dancing together, and when we see each other's faces, we smile. This is my home community and as a collective, I believe we bring positive energy to ourselves and to others. After our warm-up, we get into lines where we move across the floor practicing each new move shown by our teacher. It's not a competition and we aren't trying to dance better than others; it's a class where we're all students sharing a collective knowledge and joy of movement.

Cowering in my chair at the 2:00 a.m. Sabar party on that summer night in Dakar, I felt far away from my mom's light-filled dance class. Terror, insecurity, and self-doubt streamed through my veins, simultaneously freezing me and sending every nerve on edge. Not until I landed my final jump and heard friends and unknown neighbors cheer did I realize that they too danced to be part of the community, celebrating each other, and bringing joy through music and movement. I feel like my experiences with African dance are akin to what people feel when they go to church or win a home game in sports. The energy that everyone brings to a community event results in an identity and experience that is greater than the sum of its parts. Therefore, it is venues such as these dance parties that provide a window into a culture, in part because they have helped define the fabric of meaning that defines how a society sees the world. At the same time, dance is a universal language accessible to every human being.

Culture is like oxygen: it surrounds us often without our awareness of its crucial function to our lives. Senegal has a rich dance and drum tradition which uniquely defines it from the rest of West Africa. Unlike the Guinean government, which has fostered the development of its artistic industry for domestic and international marketability, Senegalese artists have developed individual careers but mostly only after leaving Senegal. I have seen from the United States that touring artists sponsor entire families back in Senegal. Sabar is what defines Senegal for me as a foreigner, but young Senegalese are eager to study more lucrative professions than their traditional art forms. Sabar dancers who have not been able to succeed financially within Senegal have captured devoted students and audiences in the United States and Europe, creating a demand for classes and performances that Senegal could now provide as a commodity.

I am a Fulbright Dance Fellow in Senegal, studying how to make artistic professions economically viable within the country so that artists don't have to rely on foreign travels to support themselves. More than anything else, my time in Dakar has led me to reflect on my role in African dance and in the world. Am I here to take responsibility and act upon the problems I see? Am I here to contribute my training in economics and microfinance to reduce poverty and improve the lives of the artists I know? Am I here to learn Sabar dance in order to be a teacher myself? Unfortunately in my life, the more I learn, the less I seem to know, because new information leads me to question my assumptions. Although I can't predict where dance will take me or what I will be doing in ten years, I can tell with certainty that I will be dancing because dance is something that unites me with my community in Santa Fe and my communities around the world.

I didn't end up getting the scholarship, which didn't surprise me, but sometimes it's better to go through the experience of applying and keeping those skills honed than to not try at all for fear of failure.

"Rejected by the college of your choice? Rejected by the grantor that could have taken you around the world? Rejected by the love of your life?

It's not the end of the world. There's always something better around the corner. The worst that can happen when you get rejected is that you stop believing in yourself. It's natural to feel sad, but there's no point in letting that consume you. Get up, dust yourself off, and move on. Try again, and again, and again."

—**Vidhee Garg**, Scholarship recipient at Mumbai University and Cornell University

Perseverance is perhaps the most important element of grant writing. While it isn't something that can be taught, it can be learned through practice.

Not telling everyone you know about your project can sometimes help with recovery and re-motivation following a rejection. When I first applied for the Fulbright, I told all my friends and family, and my mom told all her friends. It was widely known that I'd applied. I knew that my mom told everyone because she was proud of me and was sure that I would get it, but then when I didn't, it made the rejection a little harder.

I considered whether I should tell people that I was writing this book, but decided against it. Not because I don't think that I will end up publishing it, but because sometimes an idea or a project can be fragile; it needs time to incubate. In some ways, applying for a scholarship is like pursuing a dream. We have to overcome our insecurities and inner doubts to develop the confidence to apply at all. This is a fragile state of mind and our own demons can keep us from accomplishing something so seemingly grand. Sharing this information with others can sometimes diminish the will that you're developing, even if all the people in your life support you one hundred percent.

I think this happens because we switch from relying upon internal gratification to external gratification.

When I've completed an application, I keep that satisfaction for myself, like a little pearl of accomplishment.

Even if I don't get the grant or fellowship, I feel a sense of pride and satisfaction that I've completed the task and tried my best. When I've told people about the applications I'm working on, I think I have sought out some kind of praise that I couldn't give myself. Either I was trying to impress somebody, or I was trying to prove myself in a situation where I felt inadequate. Telling someone about the application gives me a moment's worth of satisfaction, but I'm left with a looming, expectant pressure over my head. It's hard enough to deal with my own expectations, let alone the expectations of others. The more people you tell about the work you're doing, the more people you have to notify about the results. When I didn't get the Fulbright the first time, everyone asked me about it (expecting that I got it), and I had to tell them the sad news.

Relaying the news of rejection is one of my dilemmas. On the one hand, my advisors and everybody who has helped me work on applications should be notified. But on the other hand, telling people that I didn't get a grant feels like fishing for sympathy. I don't want to bring up bad news about myself and have all the condolences and encouraging pep talks. It makes me rethink every time I'm about to tell someone about a project.

Sometimes I think about the tradeoff between the time I spend writing grants and the amount of success/rejection I get. I usually think it's a pretty good deal. In contrast to the time I have spent working on school projects and homework without much payoff at all except a grade (and learning a new subject), a grant proposal is something that can win you money. Is this not a good investment, even if it takes a little longer and a few more tries? I think I realized this relatively good use of time when I entered the Elevator Pitch Contest at Smith, as I mentioned in Chapter Eight. For a few minutes of practice over a couple of weeks, I won the contest and one hundred dollars. Then for the regional contest, I spent about an hour a week improving my pitch with faculty members and I got a free dinner and a seven-hundred-fifty-dollar second prize. Again, this seems to me like a pretty good use of time, especially considering that I've used the elevator pitch skill many more times since then. I was learning a very important real-world skill while also winning money.

The same is true if you consider how much time goes into grant writing compared to the payoff. Working on an application for a couple of months while doing whatever else you're doing can be rewarded by five, ten, twenty-five, maybe even fifty thousand dollars in scholarship money. This is a motivating thought for me when I start to get boggled down in how much time it seems like I'm spending on applications. There are great rewards at the end of the road.

Final Thoughts

My husband Okwen and I dreamt up the Go Green Africa project for the summer after we first met. We taught about environmental sustainability issues in Cameroon. We had four classes of twenty to forty eighth and ninth graders, 120 students in total. My curriculum focused on basic tenets of environmental education, including the essential science of global warming (I used sections of Al Gore's movie *An Inconvenient Truth* to help explain some concepts). As early as our second lesson, we drilled down to the issue of plastic bags, directly challenging our students' attitudes.

My second lesson for all of the classes was one in which I held up a thin plastic bag and asked the class, "What is this called?" Most people responded, "Paper," but others said, "Plastic paper," as it is called in the Pidgin English that they speak. I told them that what I held in my hand was nothing even remotely similar to paper, that what I held was a plastic bag and it should not be confused with paper in property or function.

We then proceeded to investigate why it was called paper ("Is it opaque? Can you write on it? Is it made of the same things as paper?") and, to all of their surprise, I told them that plastic is a petroleum product. I told them about how alarmed I was at age ten to see burning plastic, and how I continue to worry about the practice of boiling food traditionally prepared in banana leaves in plastic bags.

This became a central part of my curriculum. Every single student ended up writing a letter to the Ministry of Environment and Nature Protection in Yaounde, sharing the new information with them and asking that Cameroon be like Rwanda, South Africa, and twenty-one other countries around the world that have banned thin plastic bags. Okwen and I personally deposited all 120 letters to the minister's office on the day I flew out of the capital. This was back in 2009.

Jump ahead to April 2014. Okwen and I have moved back to Santa Fe after about five years of living and studying in West Africa and upstate New York. We have given birth to the baby that we dreamt about since the first weeks of our courtship, named after her two grandmothers and godmother. The Voice of Africa, among other African news sources, reports that Cameroon's president, Paul Biya, has banned the use of non-biodegradable plastic bags in the entire country as of April 27, 2014. Could we have contributed to a movement to increase awareness about the harms of cooking with and burning plastic bags that led to this massive shift? It was surely the ongoing work of many passionate people, but our students' letters must have helped. So much has happened in the short five years since we worked on this project.

I took my baby to my mother's dance class for the first time when she was one month old, watching as she observed the amazing woman after whom she is named. Without that first experience as a Kiva Fellow in 2008, I wouldn't even know this man who became my husband and the father of my child. That experience inspired me to apply for the Fulbright, and although I didn't get it on my first try, it taught me that perseverance pays off when you try again. My fellowship background allowed me to go to Cornell for graduate school, where I got a scholarship to cover my tuition and multiple grants to continue working in dance and teaching, mostly because I had built a strong profile. As I look back, fellowships have truly shaped my life.

I've learned so much from the adventures I've had and the experience of pursuing funding. I keep journals occasionally while I'm abroad, but the journaling falls off pretty quickly, leaving only fragments of my real-time experience to look back on. Memories of people I've met and poignant moments come to me years later and present themselves as pivotal events that at first seemed insignificant—like the moment I received an email from my Fulbright advisor saying that dance might work, or when I was canvassing the Smith library to petition people to vote for my Go Green Africa project.

I can't quantify my gratitude for these experiences, all I can do is pass along the bits of knowledge I've gained and offer to talk with anyone who has questions. Fellowships have shaped me into the person I am today, someone who has the ability to do what I love. All I hope is that my work in the world has made positive little impacts—chief among them, helping you achieve your potential.

ABOUT THE AUTHOR

Born in Santa Fe, New Mexico, to a family of West African dance and drum artists, Lucy Gent Foma is a dancer, city planner, and educator who has lived in Senegal, Cameroon, Brazil, as well as the southwest and northeast regions of the United States. She has received funding, through merit-based fellowships, scholarships, and grants, to conduct research and implement projects in American and African cities alike. After graduating from Smith College with BAs in Economics and Portuguese, she secured private funding and prizes to implement the Go Green Africa middle-school environmental education program in Cameroon. The following year, she was a Fulbright Research Fellow in Dance and a Rotary Ambassadorial Scholar in Environmental Planning in Senegal.

As a graduate student pursuing her Master's degree in City and Regional Planning at Cornell University, she was awarded one of five available Foreign Language and Areas Studies Fellowships to research transportation systems in Portugal. She currently works at Bandelier National Monument as a Transportation

Scholar and writes about finding funding, community planning, and parenting. Lucy lives in Santa Fe with her husband, daughter, and family.

YOU GOT IT! NOW WHAT?

The goal of getting a fellowship is to follow your dreams, right? So you can feel ungrateful and guilty when you're about to set off for your fellowship and you don't want to go. Not at all. The biggest adrenaline rush is actually getting the award. You will be on a high for days, unable to believe that you've actually accomplished your goal. This euphoria is tough to sustain. It's the nature of our emotions: we have peaks and lows and most people don't stay at either for long.

Then the reality sets in that you have more work to do: plan your trip and/ or project, contact all the people you promised to work with, get vaccinations if you're going abroad, figure out housing. It's a lot to organize, especially after you've done so much work so far. It's just like buyer's remorse, because you can be led to believe that the application *was* the work. Possibly the worst thing that could happen would be not wanting to do your project by the time you hear about the fellowship. With some of these opportunities, it can be a long wait period. I applied for the Rotary scholarship in March 2009, notified that I was a finalist in August 2009, and then found out I was going to Senegal in January

2010. I finally got to do the scholarship in October 2010, a full year and a half after I'd first applied.

Every time I go abroad, whether for scholarships or leisure, I find there's a time when I ask myself why I'm subjecting myself to the uncomfortable feeling of being an outsider. Inevitably, there's something that challenges me: bargaining with taxi drivers (the bane of my existence); finding food that doesn't make me sick or feel unbearably fat; misunderstanding instructions; the list could go on and on. I remember reading about a seemingly xenophobic man who described how he would go abroad with his wife, who was much more outgoing than he was. He usually would find some excuse to stay in the hotels while she went out exploring markets and trying new foods. The one time that he went abroad without her, it dawned on him that he actually didn't like how uncomfortable he felt while he was traveling. He posed the question, "Why do I pay all this money to be less comfortable than I am at home?" In some ways, I was disgusted by his point of view, but in other ways, I actually felt a similar sentiment. He was being perfectly honest. Unless you are going somewhere to experience a four-star resort with tons of other Americans and only American food, you're going to find uncomfortable growing pains.

As Katherine Noble explains,

> Living in another country requires tenacity. Get ready to be lost all the time, committing cultural faux pas, become very shy in speaking another language, and have difficulty making local friends. You pretty much have to come to terms with the fact that you will be speaking an error-riddled version of another language, so try to not be embarrassed by it. I now realize that this is the only way to learn another language: make lots of errors and take corrections with humility and grace. A person correcting your language is showing you great care, even though at the time it can feel difficult.

I think this is particularly true if you are a young student, because you really should experience the culture in which you're immersed. In other ways, going abroad as a younger person steels you for anything that could happen. You haven't yet shed the invincible and naïve sheen of teendom. This armor blocks some rational reasoning that tells you in advance that you will be challenged.

As a nineteen year old in Senegal my first time, I tried things that absolutely terrified me. I wasn't as afraid to try out a new language, sounding like a baby repeating simple words over and over again, or dancing in front of large audiences who would be able to discern my every mistake. In Brazil as a twenty year old, I spoke in Portuguese in front of hundreds of people and went into the countryside to spend time with people I didn't know.

I can't say that I have the courage to do these things at this point in my life, or at least I would have a lot more reservations about them now. For example, I would consider whether I would be able to find food on a regular basis if I went into the countryside. Back in Brazil, I sat on a bus for about nine hours without food and water because we got stuck in a traffic jam. When we finally reached a semi-urban town on the outskirts of Rio, street-hawkers offered some very salty and fatty crackers through the bus window, and we had to toss money out the window as the bus rolled forward. At this point in my life, I've also come to rely on my husband to do all taxi negotiations. Although his French is worse than mine, he seems to have a better rapport with taxi drivers than I do. I've also found ways to cut corners and make it more comfortable to travel, although I realize I'm missing out on part of the experience by doing this.

One lifeline that I've come to rely on is American friends. Again, I realize this is cheating in some ways. You're not completely immersed in a culture when you spend a lot of time with Americans abroad, but I've found that it's really comforting to get together with people from my own country. Not everyday, maybe not even every week, but every once in a while. In Senegal I had a couple of American girlfriends who would come over to my house for tea. We would use the time to catch up, bitch about frustrations, or revel in the amazing things we were experiencing. We never just complained about our lives. Almost all the people I've met abroad were very happy to be there, but inevitably had some problems along the way. I've had terrible luck with landlords, for example, which has required a lot of talk therapy with my mother and my friends.

How to Prepare to Go Abroad

"I like to have an 'I won't be able to buy anything there' attitude. Sometimes we get ourselves in trouble when we think, 'Oh, I'll just buy that there' and then we get in-country and we find out that we can't purchase the necessary item. Before I went to Senegal, I heard that I could have clothes tailored locally, so I didn't bring too many outfits. But once I arrived I discovered that the tailoring process takes longer than I'd imagined, so I was tuck with the same two outfits for the first month. I wish I had packed better!"

—**Artis Henderson**, former Rotary Ambassadorial Scholar

"Seek out information from a variety of sources—the study abroad office at your school, past participants of the program, and general travel-related sources. You may require special medication or vaccinations for some countries, so you'll need to see a travel medicine doctor, and they will provide you with all sorts of other helpful information. You may also need to apply for a visa, depending on the country. The program you've signed up for may require a student visa or a tourist visa, depending on the length and nature of the program. If you don't have a passport yet, be sure to order your passport with as much advance time as possible and a minimum of six weeks before you leave. If you already have a passport, make sure that it won't expire during your travel and that it has the correct amount of empty pages to meet the requirements of the country you are visiting. If you are purchasing your own flights, Student Travel Association is a great resource for students for both airfare and travel insurance."

—**Gemina Garland-Lewis**, former Thomas J. Watson Fellow and National Geographic Society Young Explorer Grantee

"I made time to travel with a friend for a week or so before I moved into my homestay—that way I got to experience Buenos Aires and the country of Argentina a little bit for myself without having to report to any program. Plus, it gave me good conversation starters to discuss the things I had seen and tried."

—Katherine Noble, PhD Student at University of Utah Department of Biology, Ant-decapitating flies

One friend who really did have a hard time abroad was a girl with whom I went to Brazil. We had been taking Portuguese together for the past two years, but would probably not have been friends had we not be living in Rio together. Her parents had been against the idea of going to Brazil from the start, which I think set her up for a disappointing experience. They would tell her, "I don't know why you chose that stupid country." I think not having the support of your parents makes any choice hard, but when you're having a hard time with the decision you've made *and* your parents don't support you, it's a recipe for disaster.

We would go and have some overpriced American food at the posh food courts in Rio's fancy malls, taking the time to talk about our experiences. I remember one particular day when I had been hearing complaint after complaint from her about all of the things she hated about Brazil. Suddenly, she stopped and said, "I'm probably not a very good friend to be around right now because all I've been doing is complaining." It was a genuine reflection, like she could finally hear herself, and she also could hear what she sounded like to me. I try to surround myself with more positive people than negative people, but I realized that my friend really needed someone to sympathize with her. Her negativity was not a constant thing; it was a product of a circumstance in which she didn't have support.

I have been very fortunate to have my parents' support wherever I go and whatever I do. Don't get me wrong, my mom cries and agonizes over many of my trips, but she supports me. This makes all the difference, as Katherine Noble attests:

Prepare to be totally out of your comfort zone—you will be meeting lots of new people, suffering through basic communication errors, and living in a different culture and city. It's completely normal to feel overwhelmed. If you prepare to feel this way, you can mitigate some of the effects. Communicate with people from home (teach your parents to use Skype!), and bring some comforting things, like a favorite book or tea.

When I was preparing to leave for Senegal on the Fulbright, I learned that there is a very common transition period into and out of an experience abroad. As we sat in a Washington, DC hotel for the orientation, we saw a graph of the peaks and troughs of the emotional rollercoaster that is living abroad.[19]

At first, you have a high period, when you're excited to be in a new country and embarking on your new adventure. Then you have a little bit of a low because not everything is going your way. You're also starting to get a little frustrated by the things you don't understand or wish you could handle better. After a few months, you've settled into a comfortable trend, and you level off into a balanced, happy stasis. Then, as you approach the months nearing your departure, you start to feel unhappy that you'll be leaving the place you've come to appreciate and maybe deal with it by thinking beyond your return home to the next thing. Right when you leave, you have a euphoric and nostalgic connection to the country you've been living in, thinking it will never be the same again. After you return home, you go through a little bit of depression (after the ecstatic feeling of being home again) because things have changed since you left and you find that your homesickness was mostly rosy and unrealistic.

Learning about these typical peaks and valleys didn't make the experience any easier, but as with most things, knowing that I wasn't the only one going through it made me feel less ungrateful and more normal.

---

19 "Re-entry," IES Abroad, accessed June 10, 2015, http://www.iesabroad.org/study-abroad/ parents/re-entry.

ACKNOWLEDGEMENTS

This book would not exist without the loving support of my family—particularly my mom and my husband, who have held me as I've cried in disappointment, and shared with me tears of joy. You two are my pillars of strength: quiet and sturdy yet ready to prop me up as I figure out my path.

Thank you to my dear mentors Marta Townsend and Donald Andrew, who instilled in me this love of and aptitude for finding and pursuing funding. I'm also grateful to my college advisor Marguerite Harrison, and my graduate advisor H. Pike Oliver, who both contributed to my success beyond their official roles.

My friends and colleagues have added significant knowledge to this book and I am honored to know you all. Thank you, Vidhee Garg, Caroline Sutcliffe, Ayla Schlosser, Gemina Garland-Lewis, Katherine Noble, Artis Henderson, James Gutierrez, Phoenix Mourning-Star, Ivan Ledyashov, Jenny Marotto Lutter, Nicole Gent, Megan Hallinan, and Amy Zeng for contributing your insights to this body of work.

Thanks to These Are Things, who designed the icons and worksheet headers, and to Morgan James Publishers, who also designed the cover.

Finally, thank you to Tanya Taylor Rubinstein and Candace Walsh, for pushing me to write the first draft of this book.

273

ADDITIONAL RESOURCES
& WORKSHEETS

For additional free resources, motivational support, and news about Lucy's current work visit:

www.LucyGentFoma.com

Check out what others are saying about Funded! and continue learning more about how to pursue your passions.

And remember!
Tell a friend about this book!

People will always remember the first person that encouraged them to pursue fellowships, scholarships and grants.

Be that person.

To receive your free bonuses, visit the website above.

CPSIA information can be obtained at www.ICGtesting.com
Printed in the USA
LVOW11s1434150416

483808LV00003B/284/P